28 for 2

28 for 28

Exploring the UK's World Heritage

Gregory Lewry

Copyright © 2020 Gregory Lewry All rights reserved

No part of this book may be reproduced, or stored in a retrieval system, or transmitted in any form or by any means, electronic, mechanical, photocopying, recording, or otherwise, without express written permission of the publisher.

#1 of 28 Tower of London
#2 of 28 City of Bath
#3 of 28 Dorset and East Devon Coast
#4 of 28 Pontscysyllte Aqueduct
#5 of 28 Ironbridge Gorge
#6 of 28 Blaenavon Industrial Landscape
#7 of 28 Castles and Town Walls of King Edward in Gwynedd (1986)
#8 of 28 Liverpool – Maritime Mercantile City (2004)
#9 of 28 Blenheim Palace (1987)
#10 of 28 Canterbury Cathedral, St Augustine's Abbey, and St Martin's Church (1988)
#11 of 28 Maritime Greenwich (1997)
#12 of 28 Palace of Westminster and Westminster Abbey including Saint Margaret's Church (1987)
#13 of 28 Royal Botanic Gardens, Kew (2003) #14 of 28 Derwent Valley Mills (2001)
#15 of 28 Saltaire (2001)
#16 of 28 Studley Royal Park including the Ruins of Fountains Abbey (1986)
#17 of 28 Durham Castle and Cathedral (1986) #18 of 28 Frontiers of the Roman Empire (1987,2005,2008)
#19 of 28 The English Lake District (2017)
#20 of 28 The Giant's Causeway and Causeway Coast (1986)
#21 of 28 New Lanark (2001)
#22 of 28 The Forth Bridge (2015)
#23 of 28 Old and New Towns of Edinburgh (1995)
#24 of 28 Cornwall and West Devon Mining Landscape (2006)
#25 of 28 Stonehenge, Avebury and Associated Sites (1986)
#26 of 28 Heart of Neolithic Orkney (1999)
#27 of 28 Jodrell Bank Observatory
#28 of 28 St Kilda (1986)

Prologue

It was a baking hot summer's day for my 27th birthday. I stood surrounded by 35 kids in a square swarming with people, and the kids, dressed in the lime green shirts of the summer school, were growing restless. I'd been left with them while our group leader went off in search of tickets. All I had to do was keep the little ones together and not allow them to fulfil their search for an ice cream van. Amongst the throng, I scanned the horizon for any sign of the group leader returning with wads of tickets in her hands. One of the most recognisable sights in London sat over my shoulder but I was staring at the modern blocks of concrete and glass that house the ticket office and a chain restaurant. Emblazoned on the side of the elephant grey blocks in silver letters, the words 'Tower of London' stood out, giving no clue to the historical significance of the 900 year old fortress across the way from it. It looked rather like the name of an office block. Perhaps it is. Underneath though, there was a little indicator of the cultural significance of the place: 'World Heritage Site'.

'World Heritage Site'. Even in tiny letters on the side of a wall, it looked grand, important, intriguing. If the Tower of London were a so-called 'World Heritage Site', I thought to myself, then it made sense for there to be others too. There must be a number of them, and so therefore a list of them spread throughout the globe. I pulled my smartphone out of my pocket, joining the kids who were all flicking and swiping on theirs, and googled *'list of world heritage sites'*. The first result was a Wikipedia list of 'UNESCO World Heritage sites' and I clicked on it, opening up a list of sites by continent. I selected Europe and then the United Kingdom and found myself on a page with a picture of Stonehenge and the declaration that there are 31 of these UNESCO World Heritage sites in the UK; 31 places in my country deemed by the United Nations' specialised agency for education, science and culture to be worthy of recognition for their cultural or natural value to humanity. The Tower of London was one, Stonehenge obviously another, but the other twenty nine? I was curious to find out.

As I discovered while waiting in the sunshine outside the Tower, there's quite a range of places in the UK listed as a World

Heritage site. Churches, castles, gardens, factories, archaeological remains, natural landscapes. I knew quite a few of them of course, as many of the UK's most popular attractions are inscribed. You will have heard of, and probably visited yourselves, Blenheim Palace, Westminster Abbey, Hadrian's Wall, to name a few. However, there were also a fair few that I'd never even heard of before. Blaenavon, Saltaire, New Lanark. Where and what are these? Why are all and each of them classed as 'World Heritage'? What does that even mean?

The questions swirled around my mind until I spotted our group leader hurrying out of the grey blocks of the ticket office. She had the tickets in hand. We roused the kids, forced the phones back in their pockets, and went in to explore the bloody history, crown jewels, and rip-off gift shops of the Tower of London.

Later, sat on the bus and heading back to the summer school in Hampshire, I returned to the list on my phone. Perhaps it was a result of being stood in the burning sun the whole day, but a slightly crazy idea had been germinating in my mind. Today was my birthday, my 27th to be exact, and I'd just visited one of these 27 World Heritage sites. Disregarding the four UK World Heritage sites outside of the British Isles (Inaccessible Island in the Atlantic sounds a tad tricky to get to), there were 27 UK World Heritage sites on the list on my phone. One for each of the years I'd been alive. Why not visit the other 26? I'd have time over the course of the next year to go around the country, ticking off the World Heritage sites as I went, and learning a little about the country I had only recently returned to after five years of living and working overseas. Why not see a bit of my own country for once? Judging by UNESCO's criteria, these were the best places to go to. I was sure that, by the time my 28th birthday came round, I'd have been able to complete the list. Let's go for it.

The thing with having these types of ideas is that they are often not very easy to realise. In practice the idea is often too laborious, too expensive, and too time-consuming. Ideas are often doomed to fail the moment you start to plan them. Still, looking at the list of UK World Heritage sites, I started to believe it was achievable. Ever the heartless trip planner, I grouped them into regions to individualise each trip that I'd have to take away from home and set about the slow, potentially worthless, but immeasurably pleasurable task of planning how to visit all of the sites between my 27th birthday on the 29th of July 2018 and my 28th birthday 365 days later.

Browsing through the Wikipedia list I noticed that I had, over the course of a childhood spent with moderately culturally curious parents and the odd cycle tour here and there in the British Isles, been to a fair few of the listed places already. That was no problem really, I'm not one to refuse a second visit somewhere unless that place is Cancun; my experience there is probably one for another book. Growing up so close to London had meant that I had already visited the four UNESCO sites in the capital, and various bike tours had led me across the Forth Bridge, past sites like Durham Cathedral, and through areas such as Dorset and East Devon Coastline. Kew Gardens recalled to me a school trip in Year 9 on which all I remember is the whole class getting incredibly excited at seeing coca leaves and marijuana plants growing. Stonehenge I had been past before, though never stopped to see. Bath, Edinburgh and Liverpool I'd all previously visited and relished doing so again.

Then there were the UNESCO sites listed that I had never even heard of before. Criticise my ignorance, but I'd never thought of making a trip to see the Derwent Valley Mills nor ever had much of an urge to see the mining landscape of Devon and Cornwall. I literally had no idea where Studley Royal Park was and though I could infer that Pontcysyllte Aqueduct was in Wales, I had no hope of pronouncing it. Still, they were on the list and so therefore had to be visited. I was sure my ignorance would be blown to smithereens (isn't that the point of travel?) and that I'd learn something valuable about my country and its history in the process. I'd at least learn that Pontcysyllte is pronounced pon-tee-salty, which I have now remembered because it sounds like a new crisp flavour.

After reading up on the UK's sites, I was interested to know how the UK's total compared to other nations. On the Wikipedia list of UNESCO World Heritage sites by country, it was no surprise to see Italy topping the list with the most sites, with China and Spain not far behind, but there was the UK, sitting high up the list with the commendable total of 31, now 32 thanks to Jodrell Bank's 2019 inscription. Being born and raised in the UK, it's perfectly normal to be surrounded by heritage worthy sites and places. While the sight of a castle or a rickety old building dating back hundreds of years may send visitors from other nations into a selfie-taking frenzy, for most Brits these are just normal places, apparent in many towns and cities across the country. Our lackadaisical attitude towards our own heritage at times is saved by the tremendous work that various organisations such as the National Trust and English Heritage do to preserve the history and culture of our nation. We never realise how lucky us Brits are.

So, without much further ado, it was time to see what Britain had to offer. A whole year to discover Britain's heritage, travelling through the country and bumping into fellow Brits, old friends, and fellow tourists along the way. Even though, as travel writer Paul Theroux once said, Britain is *'the best-known, most fastidiously mapped and most widely trampled piece of geography on earth'*, it was still a mystery to me. Through UNESCO's list, I hoped to discover not just the UK's heritage, but a little bit of the secret that makes my home nation the most wonderfully weird country on earth.

UK UNESCO World Heritage Sites #1 of 28

Tower of London

Send him to the tower! (with 35 kids)

I think I stopped looking forward to my birthdays about four or five years ago, around my twenty second celebration, possibly earlier. I've worked every birthday bar one since I turned eighteen, and now, nearly a decade later, they've come to signify another year gone rather than another year to come. Most of my recent birthdays I've worked at summer camps and summer schools; teaching swimming to kids in Connecticut every summer while at university and for the past four years, teaching English in Hampshire to students from various corners of the globe. Perhaps working with kids on your birthday, being surrounded by dozens of fresh-faced, worry-free cherubs, makes the passing of age feel heavier. Every year I grow older and they stay just as young. My year of birth slowly drifts further and further away from theirs the more summers that pass. Still, there are advantages. Spending your special day with young people means they are generally more excited than you are (something to do with the promise of cake after dinner, I suspect) and their enthusiasm does start to break down my natural resistance to my birthday. In many respects, a birthday teaching young kids is a fine way to spend the day, even if they do insist on asking how old you are every ten seconds.

For the fourth year running I was at a Hampshire summer school for my birthday and it falling on a weekend meant that instead of teaching that day, we'd be off on the bus on an excursion. Sunday 29th July 2018 just happened to be the date of the dreaded day trip to London. If you've ever tried taking one child around central London, you'll know what this means. Multiply the number by 35 and it equals a nightmare. Patrolling 35 international kids who have little understanding of the English language and even less ability to walk in a straight line is about as much of a pain in the derriere as it sounds.

At least our itinerary for the day was set to be more manageable than the previous year. We'd been hoping to walk from the river at Westminster to the Science Museum in South Kensington after a river cruise, but one does not simply lead seventy little legs for miles across one of the world's busiest cities while a cycle race is blocking off many of the central routes. As the museum was arranged as the pick-up point for the bus back to Hampshire, a kiddy train the length of the great freight trains that cross continents had to be driven through the well-to-do districts of Belgravia and Mayfair with champagne quaffing socialites looking on bemusedly. It took hours. I totally sympathised with the kids. They'd been dragged along London's streets with all the sounds and smells associated, and they were knackered. Once we got them to Hyde Park and figured out a way to trick the park toilets into letting us push multiple kids through the turnstile for one payment of thirty pence, we allowed them a well-deserved whippy with a flake and then had to shunt them back onto the waiting bus to spend an hour negotiating London's weekend traffic jams. They never even stepped inside the museum.

2018's London trip was to be different, at least certainly less ambitious. Boat along the Thames to the UNESCO World Heritage listed Tower of London then walk across Tower Bridge to meet the bus. Simple, on paper. Whether the kids were as excited as me to visit the prime example of a medieval fortress palace in Britain I couldn't tell, but they were certainly keen to receive their smartphones for the journey. Knowing that we would lose them to the virtual world on the bus, the other teachers and I had spent the previous few days in class impressing upon them that the Tower of London is internationally significant for it represents the influence of the Normans on Britain and everything in modern Britain which came from the Normans and then spread around the world. Through the Normans, British culture was bolstered by closer ties to continental Europe, the introduction of French transformed the English language, and one of the most powerful monarchies in the world was created. From protecting the crowns the royals wear upon their heads to providing the venue where various royals had their decrowned heads chopped off, the Tower is one of the most visible symbols of the British Royalty and everything that it conjures up in the minds of foreign visitors to these shores. Architecturally it's monumentally significant as it was a pioneer of the innovative palace within walls design that the Normans spread throughout England and Wales. Its walls and towers also serve as a timeline of military building advances from the 11th to the 16th century as additions from later kings kept it up-to-date. However, in truth, all the kids really wanted to hear about were the beheadings and the Crown Jewels. Gore and gold. Well, there's plenty of that at the Tower too.

So, we piled thirty five kids onto the bus, making sure to give them their smartphones with instructions to keep the volume on silent so us adults at the front of the bus could grab some peace and quiet for once (gladly taken with a few of my teaching colleagues nodding off as soon as we turned left out of the school gates). An hour or so later we were entering London at the obligatory snail's pace. When we made it to the river at Lambeth Bridge we all jumped out, almost forgetting to retrieve the packed lunches from under the bus. Chucking paper bags full of cheese rolls and Capri-Suns at the kids, we embarked on the shuffle to find public conveniences that wouldn't mind their facilities being swamped.

Walking is hard for my generation and the next. The compulsion to have a smartphone in hand as you meander along, head down and concentration firmly on the latest addictive app is too great for many of us Millennials and for those in Generations Z and Alpha. These kids had been without their phones for a whole week and a two hour drive was simply not enough time to catch up on the games and social media that soak up our time. Plus the South Bank is a rather attractive walk, the trees providing shade and colour amongst the buskers and posh burger vans, setting the Instagrammable scene if you can look up long enough to realise what is around you. I am quite happy to admit that I have zero ability to multitask and trying to operate a smartphone while walking is generally beyond my capabilities. Should I need to respond to a message or look up my location on Google Maps, I have to pull over to the side of the pavement and bury my head in my phone while stationary. The kids may laugh at me, but at least I know my limitations. Really, I am rather jealous of those who are able to juggle walking with rapid thumb movement. In turn, I also take great pleasure in observing those who cannot perform this skill come a cropper on a slightly uneven paving slab or seeing two digital zombies collide head on. It'll never get old, nor will it ever improve. This is the human race from now on. Get used to it.

I was walking at the front of the group with a few of the faster-walking kids including the front-runner for the 'Child I would most readily adopt' award. RJ was adorable 99% of the time, being unfailingly polite, mild-mannered, and having the tendency to come out with cute statements that would make the staff coo over him. However, at that exact moment, he needed the loo, and badly. He certainly was making it known, positively skipping with the desperation. As you may be beginning to realise, excursions at a summer school consist of 50% travel time, 30% toilet breaks, and 20% selfie taking in front of national monuments. Knowing RJ, he wasn't one to exaggerate. We needed a loo in London, and fast. We ran ahead of the group, slaloming through the crowds with RJ gripping my hand so that it looked as if I were kidnapping him. County Hall is the Grade 2 listed former headquarters of the Greater London Council, abolished in 1986 by Margaret Thatcher. It's a grand old building with a beautiful facade facing the water and the Palace of Westminster. Sadly, nowadays it houses tourist traps like DreamWork's *Shrek's Adventure!* and therefore deserves to have little Korean boys piss all over its toilet seats. It's a sure bet for a free tinkle should you be caught short south of the river. You're welcome.

Once RJ had finished his business, we latched back onto the front of the group as they caught up with us and crossed over one of the two Golden Jubilee bridges to catch the tour boat along the Thames. I've been on the tour boats that chug up and down the Thames a number of times and I have to admit they're not that bad. Sure, they're chock-a-block with camera-toting tourists, but they do provide a superb way to see the famous sights along the river. The commentaries, done by the boat staff rather than professional tour guides, usually have an equal balance of fact and smut to keep all ages, though only proficient Cockney English users, entertained. This particular guide did acknowledge the fact that *'if you ain't decent at the old English lingo, then you ain't got much of a sodding hope in hell of catching me chat'* and he was reasonably right. Good luck to any of our kids trying to comprehend his deluge of jokes. He made the trip up the Thames bearable though, and the boat afforded the opportunity for the kids to eat whatever remains of their packed lunch they had left at 11am. The kids also did a remarkable job of running the boat's supply of Pringles dry. Superb work. Further proof that no matter how well you feed kids, given a sum of money, they will seek out the sugariest and saltiest treats they can lay their little hands on. They have enormous appetites for crap.

After a slick clean-up operation of wrappers and crushed Oreos, we alighted at the Tower of London boat stop (known as Tower Millenium pier), ready to dive into the history of one of London's great attractions, and one of its four UNESCO World Heritage sites. While the UK may not have the highest number of World Heritage sites in the world, its capital city does have more sites than any other city in the world, just ahead of Beijing, Moscow, Berlin, Mexico City, and New Delhi (all on 3). The Tower of London was inscribed in 1988, over 900 years after William the Conqueror had it built to protect the city of London and provide him with a secure stronghold. It has served multiple purposes as a royal residence, an armoury, a menagerie, the home of the Royal Mint and the Crown Jewels, and, perhaps most famously, a prison for fallen public figures. The list of those who were 'sent to the tower' reads like a 'Who's who' of mid second millennium AD British history. Some, like Elizabeth I, were just held there for a while. Others, like Guy Fawkes, met their bloody end within the Tower's walls. As such, the Tower has a reputation for torture and death. Approaching the Tower from the water, you can sense the fear that the Tower would have inspired as you glide past the famous 'Entry to the traitor's gate' inscription on the wall. This is the second gate to the Tower and certainly the one through which no one hoped to pass. Those who had committed treason were taken by barge along the river, passing under London Bridge on which the heads of recently executed prisoners were displayed on spikes, and entering the complex through this gate. These ill-fated prisoners included Anne Boleyn, Catherine Howard and Thomas More, amongst many others who were accused of treason during the reigns of England's unforgiving kings.

As the majority of us were guiltless of any crimes against the monarchy, we made our way from the pier to the main entrance at the side of the complex. We found our way inside quick enough, paying a selfie opportunity to the less watery side of the Traitor's Gate and gawping at the funny dress of the Beefeaters, the ceremonial guardians of the Tower who were today dressed in their 'undress uniform' of navy and red as the Queen wasn't expected to pop in. The Yeomen Warders (Beefeaters being a nickname derived from their part payment of beef in the 1600s) are one of the many curiosities inside the Tower. Formed by Henry VII in 1485, they consist of 37 retired members of the armed services who live inside the complex, performing duties like the nightly 'Ceremony of the Keys' (reputedly the oldest military ceremony in the world) and making sure that the ravens never leave the tower causing, according to legend, the British kingdom to fall. However, nowadays their general duties mostly involve giving tours and posing for selfies. They also help to keep the queues of tourists orderly as once inside the complex you see various lines of people stretching out from doorways and snaking round the White Tower. The centrepiece of the fortress, it served as the keep for William the Conqueror and was whitewashed by Henry III in 1240 for no other reason than *keeping up with the Joneses* in France, hence its name. We stopped to admire its ancient beauty, described as the most complete 11th century

European palace by UNESCO, but really we were on our way to see one thing and one thing only (besides the gift shop that is): Her Majesty's Crown Jewels. We assumed that rooms full of sparkly metal and glittering stones would be most of interest to our merry mob of magpie-eyed miscreants. Inevitably the queue for the jewels experience was the longest, stretching round the complex, back through the entrance, and round St Katharine's Dock a few times. Honestly, it was a fair walk to find the end of it and when we did add a paltry chunk onto the end of this boa constrictor, we staff were met by an onslaught of complaints from the kids.

'Why we no go front?'. 'Why we last?'. 'I HAVE HUNGER!!!'

We tried to temper them with assurances of swift advance, but I didn't have much hope. After a minute or two of being at the back of a queue, you know what kind of queue it's going to be. You get your 'moderate paced movers', always inching forward milimetre by milimetre (can you 'inch forward by milimetres'?) Then there's the 'stop and start'. You wait a significant amount of time and then the queue zips forward, pulling you along like you're attached by a bungee cord, and usually revealing a whole portion of the queue that you never knew, and certainly wouldn't have believed, existed. Then you have the 'No move queues'. No matter how long you stand there, they never seem to advance. Time drips away and you spend your whole day out waiting for the couple in front displaying overly romantic public displays of affection to take a damn step forward, though they never do because the hundreds of people ahead of them aren't moving either. It's the sort of queue in which you start checking your pockets for rations.

So, we were most definitely in the latter variety of queue. Queuing with thirty five kids is a little easier than walking in the open with them but you still need to hurry them up, avoid them cutting under the ropes, and hope that members of the public don't start asking them awkward questions. They are also prone to undoing the retractable belt barriers and them snapping back. Reattaching those is like trying to win a cash prize in a TV game show. Everyone thinks they know the right solution until they try it for themselves. I was successful at the third attempt.

Eventually we made it to the exhibition entrance and after a brief bag search (bags on their front, unzipped, open for inspection - such pros), we made it into the dark corridors that provided the introduction to what we were about to behold. The pompous classical music started up, the projectors displayed pictures of royals from yesteryear, and the kids' eyes started hunting for the promised treasure. No phones allowed by order of the Beefeaters, they were forced to see the jewels for themselves. I like the 'No Photography' rules for attractions like these, even more so when click-happy tourists are forced to obey them. Many people choose to ignore the polite signs on walls banning photography, but they certainly don't ignore Beefeaters and screechy entrance staff. For me, the snap of the DSLRs ruin the experience as you always have the sensation of someone trying to photograph around you, so much so that you can't relax when you pause at an item to absorb it. Plus, it means no flash in your eyes after it hits the glass. I mean, you can Google Image it afterwards.

Of course, the most invasive photos are those of groups standing in front of (and therefore blocking) the very thing they want to prove they've visited. Occasionally, when I've had a day full of trying not to photo-bomb grinning groups, I'll give up being courteous and continue walking across people when they're having their photo taken, especially when the photographer takes so damn long to press the button. You'll see the majority of people, good-natured and considerate, stop as if an invisible barrier has been erected by the photographing party and wait until roughly a hundred shots from a variety of angles have been taken before they feel they can proceed. Often this is accompanied by an apology from the waiting walkers for happening to have the temerity to walk near a photo spot while others are exercising their vanity. I personally don't bother to wait nowadays. It's all digital film. Serves them right for holding people up with their narcissistic tendencies.

So, thanks to the barking commands from the woman in charge of the entrance, it was phones firmly in pockets for once and plenty of shuffling in the near-dark. Eventually, after navigating the maze of intro information, we arrived at the main event. The Crown Jewels consist of 140 items, all displayed at Jewel House at the Tower of London. Of the 140 items, there are 13 crowns (seven sovereign, six consort), six swords and five sceptres, all adorned with diamonds, rubies, sapphires, and other treasures possessed as a result of bloody wars and colonialism. All necessary items of regalia, though the one spoon and the one walking stick in the collection, as well as the 16 trumpets, are a tad surprising. I wonder if Elizabeth has ever had a go on one of the trumpets. While other monarchies in Europe have converted to secular coronations, the UK still retains the pomp and circumstance, though the coronation of the next monarch could signal some modern touches.

It's fair to say that you don't walk through a room full of gold and diamonds every day so in that respect the Crown Jewels are rather special and unique. You have some of the most objectively beautiful stones in the world displayed here. The Koh-i-noor diamond, for example, is one of the largest cut diamonds in the world (3.6cm by 3.2cm) and has had a fascinating history since it was mined in Golconda, India. It was ceded to Queen Victoria in 1849 after years of swapping between factions in India, Pakistan, Iran, and Afghanistan; the governments of which have all claimed rightful ownership and demanded its return, claims of which have been rejected by the British. Due to its checkered history of being fought over by men, only female members of the British Royal Family have worn it so as to avoid bringing bad luck to any man who wears it.

Still we shuffled through, glancing at the jewels while moving along the travelator. The downside of accompanying a school trip on one of these visits is that you can't really relax and enjoy the place much. Shepherding kids through exhibits requires eyes in the back of your head as well as the front and, due to the scatty, evasive nature of little ones, you need to be looking round all the time to see where they have got to. Head swivelling constantly, I patrolled the glass cabinets and stands tracking the stragglers, rounding them up whenever the group as a whole moved onto another part of the exhibit. This whole charade means that I didn't have much of a chance to admire and absorb many of the jewels, conscious that any concentration spent on any exhibit hands time to the monstrous crowd to swallow a child or two. This is where a smartphone camera would come in handy, if only they were permitted. Still, in spite of, or perhaps because of, the absence of their phones, the kids were in total awe of the shiny metal and stones.

'Woah, are those real diamonds? And real gold? How much are they worth?'

'Why? Are you thinking of stealing them and giving them to me as a birthday present?'

It wouldn't be the first time stealing the jewels crossed someone's mind. Perhaps the most extraordinary story to come out of the Tower of London is that of Thomas Blood's audacious attempt to steal the jewels in May 1671. Newly replaced after the restoration of the monarchy in England following the interregnum, Charles II's jewels were protected in a basement in Martin Tower by Talbot Edwards, the 77 year old Master of Jewel House. It was Edwards who Blood sweet-talked into allowing him to view the Crown Jewels before knocking him out with a mallet. Blood, dressed as a parson, flattened St Edward's Crown and hid it under his clerical coat while one of his accomplices, Hunt, broke the Sceptre with the Cross in two and another, Perrot, stuffed the Sovereign's Orb down his trousers. They jumped on horses waiting for them at St Catherine's Gate and would have got away with it had the crime not been discovered by Edwards' son. A chase ensued with Blood firing his pistols like a cowboy, but eventually he and his accomplices were arrested. Now, you might have thought that attempting to steal the Crown Jewels may put you in hot water with the king, however Blood seemed to utilise his Irish charm to wriggle his way out of any punishment for himself or for his men. Indeed, he was even granted £500 worth of land in his native Ireland. Perhaps Charles thought a little gardening would keep Blood from trying to undermine the monarchy, or possibly he was worried about an uprising in revenge by Blood's followers. There's even the sneaky theory that Charles, who was a bit short on cash at the time, was in cahoots with Blood. Whatever the real truth, it's quite a story, and somehow it still hasn't made it to Hollywood.

Fortunately we made it through the exhibit without any children missing or any jewels finding their way into little pockets and then suddenly we were out in the open again. For the length of time we waited, it felt an extraordinarily short exhibition, but I suppose it's quality rather than quantity that you see with the Crown Jewels. At least that's what we told the kids.

There are, as mentioned, 140 items on display in the exhibit, and possibly double that number of individual gifts available to buy from one of the five gift shops in the complex. This is what the kids had been looking forward to. The time had come for us to invade the gift shop. We'd limited the kids to around £100 each to spend, though they'd wanted to bring more of the hundreds they'd been given by their parents. That meant that each kid had enough to buy a few rip-off gifts for themselves and their family. In order to not swamp the shop, we split into three groups that entered at staggered times, but we still flooded the closely packed maze of gift tables, the kids grabbing plastic crap like Black Friday shoppers at midnight. Typically they'll pick up as much as they can, arrive at the till, have everything totalled up and then realise they're short of cash. Having a staff member on hand to facilitate payment helps, especially when little RJ dumps all the notes and the shrapnel he has on the till front. It amazes me what they pick up. The craze of the day seemed to be little toy horses and knights that retailed at around £30 each. Plastic swords and shields also sold well. The irony in all of this was that most of the kids were from China and pretty much every product they bought was made there, so really they'd just be returning Chinese products back to China via the Tower of London. Most of the profit though would be staying in the UK. Not a bad deal I suppose.

Once the kids had spent their hard unearned cash and we'd counted and recounted and recounted again the heads, we walked across the iconic Tower Bridge, marvelling at its regal towers and sky blue painted supports. For my money, it's the best looking bridge in the world. If only the other bridges crossing the Thames in Central London could be 10% as nice. Too often, London's bridges are decorated with bird shit, dull grey in colour (I'm looking at you Waterloo Bridge, you depressing hulk of concrete and bollards), and covered in either dirt, scaffolding, or both. There are exceptions though. After years of redevelopment, Blackfriars Railway Bridge is now the world's largest solar-powered bridge with passengers alighting above the Thames from the futuristic looking station. I also love going past Albert Bridge at night with its four thousand light bulbs aglow. The Millenium Bridge too, despite its initial problems, is a great example of how modern design can complement London's history. The illusion of St Paul's Cathedral seemingly being supported by the bridge gained by photos taken from the bridge's southern end has become one of London's iconic images. So, if these bridges can be beautiful, why can't the others? You can't really improve the appearance of the brown, rubbish strewn Thames, but you can do something about the bridges that cross it.

Back on the most beautiful bridge of them all, the kids could sense that we were on the final furlong and so galloped along Tower Bridge with their golden goodie bags swinging excitedly to meet the bus at the other end. Counting them on and forbidding them from eating the sweets they'd purchased at the Tower (oh what mean-spirited spoilsport teachers we are), we were off before rush hour properly set in (even on a Sunday it exists in London) and back home in time for dinner and birthday cake.

Although birthdays are your one special day of the year, they are best shared amongst as many people as you can find. Perhaps not quite as many as in the queue for the Crown Jewels (and they don't let you skip the line if it's your birthday, I did ask), but a reasonable number of people to strike up a rousing rendition of 'Happy Birthday' and to clap as you attempt to blow out 27 candles without inhaling all the smoke and sputtering spit on the icing. It can be hard to get excited about adding to the worrying tally of years, knowing full well they will only keep on ascending, but seeing thirty five young'uns munching happily on squares of triple layered sponge cake made me feel lucky that I could spend my special day with them, and optimistic for the year ahead. After all, now 27 years old and with 27 more UNESCO World Heritage sites to go to, this birthday felt like a year to come, rather than one gone.

UK UNESCO World Heritage site #2 of 28

City of Bath

Soaking up Roman Bath

Now seems about as good a time as any to introduce what I do for a living, when I'm not working on summer school day trips. I work as an English as a Foreign Language teacher, mostly online through Skype and other platforms, but occasionally face-to-face as well at a language academy. Students travel from across the globe to the UK to study the English language in order to pass university and get good employment in their native countries. While in the UK they have the opportunity to get out of the classroom (and out of the bedrooms their host families provide for them) to see the various tourist sites around. Being located in Bournemouth, the academy I was working at offers trips to places like the Jurassic Coast, Stonehenge (both also UNESCO World Heritage sites), Oxford, Winchester, Salisbury, London and Bath. Usually the academy utilises a tour company to show the students around, but during the summer the academy provides its own trips, charging students for a spot on a private bus to one of these locations. As they're running their own trips, they need a couple of teachers to go with the students to satisfy whatever requirements are set by external bodies, and so that's why I found myself waking up at 7am on a summer Saturday morning and setting off for work with a rucksack containing a packed lunch and a poorly photocopied, and utterly useless, map of central Bath.

My colleague and companion for the day, Mr Crouch, was sat on the bench across the road from the school when I arrived. He gruffed me a good morning and I was certain then that that was the most polite he was going to be towards me for the rest of the day. Not that he has anything against me, he's just one of those grumpy old fellows still stuck in a fairly dead-end job who resent anything and everything surrounding them. He's been at the academy since the year dot and signed up for all the trips he would be allowed on by the management. Whether he had nothing else to do other than complain audibly about the disparate state of today's youth to blissfully unaware lower intermediate English learners, or whether his wife simply wouldn't have him in the house on a Saturday (and I could perfectly understand her case should it be so) I had no idea, but he was an ever present on trips like these. He would lead the enforced tour of the destination and so thus had a captive audience to spout tabloid lies and Brexiteer propaganda to. All I had to do was keep my mouth shut, shepherd the stragglers, and collect my dosh at the end of the day. It was a hard job indeed.

Still, opportunities like these afforded me the guise of being paid to travel (albeit with the aforementioned company) and see a World Heritage site on someone else's dime. I decided to stick to the positive line running through my head, convincing myself that this trip wouldn't be the unmitigated disaster it threatened to be, and enjoy the advantages of taking in the glorious, regal city of Bath on a balmy summer's day. Dreamy, but we had to get there first.

'We've got the cripple on wheels today'. I turned round to face the direction that Mr Crouch was looking in and spotted one of the students crossing the road over to us with her friends. She wheeled herself onto our side of the pavement and came over to us to wait for the bus to arrive with the other students who were gathering in dribs and drabs.

'I don't know what she's thinking trying to come on a trip like this. Ridiculous. I complained of course, said she'd slow us all down, but they weren't having any of it. Said she'd booked and had to come. Crazy'.

I had no idea how to respond to this apart from acknowledging that Bath was famously hilly with its fair share of cobblestones. Still, it was more the selfie-obsessed girls from Colombia that would be slowing us down, rather than the student in the wheelchair. I just bit my tongue. It was never worth calling Mr Crouch out, just placating him took skill.

We stood there twiddling our thumbs for a while until the coach came roaring round the corner, mounting the kerb and almost skittling the students standing on the edge of the pavement. The students gathered around the coach door, but Mr Crouch waded through the crowd to meet the bus driver and board the bus first. The students then clambered on, a few kind guys offering to help carry our disabled student onboard and put her wheelchair away in the luggage compartment. She sat at the front of the coach while everyone else gravitated to the back. As everyone well knows, the back of the bus is where the cool kids sit, it surely works like this in any school bus around the world, and then the bus is filled from the back, bar the front few rows that separate the kids from the teachers sitting at the front. No one wants to sit there. It is the No Man's Land, even when the students are adults themselves. No one wants to sit next to a teacher, no matter what age they are.

Gloria was at the back of the crowd of students piling on to the bus with me. She was certainly the oldest student in our party, in her fifties she had told me in one of our classes, but you would never know it from looking at her. Though most of the students at the academy are in their early twenties or so, there are also students in their forties and fifties who want to learn English to pursue a change in career or take on the challenge of improving their language skills. Gloria hailed from Venezuela, though I supposed that she'd spent some time living abroad before. She was one of those students every teacher wishes to have a class full of. Enthusiastic, always happy, inquisitive. She was also objectively beautiful. She boarded last, just in front of me, and was pounced upon by Mr Crouch.

'Ah now, Gloria, I have a seat for you here at the front next to me. Come and sit down'.

You could see she had been placed on the spot, the argument of whether to find a seat amongst her fellow students or accept the insistence of a teacher to spend the journey seated next to him whirring around her brain.

'Come on now. We've got the best seats to see out the front'.

'Oh, ok teacher'. She swung past Mr Crouch standing in the aisle and sat down on the window seat next to his carrier bag containing a flask of tea and that morning's Daily Mail.

'Right ho, everyone on board Mr Lewry?'

'I think that's all of us', I responded positively, veneered with a coating of enthusiasm.

'You only think so? Good god. Right, I'll do a check.' He grabbed the register and trekked up the aisle, barking the names of the students out in their English mispronunciations and berating them when they didn't

respond quick enough. Eventually we ascertained that everyone who was meant to be present was indeed present and we were able to drive off the kerb and on our way north to Bath.

Our bus driver was a Scotsman with the hair and accent of Billy Connolly, and he and Mr Crouch found a good deal of common ground when it came to matters of politics and society's ailments. They swapped remarks on the poor state of roads, immigration, the best routes to take to various parts of England, and the pointlessness of taking 40 foreigners sixty miles up the road just so they can take selfies and drink Starbucks frappuccinos. All this within capable earshot of half the bus. It wasn't so much a conversation as just an exchange of views. One would whinge a little about something and then the other would rant about something else completely different. No questions were ever asked. It was simply two men talking at each other. Neither commented on the other's opinion, they would simply just state their own. It was very much as if neither of them had ears, just mouths. Gloria just sat there quietly, nodding politely and feigning interest whenever Mr Crouch chose to elaborate to her personally. I couldn't wait to get to Bath.

After miles of country roads we pulled into the coach park in Bath and everyone, as every student does on a school bus, immediately got up and started making for the exit. Not before they were shouted down though by Mr Crouch and had a dodgily photocopied map of Bath, the same that was crumpled down at the bottom of my bag, thrust into their palms. Perhaps he was unaware that every student had a phone with Google Maps on it that would provide them with a far more accurate plan of Bath. Or perhaps by giving a map to a student you can ensure yourself that they will never get lost. If they do, well, clearly they've got shit for brains because they've got a blurry black and white photocopy with squiggly lines and symbols for the locations of churches and pharmacies on their person and how could they possibly not find their way with this?

The students were technically allowed to go their own separate ways from this point, but Mr Crouch was to give a personal guided tour of the city of Bath for all those who came with him (and that would be everyone). We all gathered outside the bus and proceeded to Green Park Station Market. In fairness, it was a great suggestion. The students needed their mid-morning coffees and an opportunity to buy knick-knacks. We entered the cavernous former rail station (opened 1860, closed 1966) with strict instructions to meet outside on the steps at 11.15. As it was a Saturday, the market was bustling with fresh produce stalls and plenty of interesting second-hand and arts stands. I wandered slowly through the crowds with a coffee, watching the students as they gazed bemusedly at pork pies and jars of homemade jam. As well as the market which takes over the parking spaces inside the former station on a Wednesday and a Saturday, there are a few permanent shops within the rooms which I suppose once provided waiting facilities or ticket offices for the station when it was operational. The building space was left derelict until the 1980s when the market started up and began to showcase local businesses and producers to the public. It's a great space and one that still continues to be in demand from consumers. People want to interact with what they are buying, they want the seller (and indeed probably the maker) of the woodwork or the cupcake they are buying to tell them the story behind it. It's fantastic. Saying that, there is a huge Sainsbury's supermarket at the other end of the market where I suppose you can buy the same veggies at a cheaper price and with next to no imperfections. It's a choice that fortunately we all have, and thankfully there are those who are determined to complement their supermarket shopping with local produce from independents. The two can coexist happily together, as Green Park Station so wonderfully demonstrates.

At around 11.10 we had most of the students gathered on the steps, happier now that they had caffeine and sugar running through their veins. By 11.15 we had more or less everyone, but when the register was taken at 11.20 we realised that there was one of our party missing. We waited a while and then impatience got the better of Mr Crouch. I was sent in to hunt down Alp, the missing student, and to bring him forthwith. It wasn't an easy task. I barely remembered what the student looked like as he wasn't one from my classes and I had to find him in a large market packed with people. I set about my task with pace, sprint walking through the crowds, face-checking from vantage points, inspecting crowds gathered around particular stalls. It was all quite fun actually, like being Bond sent in to find a baddy trying to escape, but I still had to find the guy and I couldn't go back to Mr Crouch empty-handed. Fortunately, I spotted Alp in the back of a coffee shop called Beyond The Kale and was able to apprehend him in the gentlest way possible. He wasn't enjoying a coffee, in fact I don't think he'd ordered anything at all (for the best, as we certainly weren't waiting for a panini to be heated up), but he was charging up his phone. I indicated that he was rather late and that we had been waiting a while just for him, but I let Mr Crouch deal out the hairdryer treatment, which he duly performed with relish.

Suitably scolded, Alp joined the back of the group as we walked up to see some of the most beautiful and famous architecture in Bath, namely the Circus and the Royal Crescent. On the way up, which, I'm pleased to report, our friend in the wheelchair achieved with no difficulty whatsoever, we passed by the Jane Austen Centre on Gay Street where ladies dressed in Regency costume did their best to convince us to enter the centre and engage in all things Austen. The writer was in Bath for five years due to her father moving there after his decision to quit as rector of the Anglican churches in Steventon and Deane in Hampshire. In reality, Austen's time in Bath was quite a dry time for her writing wise and it has been supposed that she was deeply unhappy living there, either that or she was having too much fun in the fashionable and thriving spa resort to sit down and write. Of course, two of her most famous works, Northanger Abbey and Persuasion, feature

Bath as locations and so the city has a just right to squeeze as much money out of tourists who dream of meeting their Mr Darcy and dressing up in flouncy dresses with corsets suffocating them. We weren't to be persuaded, God knows what Mr Crouch would have made of it all, but I'm sure it's just great if your idea of England is based upon the various film adaptations of Pride and Prejudice.

A little further on and we were at the Circus. Our leader-cum-tour guide informed us all about the use of Bath stone in the architecture and we could appreciate the honey colour of the three curved buildings that make up the circle surrounding the London Plane trees in the centre. It's a wonderful example of Georgian architecture; the effect distorted by the multicoloured cars parked around the circle, but enhanced by the sunlight that tries to curl itself round the many pillars. Further on you have the Royal Crescent, instantly recognisable and a treat for the eyes. Urban architecture at its very grandest and most supreme. 150m of curved facades designed by John Wood hide individually built houses behind them (if viewed from the rear, you can see a mixture of house types and heights), but the effect from the front is outstanding, and the grass in front provides a space for the public to enjoy picnics and what-not with the Georgian architecture as their background. The students took full advantage of the selfie opportunities while Mr Crouch looked on bemusedly. My job was to harry the stragglers and so once I arrived with the Colombian chicas after pausing every five seconds for photos on the way up, we were led back down to the city centre by Mr Crouch. The promise of lunch was enough to get the students off their tired feet and follow their glorious leader once again.

The lunch venue was up to each student's own choice, but Mr Crouch was determined to have a selection of his favoured students join him in a cafe chain called Boston Tea Party. A few were coerced into accompanying him, but the majority went off in search of other nourishment. The few that joined him, as I observed from a bench across the street from the restaurant where I was eating my own packed lunch, seemed indecisive as to whether sitting down for a meal with their teacher was really what they wanted to do, especially as the cafe was packed and seating was at a premium. I had a few items left over from a picnic I'd enjoyed with a friend the day before, so I took the opportunity to enjoy a break from the group and some peace and quiet. I was joined by one of the students, an amiable young chap from Turkey, who was able to offer me his perspective on UNESCO World Heritage listed Bath. *'It's old, busy, lots of hills, nice buildings, interesting'.* I decided that perhaps we'd better focus on adjectives if he were to be in my class the next term.

Perhaps conscious of Alp's treatment that morning, everyone was right on time at the meeting place outside the entrance to the Roman Baths after lunch. We had a group ticket so sped past the queue at the entrance, through the sliding door emblazoned with the UNESCO WHS logo, and into the grand entrance hall where we collected audio guides. Each student immediately tuned into their native language despite the encouragement from myself and Mr Crouch to listen in English, but at least they were keen to learn as much about the extraordinary baths as possible. The audio guide was excellently done, with options to select a normal tour, a child-friendly tour, and thirdly the option to listen to Bill Bryson's perspective on various parts of the baths. I'm a huge admirer of Bryson's writing and so to have him accompany me as it were around the baths added an extra special element to the experience. I would even go as far as encouraging every heritage site in the UK to hire Bill Bryson to provide an audio tour. The mix of humour and information with his soft, calming voice is a refreshing antidote to the litany of facts often pompously spouted by the rigidly posh voices that do the audio guides in other heritage sites. These audio guides do have their drawbacks though; they can often be heard as you pass other people and they force everyone to walk around as if they're on the phone, but generally they're great and a fountain of information if the site hasn't chosen the lazy option of just recording an actor reading the information boards. The ones at the Roman baths are superb.

The audio guide leads you round to the left and outside to a view over the bath itself and in that moment you are transported back thousands of years to the age of the Romans. Ignore the rooftops in the distance with their TV dishes, ignore the sounds of the city streets behind you, you are here in Roman times with grand statues of emperors looking down upon the murky rectangular water feature below. Of course, if you really were in Roman times, you wouldn't have had this view at all. The terrace that gives you the first of many fantastic views of the bath was constructed in 1897 when the baths were opened to the public. In fact, not much about the Roman baths as we see it today is Roman. The baths were seemingly destroyed in the 6th century by Anglo-Saxons and subsequent renovations have given us the 'Roman' baths that we see today. Only the rough parts of the lower walls, some steps, and the bath itself remain from Roman days.

The Romans used this place as a religious shrine dedicated to the goddess Sulis Minerva and as a spa complex, however it was Bladud, a legendary king of the Britons, who is supposed to have discovered the curing properties of Bath's waters as a result of his leprosy disappearing while in the area. The water itself comes from rain in the nearby Mendip Hills where it descends thousands of metres below the earth and is warmed to temperatures pushing 100 degrees celsius by geothermal energy before rising through fissures and faults in the limestone to the surface where it emerges at a rate of over a million gallons a day at a temperature of 46 degrees. Nowadays of course, bathing isn't permitted (I had brought my swimming shorts and everything) but visitors are curious to touch the water with their hands just to check that, yes, it is indeed water.

So, even though very little of what you are seeing is

Roman, you still get that sense of being back in ancient times. Perhaps it's the actors wandering around in togas that does it. There are plenty of Roman artefacts displayed in the various museum rooms around the complex, some of the best examples of Roman Britain, with some of the most impressive items like the Gorgon's Head and the temple pediment being given deserved space to be appreciated. The Gorgon, the most well-known of which is Medusa, is typically a female with snakes for hair and the ability to turn anyone who looks at them to stone. Ironically, nowadays we know about them thanks to their stone carvings (perhaps she once took a look in a mirror), but the purpose of the stone gorgon at Bath was to look down upon those who entered the spa from a height of around 15 metres, an imposing welcome to a place of relaxation and calm. The gorgon displayed in the museum at Bath still has the ability to turn people to stone, though the curse only lasts as long as the time it takes to snap a series of selfies.

In fairness, it is spellbinding when viewed from the top of a platform that gives you an eye-to-eye view of the sculpture. Following the steps down from the platform there are even more sculptures and stone carvings to discover including the Roman curse tablets which detail the prayers and pains of citizens who had had items stolen. The prayers are directed at the goddess Sulis Minerva and ask for justice to be avenged on the naughty Roman who nicked their clothes while they were enjoying a bath in the thermal waters. The Romans invented a lot, but perhaps changing room lockers would have solved the problem. They certainly had enough coins to use in them. The curse tablets are inscribed on the UNESCO Memory of the World register, the only item from Roman Britain on this list, but still the practical joke of hiding little Remus' clothes while he's in the bath so he has to wander around covering his bits, pleading his older brother to return his modesty, lives on. The threats on the tablets though, such as *'be accursed in (his) blood, and eyes and every limb and even have all (his) intestines quite eaten away'* shows that perhaps the Romans couldn't take a joke very well.

The audio guide, both the pontifical voice of the normal tour guide and the dulcet tones of Mr Bryson, led me round the exhibits and various spa rooms. Occasionally I bumped into students, but mostly I was free to wander around at my own pace and enjoy the exhibits. When I'd reached the end of the tour I walked out into the drizzle of a summer's Saturday in Bath and found the students in huddles, all waiting to be taken back to the bus and back to Bournemouth. Mr Crouch was out there too and so we made our way back to the coach park with just a few students who had chosen to skip the baths and go shopping instead not with us. 4.30pm was the departure time and by that time we were sat on the bus, out of the increasingly intense rain, waiting for the last few students to show up. As soon as 4.30pm struck, Mr Crouch was ready to get going, even without the couple of students who were either lost or delayed.

'Right, time to go. If they're not here in the next minute, we'll leave without them'.

It wasn't an empty promise. The coach driver was Mr Crouch's willing accomplice. It took the pleading of the missing students' friends to stop the bus leaving the students in Bath. Mr Crouch attempted to direct them by phone back to the coach park, but with increasing frustration at their inability to understand compass directions.

'Turn south, walk along Stall Street, what do you mean you don't know which direction south is in. Good God! Just... Oh I give up. It's the same bloody place we got off the bus this morning. You can't have forgotten that!'

Eventually, completely soaked, the students turned up and we were able to head back down the country lanes to Bournemouth. Overall, it was an eventless journey back. Mr Crouch dried his wet socks and shoes on the dashboard, his bare feet providing a succulent pong to the bus, and he and the bus driver resumed their trade in disparaging remarks from the morning. I stayed quietly in my seat, not daring to barge in, and reflected on the city of Bath and its World Heritage status. It's been suggested that Bath is simply a tourist attraction disguised as a city. Some tourists have been heard to ask whether Bath is even open during the winter. With its Georgian architecture, Jane Austen inspired costume actors, and proliferation of tourist tat shops, it's been compared to a 19th century Britain theme park. Of course, it's not. There are people who really live in houses in the Royal Crescent and the Circus (and what lucky people they are). The Romans and many other peoples that passed through southern England really did live their lives here, though in the pursuit of pleasure rather than expansion of empire. Bath has always been, and continues to be, a delightfully pleasurable city to visit, that much hasn't changed over thousands of years, but there is a concern that it is stuck in the past compared to many other UK cities that have embraced industry and modernity. For my money, I'd rather it stayed the way it is. If you want modern development, just go to Bristol. You'll find 'development' in abundance there. Bath: you stay just as you are, you delightful little cocoon of Englishness.

UK UNESCO World Heritage Site #3 of 28

Dorset and East Devon Coast

Dinos and doors in Dorset and Devon

Once myself and the few other cyclists were onboard the chains started rattling and the Sandbanks chain ferry began making its way across the narrow strip of water to Shell Bay. Five minutes later and we had arrived at the natural oasis of bare beaches and wild gorse, a stark contrast to the millionaires' houses on the other side. I mounted my bike and pedalled off the ramp. For some reason Toto's 'Africa' always plays in my head whenever I go across the water from Bournemouth for a cycle around Studland. Perhaps it's the straight road with sand spilling onto its sides or the barren expanse of wilderness everywhere you look. It's a beautiful introduction into the Purbecks which take you up to the proud ruins of Corfe Castle and then even further up into the windy hills before rewarding you for your efforts with the Lulworth Estate. It was a route I'd cycled a few times before so I sped along the country lanes, anxious to set a marker early on in the day and beat the Saturday hordes.

18 miles later and it was now 10.30. I knew the place where I was heading for the first stop along the coast would be filling up with tourists by the second. The Durdle Door, whose picture features amongst every postcard collage along this coastline, is a magnet for every visitor to this part of the world for its spectacular setting and for the ample opportunity it provides to amateur photographers, and by that I mean selfie-takers. It's only a five mile ride from Wool, skirting through the quaint village of West Lulworth. After a while the undulating roads give way to a turning into a caravan park and soon after I arrived at a car park with a National Trust information shack and a tea van. With no obvious bike parking available, I found a wooden fence to lock my bike against, hoping that no one with a chainsaw in the back of their car had the evil desire to nick her.

From the car park it's a steep downward shuffle to the Durdle Door viewpoint and access to the beach. Like goats descending down a dusty mountainside, the other tourists and I made our ways gingerly down to two large green rubbish bins on the edge of a cliff. A slight anti-climax perhaps until you step past the giant receptacles and realise the view that welcomes you. At the left hand end of a small, sweeping bay, a pointy green hill whips its tail out into the perfectly clear waters below. The tail flicks up and then down into the water, creating a large gap, an arch that seems too big, too perfect to have been created by such an unpredictable force as the sea. It drew to mind the seat of a rocking horse sized for a giant to sit astride it. It's justifiably popular. I peeked down below to the beach and witnessed small crowds of posing, posturing people in front of elected photographers. Jumping up, raising their arms, grinning eye to eye. Towards the bottom of the cliff there was also a group of a white hard-hatted individuals with clipboards. Either a tour-group had gone totally health and safety conscious or they were there to inspect the rocks and fossils that this stretch of coast is so well-known for. I suppose, if you want to give them a grander name, you could call them 'dinosaur hunters'.

The Jurassic Coast has been part of UNESCO's World Heritage list since 2001, though it is known as the Dorset and East Devon coast on the list. Of course though, 'Jurassic Coast' sounds much more attractive to tourists so it is advertised as this across the 95 mile stretch which starts in Studland and winds its way west to Exmouth. The rocks actually come from three geological time periods (Triassic, Cretaceous and Jurassic) though of course the name, in yet another cunning marketing ploy, only uses the most well-known of these periods of time (thank you Steven Spielberg and Universal). The Jurassic part of the coastline was the part I was exploring today with a few Cretaceous interruptions; the Triassic part starts near Lyme Regis and continues westward from there. That would be coming up in a few days' time.

Cycling westward I was actually heading back in time, the relatively newer rocks starting in Studland, though with an age of around 65 million years, it's hard to define them as young. Fortunately there is a relatively new walking path that traverses the entire length of the coast. Finished in 1978, the South West Coast path has been called one of the great walks of the world, stretching 630 miles up and down Dorset, Devon, Cornwall and Somerset hills. If you were to walk the entire path, you would climb the equivalent height of four Mount Everests. I can confirm that simply walking up one of the many hilly cliffs feels like an Everest ascent, especially if, like me, you choose to take your 16kg bike along with you for the hike.

The plan was to nip off-road and take the bike along the SW coast path to St Catherine's Chapel where the road next meets the coast and cycle on to Weymouth from there. What I didn't take into account was White Nothe. Sticking up from the coast like a stubby white nose from which it is named, it rises relentlessly up into the sky, a daunting prospect when you find yourself at the bottom of it with a touring bike. I'll probably have to walk this one, I thought to myself.

Not many hikers traversing these cliffs take a bike with them, mainly because to do so would (and realistically should) be classed as insane. Added to that, a bike is simply not a necessary tool when scrambling up the near vertical side of a hill. Still, there I was. Gripping onto the drops and pushing against the unstoppable force of gravity while rolling from one muddy foothold to the next. It was a knackering task made even worse by the sensation that other walkers on this trail, husband and wife teams in matching North Face coats, were sneakily watching my progress while pretending to take breathers. I had started strongly, giddy with the false pretence of my own strength, but then made the fatal error of turning round to see how far I'd come and realising that actually I'd only just started the slope that turned into the slog of crisscrossing paths snaking up the hillside ahead of me. Steeling my resolve, I wobbled on up the hill, stopping occasionally to allow my breath to catch up with me. As the hill became steeper I realised that holding the handlebars with both hands was not the best method and so switched to right hand on the saddle post and the left remaining on the handlebars. It worked better and I was able to virtually carry the bike up the hill which, though heavier work, made it far easier to walk myself as I was no longer tripping over the pedals. Within minutes, though after what seemed like hours, I was at the gentler slopes of the peak. The couple who I had followed up the hill were sat on the summit looking down at their achievement, occasionally stealing glances in my direction. Another couple were walking towards me, about to descend. I steadied my breathing as best I could to make it appear as if carrying a steel bike up a hill were a simple task for a man as strong as I, though I'm sure the stymied huffing and puffing was more of a giveaway than just being honest with myself and them. Never again, I thought to myself, though gazing down at the next hill, and the next, and the next, and the one following that, I knew that I'd be breaking that promise pretty soon.

Fortunately White Nothe was the toughest of the set, and once I'd done three or four ups and downs I was back to the flats thanks to a crafty cut across a field to an alternative path that cut a straight line along the bank of a hill going my way. The path was just about wide enough for my thin tyres and, though it occasionally took me through brambles and the odd cow pat landmine, at least it wasn't the main path which swooped down to the sea and then rose back up at inclines greater than most roller coasters. Along the way, I encountered a few walkers, though none I supposed were doing the whole 95 miles in one go. I was fortunate in parts that the path would widen or even split into several tracks at opportune overtaking points, though I almost met a few occasions when I was engaged in a game of chicken with stomping ramblers. I was now cycling along the ruts in the ground and so hoped that walkers might part from their groups and allow me to easily split them, but there were inevitably a few groups for whom I was invisible and they required me to plough through them, flattening them to the ground with tyre marks tattooed along their lifeless bodies. In fairness, I did ring my bell to warn them.

Leaving the few disgruntled walking groups behind me, I did eventually find the tarmac and from there the zip round the coast into Weymouth was a simple matter of sitting and pedalling on pristine surfaces. Ah, how good it feels to cycle on a flat road after traversing the rocky, muddy slopes of a bridleway. With a bit of wind behind me I zipped along to Weymouth and rounded the bay jubilant with the fact that the cycling for the day was mainly done.

I like Weymouth. An impressive wall of terraced apartments and BnBs face onto a stretch of sandy beach which continues round to a harbour from where you can get the ferry over to the Channel Islands and to the continent. It's busy for a seaside town that you would assume has passed its heyday. So busy it seems in fact that cycling along the promenade is prohibited from Good Friday to Hallowe'en, a measure that seems a little heavy-handed, though probably is safer for all concerned. Keeping to the road that runs along the prom, I cycled until I reached the harbour, easily identifiable by the white tower that rises up from it. Quite what this tower with no windows was doing I had no idea, but I was curious to find out. Google Maps had said something about the 'Jurassic Skyline' which sounded promising. I was expecting a viewing platform like the excellent Spinnaker tower in Portsmouth, but this had no recognisable way of scaling it. Rolling closer through a car park I found the answer. For a fiver you could sit in a 360 degree pod that would rise up the tower and give you a view of the surrounding area. There was one issue though. The tower reception was blasting out some awful dramatic theme park music that made it seem as though Mum, Dad and little Johnny were about to embark on the Apollo 11 mission to the moon. I watched from the car park as a trickle of tourists filled up the pod, navigating their way through queue lines, ice creams dripping down their hands as they waddled, and decided that for today, it wasn't for me. Maybe another time, but I wasn't sure I could stomach the tourist shit today.

I decided to find a bite to eat and continue on the bike to Portland. Gratefully, while navigating the multi-lane traffic of Weymouth's interior, I happened upon the Rodwell Trail, a former rail line between Weymouth and Portland that had closed in 1965 after one hundred years of transporting passengers and stones, and is now a mighty fine 3.4km long walking and cycling trail. Coming off the main road, I cycled down a slope and was swept onto the former rail bed, a few hard pedals enough to send me flying past flowerbeds and through tree tunnels. It was glorious. Families cruised along in mother and duckling formation and walkers let their dogs furrow in the undergrowth as they plodded along. The trail brought to mind a similar former rail line that had been converted into a trail near my grandparent's old home in Bramley, Surrey. Stations along the line had been restored with information about the trains that once passed along the line. Tunnels under roads showed the black remains of steam engines passing through them and the trees formed a guard of honour, leaning over to touch their neighbour across from them. There are trails like these throughout the UK. Though the closing of the rail lines following the Beeching reports in the Sixties meant that many lines between small towns and villages closed down, in many cases these wonderful escapes into nature opened up traffic-free opportunities for the local population. And often, though a train service could never be financially sustained between these places, they provide an off-road walking and cycling route between places that people actually go between.

Portland is actually an island and so once I came out of the woods and to the end of the trail I had to cycle across the busy road and then continue over a bridge. Now running parallel to my right was Chesil Beach, a misnomer really as it's really more of a barrier of stones (a tombolo to those of you who like the proper name of things) that protects the Fleet Reserve from the waves of the English Channel. Still, it's a heck of a barrier at 17 miles long. I parked the bike and then scaled the mountain of potato sized stones to the summit of the pile. A vast long peak of stones stretches beyond where the eye can see and straddling the summit you can view the calm, bountiful waters of the reserve to your right, while on the other side the ocean lashes at the immovable mound of stones. I was awestruck. A tour group of English language students took their necessary splurge of snapchats and then struggled back over the summit of the mound to their tour bus. A few fishermen were sat resolutely waiting for a bite, the wind battering their little tents. I took in the panorama and then felt it was time to learn something about this phenomenon other than it's obvious physical features.

The free visitor centre was pretty much the perfect place to answer my curiosities and I wandered around the colourful and interactive displays looking at the types of nature that call this area home and the science behind why a great line of stones happened to end up between the land and the sea. It emerged tens of thousands of years ago after the last ice age and is still evolving today with the end at Portland moving eastward more than 15cm per year. The waves also affect the size of the stones with those at the Portland end measuring more like potatoes and those in the west at West Bay more like peas due to the waves moving the larger pebbles faster laterally.

Of course today Chesil Beach is more famous for Ian McEwan's eponymous novel and the subsequent film, from which the phrase 'to do a Chesil Beach' has now arisen. The less said about it the better, but I at least derived some pleasure from the location!

Portland is a curious place, described by Thomas Hardy as *'the peninsular carved by Time out of a single stone'*. It is stone that made it rich and famous, indeed Christopher Wren's rebuilding of St Paul's Cathedral used Portland stone. The eastern face of Buckingham Palace is also made from Portland stone, a high-quality and prized stone that has been dug out of the island since Roman times. In fact many of the buildings on the UK's UNESCO World Heritage list are made from Portland stone, and many others around the world too including the UN building in New York.

The excavation of this valuable resource has left Portland pockmarked with quarries, though walking along the island's western coast I happened upon the genius revitalisation of these sites. Tout Quarry is now a nature reserve and an open-air sculpture exhibition. I walked up from a lovely cafe at the far end of Chesil beach along the South West Coast path that encircles the island and ventured into the abandoned quarry, hunting for the sculptures an information board had promised. Treading along the paths past monolithic stones, you notice patterns, perfectly spherical holes and even dragons and elephants carved into the stones. I spent a happy half an hour wandering curiously around what was once a place of work since turned into a gallery for sculptors and then somehow found myself spat out onto the main road. In my search to rejoin the coast path without retracing my steps (I, like many of you too I suspect, will never simply turn 180 degrees and retrace my steps), I happened again upon a remarkable place: St George's church. You may have guessed that this rather inelegant building (a *'masculine show'* to architect John Vanbrugh's eyes) be built of Portland stone and you'd be right. Approaching it I wasn't sure what it was, but the mossy headstones in the grounds around it gave the answer away. Like the quarry, the church too seemed to have been repurposed for art (and why not, I feel). The b-side contemporary arts festival was using the wonderfully atmospheric settings of the church to showcase photos of Portland's residents using an Afghan camera box and I popped in and was promptly transported back to the Victorian era with the church crammed with wooden benches with vertical backs and little doors for each row. The church is now redundant but is in the care of the Churches Conservation Trust who had cannily balanced collection buckets on the ends of the aisles. I took a peek at the art, but marvelled more at the inside of the church. It truly was like being transported back in time, albeit with modern day tourists snapping away at its curiosities.

Back outside in the balmy late summer weather, I rediscovered the path and followed it back along the coast to the cafe where I'd left the bike. To my left, the Atlantic Ocean and the obvious signs of discarded waste from years of excavating. To my right, possibly the ugliest apartment blocks with a sunset seaview to exist in the country. It totally befuddles me how the designers of these blocks of flats (I can't call them architects) managed to build boxes with paint scabs and tiny windows to look out at such a magnificent view. Dirty windows with curtains drawn across them, overgrown grass and rubbish blowing about in the breeze. It just looked so at odds with the surroundings. How well humans manage to uglify beauty.

Walking further I came across a bunch of kids hanging out in an abandoned bunker. The stench of pot hung in the air. I could hear them yelping and yawping inside. Part of me wanted to stop by and go talk to them. Who were they? What were their dreams and ambitions? Did they go to this old WW2 lookout every day to smoke away their worries and chat shit about their absent peers? Other rather deeply inquisitive questions sprung to mind, but I just kept on walking. Something about a slightly older guy going into the hangout to simply chat struck me as something that they wouldn't understand or be willing to go along with. I do wish it were possible to find out things about the people around you more without seeming like a nosy weirdo. I often think this in train stations and in cafes. Who are you? What are doing here? What have you done today and what will you do later on and with who? It's intriguing. You could think that by someone's appearance that they would be doing nothing special at all or that what they are thinking is totally worthless and mundane. I mean, it could well be complete drivel and then you convince yourself that everyone in the world must be like that and you never wonder these things about anyone else until the next time your brain spots some kids doing something you could only have dreamt of when you were young yourself and being slightly jealous of them being so carefree and rebellious. Still, going over to a group of people and involving yourself in their evening is deeply regarded as weird. Here, and everywhere else around the world I suspect. I satisfied myself by wondering the answers to the questions I would have asked the stoned kids high up on the rocky cliffs of the stone quarries of Portland.

I was still wondering these trifling matters as I pedalled swiftly back along the Rodwell Trail which spat me out onto a murderous crossroads before I arrived back in Weymouth. My legs were tired, my brain was tired, but at least I'd covered about a third of the route. Tomorrow was another big day. With that in mind, I let Saturday night in Weymouth party on without me, and enjoyed a fitful slumber.

The next morning it was back on the bike, though with fewer hills to conquer. The cycle from Weymouth to Lyme Regis takes around three and a half hours, a fair pace for 34 miles, and follows the length of Chesil beach which is near by but not close enough to see it. Fortunately I'd seen the length of it from Portland the day before. The road led me through the picturesque villages of Dorset and West Bay where I diverted a little to spin around the harbour and take a look at the spectacular burnt orange cliff-face on East Beach, the land cut like a cake before it reaches the sea with the sand below a few crumbs off the sheer sides of the cliffs. It's a bold sight to behold. Unfortunately it was the last taste of natural beauty for a while as the country roads turned into the vicious A35 through Chideock, a village that I'm sure was once a pleasant place to live but now has lorries thundering through the middle of it. I too had to cut through, holding on for dear life as huge vehicles overtook me on the hill going out of the village. I had to grit my teeth and bear the A road until Morcombelake where I took the first opportunity I had to latch onto a smaller road that would take me through Charmouth and into Lyme Regis.

Relieved to have the worst of the roads over and done with, I swooped down to the centre of Lyme Regis, skidding to a halt outside the Lyme Regis museum and scattering the seagulls feasting on fallen chips. Lyme Regis is perhaps the best place to get a feel of the dinosaur history of the Dorset and East Devon coast. Pretty much any child who grew up in the south of England has been to Lyme Regis and has spent an afternoon fossil hunting. It's kind of a rite of passage. It's certainly not just an activity for kids though. Commercial fossil hunting is big business down in

Lyme, though generally the best season is the winter after a heavy rainfall. I was, according to geologist and tour guide Chris, in Lyme at the very worst time. Still though, he was sure we'd at least find something to take back home. In fact, we were encouraged to put things in our pockets.

'The Jurassic Coast here in Lyme Regis is a World Heritage site, just like Stonehenge. However, they're generally not best pleased if you try to slice off a bit of one of the henges for yourself. Here though, if you find it, it's yours'.

It sounds a rather blase attitude towards a World Heritage site that surely demands protection and conservation, but actually any fossil found lying on the beaches at Lyme Regis just isn't useful to geologists. Without knowing whereabouts on the cliff it came off, it's difficult to know how old it is. Essentially, it's just going to be taken by the sea at some point, so you might as well take it for your mantelpiece. It's not illegal, there are no fossil police out to catch anyone who slips a stone into their pocket. Of course, the main attraction for parents is that this solves the gift shop nightmare. Despite the plethora of gift shops in Lyme, the best souvenirs are freely available on the beach. This also means that anyone can come down on their lucky day and find a fossil that could sell for a hundred, a thousand, even tens of thousands. For this reason there are people, professional fossilists, who spend their working days down on the beach scouring the sands and stones for ancient remains of dinosaurs. Our guide Chris, complete with dinosaur skeleton t-shirt and brown leather hat, is one of them. Walking round the museum afterwards I saw quite a few remarkable fossils attributed to him and the other two guides that led us down the beach for a little fossil hunting. Some people have made a relative fortune out of it. Indeed, in 2017 a rare plesiosaur, 90% complete, was dug up on Lyme Regis beach and was sold for £90,000 at auction.

So what can you find down on Lyme Regis beach, aside from your early retirement and yacht in the Caribbean? It seemed that Chris was bigging up the discoveries a fair bit. Sure, Lyme Regis beach is famous for it, but surely nowadays with mass tourism and commercial fossilists there can't be much of worth around. Just a few bits of Fool's Gold discarded by those who know better than to pick it. The way that Chris talked about it seemed that all we'd have to do was walk a little bit down the beach and we'd all find a dinosaur each. If we didn't all find a whole dinosaur to ourselves, even in the worst time of year and at the tail end of the tourist season pretty much everyone went home with at least something. This is due to erosion. They might not put it on the tourist brochures, but Lyme Regis is home to Europe's largest active landslide. Essentially it keeps the beach topped up with fossils as the cliffs retreat. In 2008, three quarters of a million tonnes of cliff fell down in one go, keeping the geologists in trade for quite some time to come and even now more than ten years later.

In terms of dinosaurs, one of the most commonly found in Lyme is the Ichthyosaur, a dolphin like dino that could extend to 5 metres in length. Paddy, taking over the tour guiding duties from Chris, passed round a few bits of vertebrae that he'd found. The forty of us on the tour diligently handed each bit of vertebrae around the circle, and then Paddy showed us another small extract from a dinosaur.

'Now what do you think this could be?'

'A poo!' The young boy to my right called out, earning himself a look of derision from his father and a few chuckles from the crowd. He was still cute enough to get away with it.

'Actually, you're totally correct. This is Ichthyosaur dung, now see the scales there on the sides, those are the fish it ate before it died. Now, does anyone want a poo?'

He was handing it out now. A woman sheepishly stepped up from the back of the crowd and volunteered to take ownership of the millions of years old piece of poo. A souvenir is a souvenir, after all.

'Actually, it's everywhere. Not so hard to find. Dinosaurs only have so many bones, but they did a lot of excreting in their time'.

With the promise of finding more excrement, amongst other perhaps more desirable fossils, Chris and Paddy led us on to the beach and we began our search for treasure. Chris provided the commentary as we walked, and ruthlessly dismissed any value in the first few finds that were presented to him. A little further along though and a couple who had brought their own hammers for the search presented Chris with six vertebrae all joined together. It was, apparently, a valuable find. You could see the pound signs light up in the couple's eyes as Chris told them that it was the best find on any tour for quite a few weeks. With our motivation doubled, we slowly scanned the beach with our eyes as we walked along, hoping for our own Eureka moment. It wasn't easy though. I was more inclined to picking up the shiny stones and then discovering that they were actually shards of glass or bits of broken ceramics. There was once a rubbish dump at the top of the cliff which collapsed during a landslide sending tonnes of unwanted waste on to the beach. For that reason, you see a lot of metal, glass and trash from the Seventies as well as slightly older discarded waste along Lyme Regis beach. I wasn't having much luck finding the older stuff though. It was only on our walk back along the beach that I found anything of note - the imprint of an ammonite on a grey stone that fitted the pit of my palm. I picked it up, inspected it, and then put it in my pocket.

The next day I rode the rest of the Jurassic Coast, spinning through the Undercliffs National Area of Natural Beauty and down into Seaton in the dazzling sunshine of a Monday morning. Seaton is followed by Beer, the next village on the way west, which necessitated a photo stop at its welcome sign before I continued on through Sidmouth and Budleigh Salterton. Though the South West Coastal Path follows the cliffs as closely as possible, as I'd discovered earlier it's not usually so suitable for cycling so I mainly had to stick to the roads. These tend to be further inland, sometimes as much as a kilometre from the coast. The possibility of landslides I guess means that villages stay a fair distance back unless they are built in the gaps between cliffs like all the main seaside towns along the route. Cycling the coast as closely as the roads allow means having to make diversions into villages and towns along the way, sailing down the slopes to the seafront and then facing the steep climb out back to the main road. It means that 95 miles is really the minimum distance, not accounting for all the metres climbed and freewheeled. For much of the way, you could be anywhere really. I suppose the true way to see the Jurassic Coast is to walk along the South West Coastal Path. The catch is that you'd need over a week to do it comfortably and have time to explore the sights. Maybe one day, I promised myself.

Finally, with my bike chain starting to squeak, I made it to the western end of the World Heritage site, the pretty town of Exmouth where the River Exe meets the sea. I stopped at a park across the road from the beach and went in to sit down, resting my legs from the constant motion of pedalling. The park had a beach themed area and then a large playground for kids in which a giant sauropod took centre stage, its long neck begging to be climbed on despite the signs warning visitors to refrain from their desire to mount a dino. I took the fossil stone out of my pocket and inspected the pattern of lines radiating out from the centre. It seemed bizarre that it bore the imprint of a creature that had lived millions upon millions of years ago. Billions of days had passed while it lay in the same place without ever moving until today when I had put it in my pocket and cycled it 26 miles to Queen's Drive Park. It was curious that I could hold something so old in my hand, and that it was now mine. It wasn't valuable in any way, not that I knew of anyhow, but it seemed like I should look after it. So I put it back in my pocket, cycled round to Exmouth train station and got the train home. It's still in my coat pocket today. A souvenir from the days when dinosaurs roamed the seas and skies of Dorset and Devon.

UK UNESCO World Heritage Site #4 of 28

Pontscysyllte Aqueduct

The river in the sky

I'd given it 15 minutes running the eternally freezing water in the hope of it blossoming into tepid, warm and then finally hot water, but it just wasn't going to turn. With just my feet wet, I stepped out of my Airbnb's shower and put my fresh clothes onto my unfresh body. I flattened my bed head with a little cold water from the sink, washed my eyes to kid myself into believing I'd just enjoyed an invigorating shower, and then, bag slung over my back, ran out the door. It was a miserable morning in Cardiff. Within 5 minutes I was so wet that I needn't have tried to have a shower in the first place. Not for the first time that day I cursed my stupidity in not bringing a raincoat and an umbrella with me on a long weekend away in Wales in October. Screw it, I consoled myself. There's only so wet you can get and I was well on the way to getting as wet as can be.

Ironically, I had an aqueduct on my itinerary for the day. I'd be spending the morning learning how canals and countries are connected by the Pontcysyllte Aqueduct, near Wrexham, Wales. How water could be moved (and used to move) up into the sky and carried across a valley. I was pretty excited to see it for myself, especially as it was one of the UK's newest UNESCO World Heritage site. So new, (well, less than ten years since inscription) that my guidebook to the World Heritage sites in the UK didn't even include it.

First I had to get there. The 07.21 to Holyhead from Cardiff Central was surprisingly packed but the commuters left at Newport and even more departed at Hereford. This rather epic train route criss-crosses the England Wales border, a line that has remained much the same since the 8th century since the creation of Offa's Dyke. A physical divide between the peoples of Anglian King Offa's Mercian kingdom and the native British who resided in what is now Wales, the dyke runs for around 180 miles from Prestatyn to Chepstow and is reckoned by archaeologists to have been built to protect the kingdom of Mercia from Powys. Nowadays the current Anglo-Welsh border that my train was passing through like a needle and thread lies at most no more than a few miles from the dyke and at times uses the ancient earthwork to delineate the border. Offa's Dyke was nominated in 2010 for UNESCO World Heritage status by the association that represents it, but the proposal was rejected a year later. A shame as it may have protected a 50 yard portion of it from being destroyed by an ignorant landowner who in 2014 flattened part of the dyke to build stables. He later claimed to have no knowledge of the historical significance of the land he had purchased and, as a result, was not fined the £5000 for destroying a national monument. With recognition from world bodies like UNESCO, sites like Offa's Dyke get much better protection, but the dyke has always stood in the shadow of more famous border divides in the UK like Hadrian's Wall and the Antonine Wall, both of which are UNESCO World Heritage sites. Offa's Dyke Path, a national trail founded in 1971, lets walkers enjoy the dyke's route so hopefully one day the dyke will attract enough attention to get proper protection.

Guessing which country you're in on a train journey has legs, but with two and half hours to fill my time, I began looking for alternative forms of entertainment. I'd bought a large latte to takeaway at Cardiff Central and I still had the cardboard cup with me. The cup was completely white, no branding or logos at all. I had to put a pen to it.

First I traced round my fingers and thumb while holding the cup. Pleased with the result of a rather shakily drawn set of thin fingers and an overly thick thumb, I set about creating my own Welsh coffee brand. I plumped for Cwtch Coffi as the brand name, 'cwtch' meaning a loving embrace, even more than a hug and a well-known Welsh example of their language explaining concepts beyond English. 'Coffi' meaning, well, coffee.

The Welsh language is beguiling to us English speakers. On the face of it, it has little or no relation to

English despite the fact that the two languages have lived side by side for over 1500 years. They're from different language families and different histories. Welsh words are utterly unpronounceable from an English perspective. All those double letters and lack of English vowels. My brother calls it 'alphabetti spaghetti language' in reference to the pasta letters in tomato sauce we'd all eat when we were five years old. However, there are some connections, and of course modern English words for technology and the like have penetrated Welsh as they have in all world languages. One peculiar example of how Welsh has influenced English is the word 'penguin'. The OED attributes the Welsh 'pen' meaning 'head' and 'gwyn' meaning 'white' as the origin of the English 'penguin' which first appeared in a text in 1577. There are few other examples of this, but 'penguin' must be the most random word to come from Welsh to English. Of course other languages then copied the English word with their own spelling and pronunciation twists and we now have that word today to describe the adorable waddling creatures from the southern hemisphere.

Coming back to my own experiments with Welsh, I wrote 'Cwtch Coffi' down the side of the cup, between the thumb and the little pinky. Both words start with 'C' and both have 5 letters. It looked aesthetically pleasing, if I do say so myself. Once I'd come up with the brand name, I couldn't stop myself from coming up with a few Welsh-based puns on types of coffee. Brushing off my embarrassing sense of humour, I went for Fflat White and Llatte first. Due to my absolutely non-existent knowledge of Welsh pronunciation and spelling, I had no idea if these made any sense, but from an English perspective the Ff and Ll at the start of the words looked cool. Then I had a go at Welshifying cappuccino. There are no double 'C's in Welsh (although I'm sure they tried). I searched Google Maps for Welsh towns that would fit into Cappuccino but the best I could come up with was 'caerphillyccino'. Yeah, I apologise for that one. 'Abericano', a fusion of Aber as found in Abergavenny which we had just passed through and Americano, signaled the point at which I should cut my losses and run. I left the cup under the armrest for someone to find and use my idea to make a multi-million dollar coffee empire that will bring Starbucks to its knees and put Welsh coffee firmly on the map. Someday I'll go back to Cardiff Central and see outlets with 'Cwtch Coffi' emblazoned on the side. To whoever picked up that coffee cup, you're welcome. Realistically though I realise that it's probably just found its way into a bin without so much of a glance. The most I can hope for is that it got recycled.

I alighted at Ruabon. It was pissing down in biblical fashion. I sprint walked out of the station to the bus stop in the forecourt and huddled there with a few fellow passengers to wait for the number 5 that would take me within walking distance of even more water to see. At least this water wouldn't be trickling down my back or dripping off my jawbone. The bus swung in and we boarded, escaping the rain until I had to ring the bell and reluctantly jump out into the deluge once again. Once more unto the breach. The Llangollen Canal is found down the hill from the main road running through Trevor and nearby, past the information centre, is Thomas Telford and William Jessop's aqueduct.

After a decade of construction it opened in 1805 employing a cast iron trough to carry the five foot five inches deep canal 1007 feet (307 metres) across the River Dee which lies 127 feet (39 metres) below. It holds enough water to fill 16,000 baths, approximately the same number of baths that I would need to return me to a clean state after a morning without a shower and being rained upon. Aside from its vital statistics which are impressive enough, it served the important purpose of carrying coal, bricks, iron, and chemicals to the Midlands of England. The small but sufficient visitor's centre described the story of its construction and use during the Industrial Revolution. I walked in looking like I'd just dunked my head in the canal and was met by a cheery *'Bit wet out?'*

'Just a bit', I admitted. They allowed me to spread drops of water and muddy footprints in a clockwise direction around the exhibition while I inspected the info boards. A visual graphic video of the aqueduct's construction captured my attention showing every building block and iron plate floating into position to create the structure that has stood for over 200 years. Another video to my left featured local people's feelings on *'that'* bridge. A particularly deadpan young gentleman detailed his amazement that anyone in the world bothered to come to this quiet corner of Wales. He was a good example of how many Brits react to people travelling round their country, touring the various notable infrastructure.

'When they ask me where the aqueduct is, even when it's right behind them, I just point and leave them to it. Some of them don't speak English so it's just better if I point'.

In my experience, so many Brits take this view on tourists. *'Why are you here?', 'Why aren't you on a sunny beach in Spain for your hols?', 'Yeah, it's just an aqueduct, only a few hundred years old. Biggest in the world? Yeah, that's only 'cos canals ain't around nowadays. Bet the Chinese could build one ten times longer if it were actually needed'*. It's self-deprecating but also self-defeating. Britain is a treasure to travel around, and I believe that secretly us Brits know it, however much we lambast the public transport and the price of National Trust memberships.

Eventually, having read every info board twice and seen the videos rotate, the time came to venture back out into the storm. Without an umbrella nor a hood, I had nothing to ready myself with so I simply strolled out of the warm, dry info centre, the automatic doors separating, and into the exact opposite. Well, no point waiting around. Let's go and see this damn aqueduct. And, cloaked in grey and sodden wet, it was a marvel to behold. Pure engineering magic of the highest degree. Picture this in your mind. You are walking along a gentle canal, nothing untoward, past houseboats and ducks, when up ahead you see that the land disappears but the canal doesn't. It continues, without so much of a blip, across a valley to the other side far far away. All the time though, there is a perfect line of water suspended in a flat line. You could almost believe that the land either side of the water was dug away rather than the aqueduct constructed, until you spot the iron archways and stone supports grandly lifting the water high in the sky. It simply beggars belief. There is a narrow path to the left hand side of the water on which pedestrians may pass from one side of the valley to the other. It was on this path that I followed the water from land to 127 feet above the River Dee and was able to take in the grandeur of the surrounding countryside.

Having only visited the aqueduct only this one time and this one time being a mid-autumn day, I had no real comparison to make, but I'd wager that mid-autumn, with the trees a kaleidoscope of oranges, browns, yellows and greens, must be one of the most stunning times to visit. It goes without saying that the plentiful rainfall (as superbly demonstrated on this particular Friday) creates a lush, verdant landscape that can be viewed 360 degrees around, so long as you're careful not to get dizzy and trip into the canal. Peer over the side of the metal railings and you see the Dee rushing below you, a stark contrast to the barely mobile water above it, autumnal leaves drifting languidly along. After crossing the river, a football pitch is laid out to the right (surely one of the most beautiful places to play the beautiful game) and to your left a water treatment plant. Then, before you know it, you have arrived at the other side of the valley, back on terra firma and with the water continuing as if nothing had ever happened.

After taking the muddy track below the aqueduct to inspect her underbelly, there's not much else to be done except turn around and take the same route back, repeating the pleasure of walking on water up in the air. Of course, if you do happen to share the aqueduct with others on your visit (I was almost, but not quite the only soul around during my visit), you do have to negotiate a way to pass the other person without one or both of you ending up in the water. The path is just wide enough to allow people to pass sideways, unless you want to play a game of chicken with your opponent to see who clucks first and ducks into the water. I was already virtually as wet as can be so taking a plunge wouldn't have made a great deal of difference. I had nothing to lose now. Who wants a game?

There are plenty of accounts of those who have fallen in over the years and, predictably as this is Britain, the most common cause of drowning in the canal is drunkenness. Ice skating kids also came a cropper when the canal used to freeze over in winter and it appears that the canal was also the murder weapon of choice for those wishing to dispose of newborn babies, the bodies not rising to the surface for a few weeks. Despite its beauty, it's seen its fair share of tragedy over the years. Better then that I keep a hold of the railing and squeeze in when passing others. Cluck, cluck!

The Pontcysyllte Aqueduct begs you to spend all day admiring it, but with the rain continuing to fall and the time limit of a bus and a train to catch, I had to bid my farewell. Before I made it off the aqueduct though I spotted a couple of canal boats drifting towards me, the perfect picture of the '*stream in the sky*' being used for the purpose it was created for. Of course, the canal boats were filled with Asian tourists and their Canon cameras rather than goods being transported between Wales and England, but still, it shows that the canal is still in perfect working order. In order to maintain the trough it is emptied via a plug in the middle (while the ends are closed, of course) every five years. What a sight that must be to see 1.5 million litres of water pour through a single hole into the Dee below.

So, with a heavy heart, and even heavier trousers, I turned my back on the canal and walked up towards the road. A few metres up the path a thought occurred to me and made me turn around and walk quickly back to the canal. There was one more view that I wanted to see. I walked up the steps of a footbridge crossing over the parked canal boats and looked down the canal back towards the aqueduct. That view of the water continuing its innocent way from land, across valley, to land once again really is extraordinary, and I can see why, even if the locals don't, the reason people come from all over the world to see it and why it is a UNESCO World Heritage site. It was well worth getting a little wet for.

UK UNESCO World Heritage Site #5 of 28

Ironbridge Gorge

A bridge to the future

When you think of the great bridges of the world, a picturesque Shropshire village on the River Severn doesn't usually come to mind. The Golden Gate Bridge, the Sydney Harbour Bridge, Tower Bridge in London: they all originate from that small Shropshire village that you never thought of. Before 1779 you either had to cross rivers in a boat or try your luck with stone or even wooden constructions. However that all changed thanks to a series of men called Abraham Darby.

There were actually four men called Abraham Darby, all Quakers and all related, who lived at various points during the 200 years between 1678 and 1878. All four influenced the iron industry around Coalbrookdale, just up the road from where the village of Ironbridge now sits upon the Severn, but two, the first Abraham

Darby and the third, had the most significant effect upon our modern industrial world. Abraham Darby I developed a new method of producing pig iron, so called because the shape of the moulds resembled a litter of piglets being suckled by a sow, by using a blast furnace fuelled by coke rather than charcoal. Coke had the advantage over charcoal in that it generates intense heat and is nearly smokeless. It also, crucially, made the production of iron cheaper. Then Abraham Darby III, the grandson of the first, though he was born 33 years too late to meet his pioneering grandfather, used this iron in the construction of the world's first iron bridge, the very bridge I was here in the Shropshire countryside to see. Opened on New Year's Day 1781, it set the precedent for metal bridges around the world, but at first it simply provided a link between two parishes on either side of a deep gorge. Really it was an experiment to see if this type of material could be used in such a way. The proof in the pudding came with the floods of February 1795 when the bridge was the only crossing over the Severn to survive. All the other stone and wooden bridges suffered significant damage, but Darby's bridge was as strong as before. From then on, metal was the material of choice for bridges and other infrastructure around the world. It's so ubiquitous that we barely stop to question where the idea came from, but I was about to find out.

To get to the start of iron's story, I caught the bus connecting Shrewsbury to Telford, a wonderfully winding country lane kind of bus ride along roads only inches wider than the bus itself. We followed the banks of the Severn for a while before I alighted outside the village Co-op food store. The Museum of the Gorge is located here and I'd planned to go in, but as the rain had finally paused for a breather I seized my opportunity to see what I'd really come here for. The bridge is only a few hundred metres along the road that lines the river, past welcoming village pubs, cute cafes and the opening to a single track lane which is simply named 'Paradise'. Avoiding the temptation to cross the road and take the easy path to Paradise right at this moment, I continued on and followed the rise in the road that offers a first glimpse through the trees of the world's first metal bridge.

Except today it didn't offer that view. Unfortunately for me, though luckily for the bridge, it was covered almost completely in scaffolding and sheeting as part of a multi-million pound conservation project by English Heritage. The largest conservation project in EH's history, the bridge is still attracting visitors during the works and still allows pedestrians to cross it as it has done for the past two hundred years. It looks like a huge project. Getting closer to the structure I could see a vast network of metal covering the bridge and metal railings closing off most of the path across. Though of course the romanticism of the bridge is lost through the crude blandness of scaffolding, the surrounding area still gives an idea of the grandeur that inspired artists to come and put brush to paper. The sides of the land descend dramatically down into the Severn, rocks and land partial to dropping when the time comes. The village of Ironbridge looks down upon its eponymous crossing, most impressive of all the church of St Luke which occupies a grand position half way up the side of the forested hills.

This was my view as I surveyed the surroundings from the village end of the bridge. Behind me was the ordered mess of scaffolding and plastic sheeting that covered the bridge underneath. The road across the bridge was mostly rubble fragments of tarmac scattered around the deep incisions hammer drills had made into the road surface. There was still a pathway open to the left though and it was along this narrow strip that the very few tourists in Ironbridge were plodding along, stopping occasionally to snap the view and trying their best to ignore the destruction within the temporary fencing panels and corrugated iron sheeting behind them. I was tickled by the irony in iron and steel being used to hide the view of Ironbridge which itself was the very first example of iron being used to construct something. Still, it's for a good cause.

A walkway that had been constructed using scaffolding ran alongside the bridge, from one end of the land to the other, but it too was closed. Apparently work on the bridge made it too invasive to use. I supposed it went a little way to appeasing summer visitor disappointment. No matter how much a monument needs restoring and how much it deserves to have a few million thrown at it, it's always sad to see a site like Ironbridge covered up. Take the restoration of Elizabeth Tower, home of Big Ben, for example. Ugly white sheets barely covering the network of scaffolding are wrapped around the best-known symbol of London. Just a little colour or the image of the tower could do a lot to make this temporary scar on London's skyline a little more bearable. They could have even sold it to advertising and made a few bob; anything would be better than what they've got.

There was a tour of the bridge due to depart five minutes after I arrived but I supposed the sodden conditions on this Friday afternoon probably meant that it would be cancelled. Either that or I'd be doing the tour by myself. This wouldn't have been so much of a problem for me. I can recall a city tour around Riga where it was just the tour guide and I, but I felt rather sorry for the Ironbridge guide who would have to recite their whole script on Ironbridge just for my benefit and in return receive the miserable collection of coins I had in my pocket from all the change I'd received off bus drivers that day. So I told myself that the tour would be cancelled and really, who needs a tour of a bridge this tiny? I'd make my own tour starting from this end of the bridge and finishing, well, at the other end of the bridge over the river.

Keen to take in as much of the bridge that was visible to me, I walked as slowly as I physically could across the 6000cm length of Ironbridge, tip-toeing up the path to the summit in the middle and taking in the view of the river eighteen metres below and the green foliage dominating village cottages along the riverbank. It's a lovely place to be. While not spectacular to our modern eyes, people at the time declared it a *'wonder of the world'* and a *'stupendous specimen of the powers of mechanism'*. Nowadays, it's more about the fact that it's the first of what became many, rather than the greatness in of itself.

Satisfied, I completed the second half of the crossing over to the other side, still shuffling slowly like a penguin. I had two and a half hours to kill. Thankfully the old toll house at the other end of the bridge has been converted into a little, two floor museum which, with a friendly 'Hello!' and the passing of not even one penny, you may enter as I did and discover the info behind the iron. With profiles of important people involved in the financing and construction, a timeline of its journey from its beginnings to the present, and a few scaled models and looping videos, the museum contained more or less all you needed to become somewhat of an expert. Of course, like with many of these places, I watch the videos, read the boards, and inspect the models, but when I walk out, all but a few random, inconsequential facts drain out of my brain almost instantly. Notes and photos are essential, plus a leaflet if there are any lying around.

There's a certain order to boards and displays in museums of course and occasionally you find that either, through relatively slow or quick reading or general disinterest, you catch up with or get caught up by the group in front or behind you. Today I was the meat in the sandwich being squished for time by the couple behind me and the group of elderly visitors in front of me, one of whom was dragging one of the museum's cushion seated chairs along with him to sit down upon at the foot of every info board. Every time I'd skip past them and read the boards in the wrong order they'd follow me and resume their positions in front of me, as if I somehow knew a better, jumbled sequence to reading the boards. I zig-zagged through the exhibition, desperate to have a board to myself but each time they'd up sticks and join me. In the end, I just waited downstairs for them to finish and then, when they'd had their fill, I went back upstairs to read the boards in peace.

The most interesting information came in the form of costs, both to the builders of the bridge and to those who used it after it had been built. Like many great projects, the bridge cost a lot more than was budgeted, £6000 rather than £3200, about £1.5 million in today's money. It was Abraham Darby III who had to stump up the extra cash to have the bridge finished, a financial burden that he carried for the rest of his life. Though, thanks to his grandfather, iron was now much cheaper to produce, the major cost was on the 378 tons of iron used to build the bridge, bolstered perhaps by the delicate filigree ironwork that gives the bridge its beauty along with its utility. The other major cost was labour, and this already monumental cost must have been increased by Abraham's Quaker roots which taught him to treat his employees well (he even bought farms to feed his workers and built houses for them) and to pay them higher wages than those offered around the local area. On the list of Darby's personal accounts £15 worth of 'celebratory beer' is listed which equates to over a grand today - not a bad bar tab for the last day of work!

Of course, considering the cost (and the amount of

beer they must have drunk after completing the bridge) there was a toll payable to use the bridge. No one was exempt. Prices were determined by the number of horses pulling the carriage and by the breed of animals in the party. Passing soldiers had to pay the toll and even the Royal Family weren't treated as an exception. Indeed, when Prince Charles came to celebrate the bicentenary of the bridge in 1979, he paid a symbolic toll of half a penny to cross the bridge. He left the horses at home and crossed on foot, the cheapskate.

Nowadays of course it's free, but the bridge and the ten related museums in the local area attract enough visitors to replace the lost industry with tourism pounds. Indeed, there were plans in the mid 20th century to sell the bridge for scrap and it was only thanks to the creation of the Ironbridge Gorge Museum Trust that it was saved. Thousands of pounds were raised to avert the council's plans to demolish it and the £20,000 that the council were going to use to demolish the bridge was actually redirected to preserving it. It has been on UNESCO's list since 1987 and over half a million visitors visit the area each year, a sign that it was certainly the right decision to keep this icon of the Industrial Revolution, the kindle that ignited the irrevocable change that Britain experienced from being a rural nation to an industrial one, a change all four corners of the world followed.

Where once a peaceful, tranquil corner of the English countryside lay, furnaces and smoking chimneys erupted in the 1800s and Coalbrookdale became a hellish land of fire and intense heat. Walking through the village nowadays, it's almost impossible to believe. I walked back towards the Museum of the Gorge but the improving weather and the gorgeous autumnal woods enticed me to skip the information boards in favour of a walk up towards Loamhole

Dingle and past the former furnaces that are now dedicated to educating visitors about this age of intense transformation. Across the road from me I spotted again the tiny road leading off the main thoroughfare simply named 'Paradise' and decided that I would, after all, take the road heading heavenwards. It was a steep track running up the side of the valley with houses wedged into the earth and the road about as thin as it possibly could be to allow a car to fit through. It elevated me onto a ridge that passed by houses on the right, normal houses with normal cars and normal front gardens but with the enviable addresses: '34 Paradise', '33' Paradise', '32 Paradise'... Facing the furnaces of Britain's burgeoning industry, it can't have been much like Paradise in the 1800s, but I suppose coming home after a day suffering the intense heat of the fires would make it seem so. I continued along 'Paradise' until I reached number 1 Paradise and found myself at the main road.

Number 1 Paradise, I can reveal, is actually a YHA Youth Hostel rather than God's modest abode, but the building itself is suitably grand (for Paradise that is, not for a youth hostel). It was the Coalbrookdale Literary and Scientific Institution back in the mid-1850s when it was constructed but now is only available to groups to exclusively hire the boarding facilities. A little further on up the main road I came to another repurposed site, one that actually lost its purpose entirely very recently. Beyond the iron gates with 'Coalbrookdale' emblazoned in gold upon them, Abraham Darby I first smelted iron ore with coke in 1709. A sign, titled *'The birthplace of industry'* told me so, but was wrong in stating lower down that *'today it makes the fine quality castings for the world-famous Aga-Rayburn cookers'*. Since November 2017, the grand iron gates have been shut after Aga Rayburn ceased operations at the foundry, the US-owned firm stating that the base was no longer economically viable. Over 300 years of industry on this very site came to an end with the last 42 workers hanging their boots on the gates as they left work for the final time. Though the site had been empty for a year when I visited, in all likelihood it will be repurposed again, most likely as a tourist attraction. Given that Ironbridge and the surrounding area already has ten museums (yes, you read that right, ten museums!), it may be, in my humble opinion, a case of stretching the dough too thin. Perhaps though that's all there is now. Kiddy-friendly museums, dainty tea shops, artificially authentic pubs, quaint B&Bs; these are the industries of areas like Ironbridge in the 21st century. Thankfully, the area that the foundry is in is part of the World Heritage site and so to keep that status the repurposing will have to be in accord with the heritage guidelines. Whatever happens to it, the WHS status should keep it from being totally destroyed.

There is more good news too. Where once industry scarred and dirtied the valley, nowadays nature is retaking control of the landscape of Coalbrookdale and there are a variety of trails to walk along to discover the woodlands and streams beyond the village and its many museums. A disused railway line bridge travels over a pond brimming with reeds and lilypads, blending the worlds of industry and nature together. Keen to get off the road, I plunged headfirst onto a path that wove me through the trees and up into Loamhole Dingle, an oasis of forest paths above a stream. I spent a good amount of my cooped up energy from the various train and bus rides that day jumping over fallen tree trunks and scampering down the sides of the valley, before realising that I'd better get a move on if I were to catch my bus back to Shrewsbury. Never one to turn around and simply walk back the way I have come, I attempted a full circle and this led me along the railway line, past the very tempting Green Wood Cafe that was somewhere below me, submerged in the woods (I'll return, I promise, it sounds wonderful) and onto Darby Road where the weather was now whipping up something like a blizzard but with leaves. It was like trying to walk into the direction of a huge hair dryer blowing out blasts of cold air and sending thousands of leaves to attack me. The weather, having behaved itself so well for the past two hours, was now determined to wreak havoc upon my day once again. Even so, I made it down the road and even had a peep at the Darby's houses, Rosehill House and Dale House, which are now, as you may have guessed, also museums. Well Coalbrookdale, if you've got it, why not flaunt it, hey? The houses are really nothing more than houses but you can see how the Darbys lived and take a look at a bit of memorabilia, if that's your cup of tea.

The bus picked me up again from the car park and took me safely, though a little precariously at times, along the narrow country lanes back to Shrewsbury. I'd been keen to try to fit in a little sightseeing in Shrewsbury to round off the day and so took a quick walk round The Quarry which is anything but a quarry nowadays with its tree lined promenades and rolling lawns. Shrewsbury enjoys beautiful green space round much of its city centre, and with lovely architecture and a fine range of watering holes, it's a very decent place to spend an evening after a hard day touristing. In spite of having such a selection on offer, I lazily plumped for Montgomery's Tower, part of the Wetherspoon chain of pubs admittedly, but still it had charging points, cheap ales, and fish and chips for a bargain. It also enjoyed the curious location of being below a gym, in many ways the perfect complement to a workout I suppose is a Wetherspoon beer and a burger deal. Convenience is the key. You wouldn't want to lose too many calories now, would you?

I ordered at the bar and found a table right in the corner by the window from where I could make some notes about the day and people-watch a little. All sorts come into Wetherspoon. Teenagers on awkward dates, pensioners wanting the cheapest pint available, middle-aged couples whose idea of a night out is to sit silently in front of each other and wait desperately for their food to come. In essence, it's Britain in a nutshell. If you had just one day to observe the British, you'd go to a Wetherspoon for sure. My only worry is that many people who visit the UK as tourists get lured in by the cheaper prices of the food and drinks and leave thinking that they've been to a proper English pub. They haven't. There aren't any 'real' pubs where you can order your food via an app or get a pint for under two quid.

So I'm in the Spoons, writing a few reflections on my day, when I look up and notice that the elderly couple on the table in front of me have started a Skype call on a tablet.

'Hello Katie, how are you my darling? And Charlie too, how are you sweetie? Being good for mummy and daddy? Lovely. Oh, that sounds wonderful sweetheart. Oh yes, and here's granpops too...'

It struck me in that moment watching grandparents interact with their grandchildren however many miles away, that while bridges like Abraham Darby's once connected people, today technology provides the link. Darby was a pioneer. He built a bridge in the sky where once it seemed impossible, starting a trend that has connected humans physically ever since. Now satellites are our bridges in the sky, connecting us with loved ones, enabling trade, simplifying communication between communities. 200 years later, we are still trying to find ways to bridge the gaps between us - and we, as humans, are succeeding. It takes a man, or rather four men, like Abraham Darby to take us to where humanity is today. Not just geniuses, but realists and hard-workers too. Every metal bridge in the world today is the child of that little, scaffolding covered structure that crosses the River Severn connecting the parishes of Madeley and Benthall. It felt rather appropriate that in Shrewsbury, the birthplace of one Charles Darwin who had a few decent ideas himself regarding human connections, that I would see the modern point of a line that stretches back as far as humans have been around and has New Year's Day 1779 as one of its milestones. The day that Darby's iron bridge became reality is a day that humans took one big step closer to becoming united.

UK UNESCO World Heritage Site #6 of 28

Blaenavon Industrial Landscape

Welsh state of mine

I'll be honest. I wasn't particularly enthused by spending my hard-earned Saturday in an 'Industrial Landscape'. Most Saturdays I like to get out on my bike for a bit of a cycle and a football game, perhaps a pint in a pub and something reasonably unhealthy for dinner. That's my idea of a Saturday well spent, as I guess it is for many guys around the UK. As it was I was in Cardiff for the weekend and, as Blaenavon was a quick train trip to Newport and an hour bus ride away, I thought I'd spend the morning checking out the World Heritage listed town and its industrial remains before heading back to Newport for the Football League 2 clash against Stevenage Borough. I enjoy going to see a game whenever I'm somewhere away from home. There's only really one thing to do on a Saturday at 3pm and football is always an interesting insight into the city, town or village you happen to find yourself in. For 90 minutes you can find yourself wrapped up in the fervour of supporting your adopted team, experiencing the highs and the lows of the local populace, hearing not entirely unique chants about local rivals, all surrounded by thousands of local people who have often lived in that particular town for the whole of their lives and have known little aside from going to school or work Monday to Friday and to the stadium on a Saturday. I've been to see football games of all qualities everywhere I've been around the world and would wager that there isn't really a better way to dip your toes into the modern local culture and check the pulse on the local community away from the tourist attraction that you're visiting the town for. Plus, you get to watch football at the same time. It's one thing I always look out for when going somewhere new. First though, off to see the mines and furnaces.

Plan sorted, I hopped on a mid-morning service to Newport (it was a Saturday after all) and switched onto the X24 bus to Blaenavon. It was as simple as that. Britain's buses, depending on where you are, have really come on in the last few years. Leather seats, free WiFi, USB charging points; they're often smart, whether double decker (and you always hope it will be when you're waiting for it to come) or single. The X24 was no exception with all mod cons available. Whether the handful of pensioners joining me on this journey appreciated the ability to top up their ailing smartphone battery or stalk their exes on Instagram I wasn't sure, but it sure was nice to have that option for them.

After Cwmbran, the bus route gets more and more rural until you're riding high along one side of a gorgeous valley. The Brecon Beacons aren't much further north. Little houses painted in pastel colours dot the landscape, fields of sheep cling to the near vertical sides of the mountains. It's a dramatic picture, and within its palm the town of Blaenavon is nestled.

The bus dragged itself up to the centre of the town and dropped me off by the designated Blaenavon World Heritage site information centre. Housed in a former school, the information centre is about as perfect as these things come, and, thanks to the Welsh Government and lottery funding, it doesn't cost a soul a penny. I was welcomed in by a gangly man who handed me a map and gave me an idea of what I could expect to find in the information centre. When I was finished with questions he sat back down and resumed whatever he had been doing on his computer. Every time I go to a museum or information centre and see the receptionist on the computer, I wonder what they must be doing. I imagine replying to enquiries and arranging events for the museum or info centre is all within their remit, but once this is taken care of, what else is there for them to do on a computer? I may be completely wrong, maybe there's a whole tonne of secretarial tasks for them to perform, and they always do seem to be preoccupied with whatever it is on their screens, but I do wonder whether it's a case of looking busy while watching something on iPlayer. The same with those people who sit behind Bureau de Change desks in airports and train stations or anyone in fact who has a sit-in-a-public-place and-answer-inane-questions kind of job. I remember once walking past an information desk in a train station once, perhaps it was London Victoria, and seeing that the person behind the desk was engrossed in an episode of Poldark, so much so perhaps that you'd possibly have to wait until the end of the scene before they'd pause the video and look up at you. This is all in addition to the sales assistant who work in rarely frequented shops like jewellers, posh shoe shops, bathroom showrooms and the like, who, whenever you look through the window on your way past, are always with their phone in hand and their thumbs tapping away. To be fair, who can blame them? I'd be dead bored too.

I sat down to watch a couple of videos in the first exhibit before walking through into what must have once been the school hall. The first video detailed the history of the landscape and its wider importance to Wales becoming the first industrial nation in the world. The second video must have been a tape made by UNESCO for it spanned across the globe explaining the history and importance of World Heritage Sites. Blaenavon seemed awfully proud of their World Heritage status (and why wouldn't you be?). It wasn't just the information centre that was free, it was every attraction within the site: the Ironworks, the National Coal Museum at Big Pit and various other smaller sites, all except the brewery of course. Still, at £2.50 I would reckon it's a snip, although I ran out of time before I could visit it. Having World Heritage status is a big deal. It's the recognition that your little part of the world is a fundamental thread in the fabric of human culture and history. It attracts a huge amount of visitors that may never have considered visiting before and that has a positive economic effect for the whole local economy. As a harsh post-industrial landscape, Blaenavon did face some scepticism for its lack of romance compared to other World Heritage sites, but more than £30 million was spent on turning the town into a one-stop step-back-in-time mining experience. Five years after its inscription in 2000, visitor numbers had doubled, property values had risen, over a hundred jobs had been created. Blaenavon is an exceptional example of how tourism and heritage can power economic development. If you just compare pictures of the high street before WHS and after, the difference is staggering. Where once you had most of the shops boarded up, now you have a coffee shop next to a chocolate shop next to a shop dedicated to cheddar cheese. Even when it was pouring down later on in the day, I felt compelled by the cute, bright window fronts to take a sodden walk up the main shopping street. And getting me, of all people, to check out shops is impressive, I'm just saying.

I stepped warily out of the warm environs of the visitor centre and was met by a fierce wind hurling leaves, twigs and raindrops in my general direction. Next stop on the free map given to me by the man behind the computer was to be the Ironworks. It was only a ten minute stroll up the road but I must have looked like I'd survived a hurricane when I walked into the tiny gift shop to register my attendance. That was after I'd negotiated the variety of signs informing which door to use (or rather which door to not use). Still, it was a warm welcome from the ladies, one of whom managed to frighten the bejesus out of all three of us when she pressed a button on a remote causing a burst of dramatic classical music to blast out from every corner. In truth, they don't need dramatic music to run shivers down your spine when you see the Ironworks. There are few historical sites nowadays that really transport you back to the past as vividly as the Blaenavon Ironworks does. For one thing, though riddled with moss and nettles now, the furnaces look as though they've only just cooled down. Stepping into them as you can, you feel your feet fry at the thought that once upon a time on the same spot 1500 degrees celsius burned to create the iron that would travel around the world and make Blaenavon rich. To bring temperatures above volcanic lava levels, steam engines were used to blow air into the furnaces using a system of pipes; enough air to fill a hot-air balloon in just seven minutes. The furnace in return gave off putrid gases that were recycled ingeniously by burning them in the boilers that powered the blowing engines. The captured energy meant less costs and therefore higher profits for those in charge.

Next to the furnaces stands the balance tower, used to move raw materials between the lower and upper yards with an ingenious technique that utilised the weight of water to outweigh the tank full of material and send it up in a see-saw effect to the upper yard.

The lovely ladies in the gift shop had warned me that due to high winds the path up to the upper yard was closed off and indeed there was a yellow tape across the path, barring access to anyone. Still, just being at the foot of the balance tower was enough to appreciate the scale of the structure, an intimidating coal black hulk of bricks with three lozenge-shaped gaps running up the middle. Now surrounded by lush green countryside, it must look a little different to how it was in the past, but it didn't stretch the imagination too much to picture having to spend all day measuring the materials (coke, iron ore and limestone), tipping them into the furnace, draining the waste slag into trams once the iron melted and then tapping the molten iron.

The workers were typically unskilled migrants from central England, west Wales and Ireland and were housed in small terraces that still dot the landscape of Blaenavon. Some of these houses are located just up the slope from the furnaces and are now open to the public to stoop their heads and enter. The houses are kept in a condition as true as possible to how they would have looked back in the 19th century with beds, furniture, and even a little shop from which the workers could buy produce. There were even human figures, dressed and wigged, to bring the scene to life. I was wandering around the top floor of one of these houses, trying to read the information boards in the near darkness (no lights for some reason), when I heard a family with a toddler enter and start to explore, thinking they were the only ones in the house. It took almost every fibre of my being to dissuade myself from jumping out at them from behind a door. Still, even when I tried not to scare them, I succeeded - the father jumping slightly when he walked into the room I was in, exclaiming *'Oh! You're a real person!'* to which I could only respond *'Yes, and what are you doing here in my house?'* They promptly departed.

For the real inhabitants of these houses, conditions would have been better than most other jobs available to the general population at that time, though of course children were put to work from an early age and drunkenness was an issue. Still, Blaenavon's population rose rapidly and in 1851 a census showed that more people worked in industry rather than agriculture making Wales the first industrial nation in the world. Of course, Blaenavon was a large part of this. If this wasn't significant enough, Blaenavon was also the site where Sidney Gilchrist Thomas and his cousin Percy Carlyle Gilchrist found a way to remove phosphorus from molten iron. By lining a Bessemer converter with bricks of burnt, crushed limestone and tar, they were able to transform the molten iron into steel at an economic price and therefore meet the world's increasing demand for cheap steel. The cousins' experiments actually spelt the end for Blaenavon ironworks as countries such as Germany and the United States could now use the same invention to transform their own phosphoric iron ores and thus Blaevanon's product was no longer in such demand. Such is life - shooting yourself in the foot with your own ideas.

Not to fear though as by 1880 the Blaenavon company had moved on to concentrate on coal. Big Pit, a former iron mine, became the most important colliery in Blaenavon. Its transformation signalled Blaenavon turning its hand to coal and it was a massive success for over three decades between the 19th and 20th centuries. Over a thousand miners were working at Big Pit in the early 1920s and it was a significant part of the Welsh coal mining industry that was producing over 57 million tonnes of coal by 1913.

Going to the coal face every day was the reality for many men in this part of the world at this time. Nowadays the mine is home to the National Coal

Museum and working down the mine is a thing of the past in this part of the world. The modern day coal face could be seen on my walk between the Ironworks and Big Pit. I passed through the Gilchrist Thomas Industrial Estate, home to offices of companies that offer ethical packaging solutions, biotechnology, database management and caravan repairs. The offices looked smart, though characterless. Warm and perhaps even comfortable, though with little physical work except removing files from the filing cabinet. It was a Saturday so I supposed that everyone was enjoying their weekends, work being able to be left alone for two days before resuming it. Jobs with pensions, health insurance, workers rights and a fair salary. It's amazing to think of how the meaning of 'work' has changed in the space of a hundred years or so.

I was on my way to experience what mining life was really like, or at least get a sense of it. I'd heard that Big Pit offered tours down the mines and I suppose like many tourists I somehow thought this would be a fun way to spend a Saturday afternoon. It's amazing to think nowadays people willingly go down the mines to see the dreadfully dark and dangerous work that used to be done by thousands of men, women, and children. I'd been down a mine once in my life before and upon exiting it I had vowed to never ever go down a narrow hole into the heart of the earth again. I was about to break that promise. In full honesty though, I was expecting Big Pit to take health and safety a little more seriously than Cerro Rico (Rich Mountain) in Potosi, Bolivia. While the city of Potosi is also a UNESCO World Heritage site like Blaenavon, the tours of its mines are rather different. I remember being driven to a market in a beat-up minibus before we went to the mine entrance to buy 50% proof alcohol and dynamite to appease the Gods and keep the miners sweet (and rather oblivious to the effects of working underground in one of the highest cities in the world). With no encouragement needed, the miners would take our dynamite and blow holes inside the mines for the entertainment of us tourists. We spent about an hour in the company of a female miner who led us through the rabbit holes that had us scrambling up and slipping down shafts with no ladders, ropes or lights. It was, looking back now, pretty terrifying and actually rather risky. There were no emergency procedures, no exit routes, no one to save us if part of the mine happened to cave in. You'd have to have a thick wallet to pay me to go back in there.

I was expecting a slightly less nerve-wracking time in Blaenavon. As it was though, I was positively whisked to the mine as soon as I entered the Visitor Centre and made to sit and wait for my turn to enter with a group. There were about twenty of us sat in a zig-zag formation of wooden benches that wound its way up the room to a door through which I supposed we would pass to face our fate. The waiting room was rather tense for a tourist experience. We sat in silence, each of us I supposed having no idea of what we were letting ourselves in for, until a portly, orange jumpsuit wearing gentleman popped through the door and ushered us to join him. *'Come on you lot, let's go'*.

We shuffled forward as a pack and entered a large semi-circle enclosed by other miners similarly jumpsuited. *'Right you lot, welcome to Big Pit'*, a gruff Welsh accent emanated from the middle miner in the semi-circle. He had the look of a man who had seen shit in his life.

'Now some of the rules of coming down the mine. Put all your wallets, phones and watches in this bag. You can't have 'em down there'. He waved a red cotton sack.

A few of us smiled wryly, a few others crossed their brows in confusion, but surely we'd all seen this trick before. Flog them on ebay before we all got back, that sort of joke. Very droll. We all remained still, waiting for the joke to burst. But no, he was serious. Without any explanation of the reason why (and none of us dared to question him for fear of retort), he came round to each of us and we willingly dumped our valuables into the sack without comment. It felt slightly like being mugged at gunpoint, though the only weapons the miners had were their headlamps and sarcasm. Relieved of possessions, we were then lined up to receive a tool belt with gasmask attached and a helmet with a torch powered by a thick wire stretching from a battery in our belt. The half dozen or so miners around the semi-circle took us individually to do these belts up around our waists for us and interrogate us on where we were from. Coming from Bournemouth with its Court Royal hotel which is exclusively for the use of Welsh miners, I think I was given an easier ride than some of those who hailed from other lands. The miner who was wrapping the tool belt me at the same time knew of the hotel, but had never stayed there himself. It's only open to mineworkers and occupies a stunning position on the West Cliff of Bournemouth, just along from the Marriott hotel. You could say it's one of the perks of the job. Certainly, considering the job they used to do, the former miners who get to spend a sunny week in the balmy summer air of the English south coast don't half deserve it. The dark, dank mines must feel like another planet when they're on a sunbed on Bournemouth beach.

Belted up and ready to descend, we waddled our way to the lift that would send us 300 feet below the surface. We crammed into the metal cage, lights flashed, buzzers sounded and then the floor around us rose up and we were lowered down, down, deeper and down, the sound of heavy rain falling through the shaft making it feel as though we were behind a waterfall. Once at the bottom, we tentatively stepped out and formed a circle round our guide. Bill was a miner for many years at a mine near Big Pit and he knew the business as well as any man. Receiving a tour from an actual former worker brings to life the place you are visiting. Imagine receiving a tour of a castle from a knight who used to live there or a tour of a sports stadium from one of the athletes. It makes a huge difference to just hearing from someone who has memorised a reel of facts. Nowadays Bill leads tours down the mines, and gets paid to do it, but in the past he would have come down the lift with his tools to chip away at the coalface, extracting the black gold and having it sent to the surface via horse and cart. We jokingly say 'back to the coalface' when we finish our lunches in our smart work canteens and go back to our comfy desk jobs, but not so long ago people like Bill were literally going to the coalface to work. Hard though it was, their work was rewarding. With a close band of friends, decent pay and housing, and the knowledge that they were powering homes across the country, the miners were rightly proud of their toil. Bill showed us through the mine in his understated manner, but you could tell that he was proud of the work that was done deep down below the earth. When Thatcher closed the mines in the 1980s, a whole workforce was suddenly stripped of a purpose. It took Bill a lot to even say the former British Prime Minister's name.

Like ducklings behind their mother, we followed Bill deep into the mine, stooping every so often to avoid hitting our helmeted heads on the wooden beams that support the earth above. When you see the hotch-potch mess of beams, supports, and wires, you can't help but think that the tunnels are one tourist swinging their butt into a support away from collapse, but in reality they're as safe as can be. I suppose we are rather conditioned to seeing smart roof coverings when we travel on the Underground and we think very little of being under tons of earth while waiting for a delayed Piccadilly line service. Inside the mine though, you are very aware that there are many metres of earth between you and the surface. Still, most of the time in the mine you're too preoccupied with not smashing your head on a beam to worry about these trivial matters.

Bill stopped us every so often to explain various aspects of life down the mines. He showed us the former communication system which utilised electric wires to send coded signals to other parts of the mine, but has now been replaced by the modern emergency phones that are scattered round the mine. We got an unplanned demonstration of these as a man from another tour group had fainted while following his group and a nurse from our group had stopped to lend aid. We had to wait a while for her to catch up with us, the miners calling each other on the radio phones to update on the situation. Bill explained many of the obvious and non-obvious dangers of working down the mine. One of the less obvious is the risk of carbon monoxide in the air and for this they used canaries. Should the canary start having difficulties breathing, the miners could tell that there was a dangerous gas in the air and to get out quickly. Fresh air was obviously very important and so fans were utilised to keep a fresh supply of oxygen circulating around the mine. Air doors were used to control the airflow and these were operated by children known as door keepers. If their lamps happened to become extinguished, they would have to work in complete darkness. Bill stopped us by one of the air doors and invited us to experience something that very few people alive today have ever experienced. He instructed us to turn off our headlamps and, when all our headlamps were off, he turned off his, plunging us into absolute pitch black darkness. I put my hands in front of my face, but couldn't see a thing. There was zero light from anywhere. It was extraordinary really, probably the first time in my life that I have ever experienced not being able to see anything. Of course, we have all experienced darkness, but usually there's a little light from somewhere. Under a door, the alarm clock, a hole in the window shutters. Here though, there was nothing. I could have been dead for all I knew.

Thankfully, after a minute or so, Bill turned his light back on and we switched our headlamps back on too, a little spooked and reeling from our experience. Bill then showed us the actual coalface, where we could view a slither of coal in the earth which would have only been accessible by laying on your side and chipping away in a most awkward position. The lengths humans go to. Nowadays though there are electric saws to do the work, and we were able to see a monster of a saw, the electric equivalent of a mega crocodile that must have been over three metres in length. Work that used to take days or weeks, now takes mere minutes. The game has completely changed where there is still mining in the world, but there is still a lot to be said and respected regarding the humans who came down the mine for 12 hours at a time with just the basic tools.

Bill took us to see another helper down the mine, one whose job nowadays is done by machinery. Horses, known as pit ponies, were used extensively throughout the mining sector to haul the freshly won coal on the underground mine railway. While the miners got to go above ground at the end of their shift, the horses would live in the mines in specially built stables and very rarely be taken above ground. Their work meant that fewer women and children were used in the mines, especially after the Mines Act in 1842 which made it illegal for women and children to work underground, though of course many continued to do so as there was very little enforcement. Bill spoke fondly about the horses, and dispelled any myths about the mistreatment of them. Indeed, they were often great companions for the miners and treated like true friends, a part of the strong brotherhood that formed within the mines. It can't have been a good life for any animal, human or otherwise, down the mine, but the horses were crucial to the success of the Industrial Revolution and to the prosperity of the region.

The tour was meant to last around 50 minutes but because I didn't have my watch on, I had no idea of the time when we eventually took the lift back up and resurfaced. In truth, I was just relieved to be back on the surface of the earth. I said it in Potosi, and I said it again in Blaenavon: I never want to go down a mine again in my life. We took our belts and helmets off and our valuables were returned to us, Bill eventually offering us the explanation of why they were taken in the first place. Government law restricts any battery operated device from being taken down a mine due to the risk of fire. And there was I thinking that they'd just sell them on ebay. I took a look at the time and realised that if I were to see the football match in Newport that afternoon I'd have to leave now and go very quickly down the hill to Blaenavon to catch the bus. Caught in a wave of indecision, I weighed up my options and what I really wanted to do. As much as I wanted to see a game, and it had been my plan all along, I also wanted to continue exploring the various parts of Big Pit. There were the mining galleries, the historic colliery buildings, and the Pithead baths to see still. I'd barely scratched the surface, pardon the pun. So, I did something that I'd very rarely if ever done before, and decided to not go to a football game. You know a place must be pretty good if I've chosen it over watching a footy match.

I was pretty peckish though so my first point of call would have to be somewhere that served up grub. Up the hill from the mine was the Pithead baths with a canteen attached. I hastened there, walking against the billowing wind, and entered to find myself transported back a few decades, or at the very least back to my school days. It was your classic school canteen. Grab a tray, have something brown or grey dolloped on a plate, pay the frowning dinner lady and go sit down at a table surrounded by the cacophony of screaming kids. I'd never imagined these sorts of places still existed, and in a strange way it was rather heartening to find a place that hadn't modernised entirely. Sure, you could pay with contactless and order a cappuccino, but there was something in the tiled walls and the tastelessness of the lamb cawl that I'd ordered that seemed rather appropriate, very little had probably changed since the miners last dug down Big Pit in the 1980s. Most of all I enjoyed the splendid view out the brown panelled windows. The clouds were racing across the valley, the wind whipping the Welsh flag on top of the Big Pit winding tower and howling at the windows. The group on the table behind me were chattering away, amateur photographers on a photography course I assumed as one of their party was assigning them tasks and themes to work on.

'I want five, no ten, no seven pictures on the theme of height and power. Take only the seven, no five, no ten shots. No more. No deleting. Only unique shots. Right, everyone wrap up. Out we go.'

Cue the scrapping of table legs on the floor. I watched them wander outside, adjusting the settings on their DSLRs and looking around for inspiration while their hoods and hair flew about their heads.

Moments later I joined them outside to inspect the explosives magazine and the baths that were built in the 1930s to improve the working conditions of the miners. Though their European counterparts had enjoyed a shower after work since the 1880s, it took much lobbying to force the government to start building similar bath houses in England and Wales for the miners. The benefits were obvious. No longer did the miners have to attempt to clean themselves in a tin bath in front of their home fire, they could shower with their colleagues and put on clean clothes before heading home. The exhibition takes you through the showers (with the sound of men showering and singing played in the background) and the locker rooms, which share indelible details about the men who used to work down the mine. You get an incredible amount of detail, from their family history, to the music they liked to listen to and the achievements they enjoyed. It struck me multiple times that these men worked incredibly hard for the cause of ensuring that people had heat in their houses, coal to power the trains, and every other one of the multitude of uses for the black gold that they were literally digging out of the middle of the earth. I suppose they had little choice really, but it was quite a selfless act considering the dangers and the health implications. Deaths were not a rare occurrence. It must have taken a lot of mental strength to face up to going down into the darkness of the centre of the earth every day, the lift taking you down to a lengthy shift of hard toil for little reward.

The mining galleries reminded me of this once again with its audio-visual tour of life down a mine. I suppose that it serves as an option for those who want a taste of the mining life, but don't want to do down Big Pit to get the real deal. Videos led us through constructed walkways that showcased mining instruments like the cutter/loader which bores holes into the earth, cutting away the coal with its tungsten tipped picks attached to a revolving drum. It's the machine of nightmares, but the sheer effectiveness of it transformed mining in the 1970s. We also got to hear and see simulations of dynamite being used in the mines, harking back to my experience with real dynamite in Potosi. Again, the message was clear. This is a job you would not wish on your worst enemy.

However, once again, the camaraderie between the men was emphasised and it was clear to see how much pride this town and many towns across Wales took in their crucial part in powering the industry and homes of the nation. Of course, nowadays the coal industry in the UK is no more, and we are more interested in green energy than in non-renewables. One of the final information boards in the comprehensive National Coal Museum raised my eyebrows in interest. The UK imported 8.5 million tonnes of coal in 2017 and there are still reserves of coal around the country accounting for 3.5 billion tonnes. With oil always a constant uncertainty and gas importation rising above gas production, the information board asked whether there is a future for coal in the UK.

Back in Blaenavon, cosied up in a traditional pub in the town centre with a pint of local ale and drying off after being caught (once again) in a deluge of rain, I considered this. Could King Coal really make a return? With all the technology we have at our disposal, there would be little need for human involvement, certainly nothing on the scale of what humans (and horses) were doing a hundred years ago. The demand for energy will never cease and I suppose we have to be open to all options. However, doing a little Googling about this topic, I saw a news story from 2012 that indicated the way the trend might go, and the way that I personally would like it to go. In order to power the museum, they installed 200 solar panels on the roof of the main museum building that will contribute 6% of the total energy demand. Not a great deal, but a start, a sign of changing tides. Of course, the irony of a former coal mine being run on solar power smacks pretty hard, and not all the miners were exactly pleased at its announcement, but I find it a positive step. When children go on their school trips to the National Coal Museum and see the modern solar panels next to the old machines for mining coal, they will see how far we have come and how important the transition from fossil fuels to renewable energy sources is. It's great to celebrate the endeavours of the coal miners, but in my view coal has had its day. Our responsibility as citizens of this earth was always to protect it, but certainly, given our changing climate, now more than ever.

With those sobering thoughts, I downed the last of my pint and caught the bus back to Newport.

UK UNESCO World Heritage Site #7 of 28

Castles and Town Walls of King Edward in Gwynedd

Back to uni and the castles

'Yo bro, any plans for half term?'
    Not really why?
I have a proposition
    Ok
A road trip of sorts
    Haha ok

And that's all it took to persuade my younger brother to join me on an expedition to North Wales to see the quadruplet collection of King Edward's castles in the ancient Welsh kingdom of Gwynedd. Built by England's king at the time of his invasion of North Wales in 1282, the castles asserted the power of the colonisers and fortified the English immigrants against the Welsh revolts that followed. Now the English, in the form of my brother and I, were set to return and see what nearly 800 years had done to castles that UNESCO considers to be the "finest examples of late 13th century and early 14th century military architecture in Europe." In truth, convincing Ben to join me wasn't the hardest sell of the century. Not only is he a self-proclaimed history buff, he also spent three years 'studying' (read 'drinking') at nearby Bangor University and this trip offered a chance for him to revisit the glory days he had left behind two years before. He also has a car, which would be rather essential given the fact that North Wales is a pain to get to from anywhere, let alone Bournemouth, and once you're there getting around isn't that simple. So, we selected four days over his half term break (he works in a school for special behavioural needs), booked a couple of single rooms (there was little chance of us repeating family holidays from our childhood sharing rooms), and left it largely at that.

Late Saturday afternoon I get a buzz at my apartment front door and Ben walks up the stairs. He's been playing a lacrosse game in Southampton for the local Surrey team he captains, a sport he picked up while at Bangor Uni, and he's a sweaty, bruised mess. I shove him in the shower and set about making a vast pasta bake that will go some way to satisfying his voracious appetite. He's a big boy. When I left for university myself Ben was fourteen years old and was around my shoulder height. Then over the three years I was away in Norwich, he grew and grew and grew. Every time I'd go back home I'd barely recognise him, mainly because instead of looking down at him, I was now having to crane my neck fully backwards to see anything beyond his chest. With a metal lacrosse stick in his hands, he's not someone you would readily cross. Yet he's still my 'little' brother.

The next morning we set off from Bournemouth with the aim to cover over 300 miles in his little Toyota Yaris. Rattling and constantly complaining with weight and distance asked of it, this Yaris has been much loved in our family. Once my mother's car, both my siblings and I learnt to drive in it and now it belongs to Ben as he needs a car to get to work. It was the first time I'd been in a car with him driving. I suppose it is part of being the older sibling that you grow up doubtful of the abilities of your younger siblings to do adult things like driving or getting a job. To me, Ben was always the little brother who I had to help and guide. He was the one I used to pick on for his lack of common sense or his lack of confidence. Now that he towers over me, those teases have gone, but I still find it weird that he's all grown up, both literally and figuratively.

He'd pumped up the tyres and wiped the bird shit off his windscreen by the time I was packed and ready to head off. I was impressed. The drive was monotonous as it often is on the motorways of England, but we inched north on Google Maps and by the time we stopped for petrol and a feed just north of Banbury we were making good time. As we got closer to the northern Welsh border I could feel Ben's excitement to be back increasing to palpable levels. He was starting to talk in a Welsh accent and we'd started a game of making the rudest puns possible from the funny names of villages we were passing through. He even recited a few lines of the Welsh national anthem, Land of my Father's, off by heart.

'So how many of these castles have you already been to?', I enquired. All of them apart from Harlech was the response. Apparently we'd been to Bangor as kids and had visited Caernarfon castle and a few other local sites like Snowdon and Llandudno. *'Don't you remember going up Snowdon on the railway and the day it poured down in Bangor and the tour we took of Caernarfon and the joke the guide made about charging people £2.50 every time we spotted a Caernarfon arch?'* It seems that, despite being four years younger, Ben had a better memory of family holidays in North Wales than I. Really, except a few hazy memories of castle walls and walking round dull museums with my feet squelching in sodden shoes, I had barely any recollection of having already visited much of what we were back in Wales to see. Considering the little I recall of family holidays, it begs the question really of what the point is of taking kids like me on holiday at all. For some people, family holidays as a child are the key moments in the highlights reel of their lives. It seems that many people really remember very clearly the resorts and beaches they spent their Easter and Summer holidays at, but I am not one of them. Some extraneous details come to mind, but where or when those holidays were and what age I was I have virtually no idea, let alone what activities we did. It's not that we did boring things on holiday as a family. I think we must have had excellent holidays every year as kids. We went all over the south of England, to the Channel Islands where my grandparents lived, to France and the United States. Often we were joined by aunts and uncles and cousins, and often we explored local beauty spots, historic sites, and local museums and restaurants. Still, as hard as I tried to remember, I was pretty surprised to learn that I had already been to large parts of this UNESCO World Heritage site already. Then again, as a consolation to my poor memory, it's always nice to go back, especially if you can't recall

going there before in the first place.

After crossing mile after mile of indistinguishable English countryside it was a relief to pass into Wales and see mountains emerge on the left hand side of the car. Not only does the scenery change when you enter Wales, but the road signs do too. You get a taste of it round the border but once you're in it's a world of double l's and f's, and a black hole for vowels. Sensing his return to his Welsh heartland, Ben was in high spirits and introduced me to the wonders of Welsh pronunciation. 'Llandulas', 'Dwygyfylchi', 'Llanfairfechan' (feels so good to say), Abergwyngregyn (a personal favourite), and Llandygai are amongst the names of towns signposted off the North Wales Expressway that are simply unpronounceable coming from English. Cymraeg is a source of great pride for the Welsh, and, with English as the majority language, it means that Wales is a bilingual nation. This is most vividly seen in the road signs that we were passing by now on our way to Bangor. It's a Celtic language, perhaps the most spoken still in existence, with some borrowings from Latin and English, but generally to the English speaker it is almost completely different. Fortunately for Ben, his course in Film Studies was taught in English, but he lived in North West Wales for three years, a part of the country with more Welsh speakers than most, and so heard a fair bit of it and had to get to grips with pronouncing the place names. He even showed off a little, giving the full name of the UK's longest village name ('Llanfairpwllgwyngyllgogerychwyrndrobwllllantysiliogogogoch' if you're wondering, and yes I did have to copy and paste that) though I have no idea whether he pronounced it correctly or not. Still, whether you can pronounce Welsh or not, it's great fun to get your tongue around the lack of English vowels. It's ripe for a few good puns when you've been cramped in a car for five hours anyway.

'Now Ben, before we arrive into your former university city, were you ever barred from any food outlets or public houses? Are there any outstanding crimes that you committed that I need to know about?'

'Maybe one or two places may have chucked me out, but I'm sure they'll have forgiven me by now'.

'Right, ok, and is there anywhere in Bangor we should specifically not go?'

'The two Welsh pubs. They don't like English people'.

'Really? Like, they won't serve us because we're English?'

'You wouldn't even get in the place. And if you did, you wouldn't get out alive'.

And so, feeling slightly more anxious now, we entered the university city of Bangor, views of the Menai Strait and Anglesey reminding me that we really were on the edge of the UK.
We were staying in university accommodation, by that I mean we had an en-suite single room each in a flat of eight or so rooms with a shared kitchen. It wasn't exactly luxury, but seemed a far cry from the student flat I lived in while in my first year at university. This flat was spotlessly clean and had card key access, to name just two differences. We'd purchased a large pizza from Asda in the hope that there would be an oven and, thankfully, there was. Though there was just a cardboard box with an assortment of kitchen implements available and no sign of anything to clean our plates with after we'd finished. Full marks for the 'student experience' though. Supermarket meat feast pizza, plastic plates, and a sink full of dirty bowls and cutlery presumably donated by our new flatmates. The memories of student days were flooding back.

Ben was keen to show me around a little after dinner so we walked around the main university building which is a marvelously beautiful structure finished in 1911 giving the university a prominent lookout over the valley that Bangor is nestled in and a little magical feeling with its resemblance to Hogwarts. Ben confirmed that the 'Hogwarts feel' attracted more than just a few students from the UK and further afield. I was in his hands for the evening and thankfully there were a few drinking holes that he fancied reacquainting himself with, those with friendly attitudes towards English speaking students of course. Our first stop was the Belle Vue, the posh kids pub as Ben introduced it. Monday night meant quiz night, but we'd missed the start so just sat and let the questions wash over us. They weren't particularly taxing. What was hard was dealing with the constant 'bantering' between the quiz hosts. They barely put the microphones down between questions making you feel as though you were the audience to their own personal conversations. We moved on quickly to Paddy's after we'd finished our beers, a much quieter bar despite being Irish-themed. They didn't seem to mind English customers too much either. As we walked back though, Ben pointed out one of the the 'Welsh-only' bars. It was adorned with the dragon flag of Wales and its name was in Welsh. Ben was insistent that we didn't go in, but I couldn't help but feel that a Welsh pub in Wales was quite entitled to fly a Wales flag and focus its attentions on the local populace rather than the students who spend three years of their life in the city and then move on. Bangor had a population of around 18,000 in the last census, but that included over 10,000 students at the university, most of whom come from outside Wales. It truly is a place that thrives (and possibly survives) on account of its university population and there are more cheap supermarkets, greasy takeaways and pound-a-pint pubs that the students could ever possibly need. I can sympathise with the locals who are a minority in their own city. Of course, students with thousands of pounds worth of student loans each and little in the way of taste when it comes to alcohol and food make easy pickings for savvy local businesses, but I guess not everyone can benefit from this. The locals need their shops and pubs too, and fair enough if they'd rather not share them with students. Everyone needs their own space.

One of the many, many differences between Ben and I is our approach to the morning. I'm a firm morning person. I generally jump out of bed at 6am and feel alive straight away. It's probably something to do with waking up most days to talk to English students for a few hours. Ben, on the other hand, does not do mornings. I was lucky to get a 'morning' out of him as we met outside our rooms at 8am and walked out in the Monday morning sunshine to find some brekkie.

The day promised more insight into Anglo-Welsh relations, though from a perspective stretching back to the 1200s. With a double castle day ahead of us, Ben and I fuelled up at Mike's Bites with a Full English, though of course it wasn't called this. Rather, they called it 'the Seven Deadly Sins' in this cafe, though in truth, due to its size, it was really just one: gluttony. There was even an eating challenge available, a monstrous amount of fried breakfast that included a whole pint of tea. Brits love tea and they love pint sized quantities of liquids, but I've never seen a Brit down a pint of tea. There were a few 'victors' names on the wall with their times and a tally of the number of people who had attempted the challenge. 38 challengers, only five had succeeded.

Harlech Castle was first on the list of King Edward's Gwynedd castles that we were planning to see. It's the furthest from Bangor and requires some skilled driving to get to with the winding roads that pass along a hillside. The breakfast seemed to energise Ben and he was in a better mood, adopting once again his Welsh accent, as he drove us out of Bangor and past the most stunning scenery to Harlech. On this particular sunny morning it was a gorgeous drive, though a little hair-raising when a 4x4 comes tearing round the next bend towards you. The final leg into the village of Harlech along twisting country roads that are cut into the side of a hill was memorable not just for the scenery but the many close calls we encountered with oncoming vehicles. It seems almost inconceivable that you are going to pass that Land Rover or that RV without scraping the side of your car or losing a wing mirror, but somehow you always seem to escape without a scratch. I swear cars can breathe in and make themselves thinner. That's at least what I was attempting to do everytime we squeezed past another car coming the other way. The landscape around North West Wales is stunning, like God pinched up a green tablecloth, dotting sheep as He passed. It could well be mistaken for New Zealand's North Island, and could well have served for the setting of those Lord of the Rings films. Dramatic and foreboding, but begging you to explore it.

Harlech Castle is perhaps the most picturesque of the four listed castles, though I say that knowing full well that there are good arguments for the other three. My vote goes to Harlech though for the fact that it is set 60 metres up from the flat plains leading to the sea below, embedded on the edge of a rocky promontory that lends it spectacular views of the surrounding mountains, forests and the Irish Sea. On a day like ours, with blue sky blurring the border with calm waters, and the green of the mountains gleaming, Harlech Castle couldn't have been surrounded by a more beautiful background anywhere else in the world.

Harlech took six years to build and must have been

the most challenging, given its location on the rocky edge of the land looking out over the sea known as the Harlech Dome. Like all four castles, the designer was master mason and military engineer James of St George who hailed from the cultural region of Savoy, located in the Western Alps and now shared by France, Italy and Switzerland. The castle of St. George d'Esperanche in Savoy is where he gets his moniker from. James perfected the concentric 'walls within walls' design of the castles in Wales, indeed he is responsible for 12 of the 17 castles that Edward I had built, and he was deemed an irreplaceable asset so much so that he was given a life salary of 3 shillings a day by the king. Despite the king never living at Harlech, James and his wife Ambrosia took advantage of the castle's comfortable rooms and lived there for a time, James serving as constable of the castle for three years. Nowadays, walking round the castle, you can see that only the shell of the compact castle is left and that the outer wall is in ruins, much lower than it would have been in the 13th century. The wooden floors and roofs have of course disappeared and as such it is hard to imagine the castle being used as a home and defence against Welsh sieges led by Madog ap Llywelyn and decades later as the home of Owain Glyndŵr who took the castle out of English hands for five years during the Welsh revolt during the time of King Henry IV. Harlech also played its role in the War of the Roses as the last Lancastrian stronghold and site of the longest siege in British Isles history, a period of seven years memorialised in the song 'Men of Harlech', which was playing throughout the visitor centre as Ben and I entered.

After purchasing our Castle Explorer passes that would permit us entry into all four of the World Heritage listed castles, we moved into a small theatre that projected a short history of Harlech Castle and the battles it has been involved in. As the wall display outside the theatre so succinctly displayed, there are five key dates in Harlech's history. 1283 when building started, 1404 when it became Owain Glyndŵr's royal court, 1486 when the Yorkist siege inspired 'Men of Harlech', 1647 when it was the last Royalist stronghold in the English Civil war and 1986 when it became a World Heritage site.

Nowadays, after long battles and sieges attempted to gain access to this prized site, visitors are able to stroll across a modern timber bridge from the visitor centre and enter the castle freely through the front door, passing through a multitude of defences designed to keep foreigners out. Grooves for three portcullises can be seen as you walk in, as well as beams to bar the doors, and arrowloops and murder holes to keep uninvited guests well away. Once inside, Ben and I climbed up to the wallwalks to take in the spectacular panoramic views and look down upon the elegant courtyard, with its remaining walls outlining where once there had been a Great Hall, a kitchen, a granary and all the other necessary amenities for a fortress. Walking round the edges, we peered down the shafts of the corner towers, now stripped bare and floorless, the only occupants being the crows who occupy their time by chasing each other from one perch to the next. Walking around the walkway that traces the upper walls, the scenery felt as though I was inspecting a model railway setup, with the trainline running below interrupted at an acute angle by the road and the two carriage trains on the line pausing at a small station with an ornate footbridge. Tiny cars moved slowly along the wide roads and pinprick people went about their business near the school near the train station. Perhaps every model train set is modeled on the North Wales landscape. Green velvety mountains, verdant plains, little marinas for sailing boats, and a scattering of castles surrounded by attractive towns and villages. From this height I could even see perfectly how badly Ben had parked the car, a foot free to the right and the wing mirror hanging over the line on the left hand side. He didn't take too kindly to that observation.

We decided to be brave and take the 127 step descent down to the Water Gate, the secret to Harlech's success as a fortress against the various long sieges waged against it. During the Welsh revolt of 1294, Irish ships kept the English supplied via this passage that leads down to where Tremadog Bay would have lapped against the foot of the castle rock. The Irish are also key to Welsh mythology surrounding Harlech. Brân the Blessed, Brân meaning 'crow' or 'raven' (no wonder they fly around here in numbers), was a giant and ancient king of Britain who was mortally wounded while fighting in Ireland and subsequently had his head chopped off. The story goes that Brân's severed head was still able to talk and he entertained the survivors at Harlech Castle for seven years after their return from the battle across the Irish Sea. Later, when Brân's head fell silent, they followed his instructions to bury the head facing France at the site now occupied by White Tower, the centrepiece of the UNESCO World Heritage site of the Tower of London, where ravens are still kept today in the fear that should they leave, the kingdom will fall. This connection between Harlech and the Tower of London is a little hard to prove and is perhaps fanciful, but makes you wonder whether Edward I chose Harlech not simply just for its location, but also for its symbolism with its association with an ancient king of Britain. We can only wonder.

With our fill of Harlech history, and the 127 steps up and down from the Water Gate having stretched our legs, we made our way back to the poorly parked car and set off back along the tree-lined roads. We were heading to our second castle of the day, Caernarfon. While Harlech is a small village with a castle occupying an imposing position above the plains and beaches below, Caernarfon includes a bustling town within and outside of its ancient town walls and is set at sea level, protecting the southern end of the Menai Strait.

To get there we had two options. Either we follow the main road, the A487, back the way he had come, or we could head into the interior a little more and pass along the smaller roads to reach Caernarfon. With a little arm twisting, and the promise that I would direct him, I managed to convince Ben to take the road less travelled. We diverted at Penrhyndeudraeth (or Penrhy followed by a series of mumbles as I relayed to my driver) and took the A4085 through the villages, past Llyn Cwellyn (a lake) and on the tightest roads possible where we utilised the RV in front as a battering ram against any oncoming vehicles. It was edge of the seat stuff but breathtaking. Mountains all around, rivers passing through, brightly-dressed hikers consulting paper maps: the classic Welsh countryside picture. It required quick reactions and the skills of a rally driver, especially with me trying to distract Ben by offering him a biscuit at the most inopportune moments. *'Biscuit, Ben?'* I'd innocently enquire just as a lorry would appear round a corner metres in front of us or during a particularly winding section of road. I'm lucky he didn't unbuckle me and throw me out of the passenger door while tracing a curve.

We made it to Caernarfon with both of us still in the vehicle and without pangs of hunger for lunch (that big brekkie was still being digested) so headed straight for the castle. You pass through the town walls and walk along streets lined with souvenir shops and pubs before you arrive at the foot of Caernarfon Castle where steps lead you up to the entrance. Not quite the spectacular entry point of Harlech, but once inside the courtyard opens up and you see before you the high wards and polygonal towers that connect to give Caernarfon its figure of eight shape with the upper ward to your left and the lower ward to your right as you walk in. Despite trailing slightly behind Conwy Castle in terms of visitor numbers (around 200,000 a year), Caernarfon felt as though it was the busiest of the four castles with kids off for half term running around on the lawns and being shouted at by their parents. The castle certainly tries to attract the younger visitors with the Eagle Tower hosting exhibitions on the Princes of Wales (the current Prince being Charles, the first son of Elizabeth II, who was invested in the castle in 1969) containing huge chess-figure-like statues of past princes and a room containing tablet devices that connected to a hologram game that sadly didn't seem to be operable, despite the desperate attempts of the kids that swarmed around it.

Caernarfon Castle was started in 1283 though it was never completed as planned despite fifty years of work being done to it. Parts like the Queen's Gate and the King's Gate were never finished despite the vast amounts of time and money spent on it. Walking along its walkways though and exploring the various towers, it feels far more complete than Harlech, though the interior buildings like the Great Hall are little more than foundations nowadays just like with Harlech. Many of the windows, unlike at Harlech, have glass panes in them, though this may be just to stop bow-and-arrow wielding kids from reenacting the defence of the castle during a siege. The castle was targeted by the Welsh and was taken in 1294, though it was quickly reclaimed by the English and repaired at huge expense. The early 1400s saw sieges led by Owain Glyndŵr's army with support from French troops, though it was the relative peace between England and Wales instilled by the ascension of the Tudors to the throne of England that led to the decline in importance of castles like Caernarfon in the 1500s. It was garrisoned by the Royalists in the Civil War despite the wooden floors and roofs having rotted away. This was the last action that Caernarfon saw and it was almost dismantled in 1660, but has risen to prominence in the last century with the investitures of the last two Princes of Wales.

While Harlech has the story of Brân's talking severed head, Caernarfon has picked up on the modern fascination with myths and legends by focusing on the legend of 'The dream of Macsen Wledgig', supposing that Edward manipulated Welsh mythology to stake his claim to being the rightful ruler of Wales. It's a compelling theory borne by historians who look to Caernarfon's banded coloured stone walls and see similarities with the Walls of Constantinople which Macsen Wledig, Roman emperor of the Western portion of Europe when Roman troops departed this part of Wales, has tenuous links to. Known as Magnus Maximus in Roman circles, the story goes that he had a dream of a beautiful girl in a castle by the sea. Messengers sent across the Roman Empire reported finding this fair maiden in Caernarfon. She was Elen, daughter of a British king. Macsen journeyed to Caernarfon to meet her and they fell in love, creating a dynasty whose descendants supposedly included Constantine the Great (hence the banded coloured walls Edward had built), King Arthur, and the princes of Wales. Edward drew upon the similarities between himself and Macsen to prove to the Welsh that he was the rightful Prince of Wales having defeated the local Welsh princes in his colonisation of North Wales. Both Macsen and Edward were from foreign lands, both ruled vast empires, and both Macsen and Edward's family had a taste for the Welsh women.
Though it stretches mythology close to breaking point, really it was a superb work of propaganda that ensured a peaceful future for the time being along with his network of castles that protected the English stronghold in North Wales. The first Prince of Wales was Edward's son, born at Caernarfon Castle, and since then the tradition has been for the eldest son of the monarch to hold the title of Prince of Wales, as

they do today.

Not satisfied enough by old places, Ben took me to one of the oldest inns in Wales for lunch. The Black Boy Inn has been serving beer to patrons and housing them in accommodation since 1522. It's just within the town walls of Caernarfon and aims to retain as much traditional Welsh pub spirit as possible. Stone walls, dark wooden beams, and creaky wooden chairs, it's the perfect place for some pub grub amongst heavily-accented locals and a roaring fire. We both ordered the same Lamb kofta baguette (sometimes we are similar like brothers) and ate them, all the while looking for the gollywogs that Ben said were present in the pub (there weren't any as far as I could see). Now, I know you're wondering about the name of the pub and where it came from. Well, thankfully the beer mats on every table were happy to oblige with the details, probably because it's something you should make clear if you're going to call a pub 'the Black Boy Inn' in the 21st century. According to my reliable source (a beermat), the black boy in question was Jack, a young man captured in Africa and transported to Wales in the mid 1700s. It seems he led a rather idyllic life in the Welsh hills, working as a gardener, getting hitched to a Welsh lass and fathering seven mini-Jacks with her. Of course, being the first black man in the area he was quite noticeable, but he became fluent in Welsh and is to be found today in Ynyscynhaiarn churchyard near Criccieth. There are a few other theories as to how this inn got its name, a black buoy in the harbour and Charles II's nickname amongst them, but Jack's story is my favourite and so it's the one I'll choose to believe. Isn't that how history works?

That evening we decided to hit a few more of Ben's bars in Bangor, starting with Bar Uno, the student's union bar based on the campus and just a short hop from our accommodation. It was surprisingly quiet.

Surely students still drink on a Monday. They do, just elsewhere, Ben replied. With prices hovering around £2.50 a pint, perhaps there are other, cheaper bars to go to. You can't even get a coke for £2.50 where I live. It's incredible how much prices can vary in the UK, and nothing demonstrates the divide more than the price of a pint. Research done on this (and why didn't they ask me to conduct it?) has found that a pint in Carlisle costs on average less than 50% of a pint in Brighton. It's noticeable that the further north you go, the cheaper food, alcohol and many other things get. The prices even change between big restaurant brands. Of course, the brands claim local costs and market conditions as the reason why their prices are different and there is a difference between wages between the North and the South, but it seems crazy that the cost of a Gregg's sausage roll can be 30% more 200 miles down the motorway. The North/South divide is clearer than ever. Just look at the huge blue motorway signs that display distances to cities on the roads passing through the Midlands. As you drive up you get 'The NORTH' and when you drive down you see 'The SOUTH'. It's almost as if we live in different countries.

Regardless of the prices, we were only in the union pub to line our stomachs in preparation for what could be termed as Bangor's piece de resistance for all Ben had hyped it up. Some weeks back when we'd been planning the trip, Ben had introduced me to a 'Fat Frog'. What on earth is that, had been my response and seconds later Ben sent me a photo of numerous pint glasses filled with a glowing green liquid. It looked like the liquid you get in a lava lamp. Now, sat in Rascals bar with a rowdy crowd and a racing car hanging on the wall, Ben had placed a pint of this luminous liquid in front of me and was expecting it to be drunk. Temporarily placing any cares for the state of my digestive system in the back of my mind, I took a sip and was pleasantly surprised that it wasn't totally revolting. It wasn't exactly refreshing though. A combination of three alcopop flavours, it was certainly a method for doing away with the next-to-impossible choice between a Tropical Fruits VK, an Apple and Mango VK and whatever the hell flavour the 'blue' VK is. VKs were a staple of my drinking diet while a fresher at uni, but we'd never had the idea to combine three flavours into one pint glass and call it a 'Fat Frog'. We used to order them four or five at a time and down them in a 'boat race', the idea being that you'd race the other half of your sports team to see which half of the team could down their bottles quickest. I wasn't going to be repeating any feats of making alcohol pour down my throat. It was an achievement to just finish the fat frog which I did, in the end.

Buoyed by mounds of liquid sugar, we bounced down Glanrafon Hill (alternatively known as Bitch Hill, according to Ben, on account of its unfriendly gradient) and entered the hustle and bustle of The Harp pub in the centre of town. There was a reason it was rammed. Monday night is pound pints night. Yes, you read that right. One pound for one pint. For someone who regularly pays five or six pounds for a humble pint of beer, obtaining a drink for a fraction of its usual price felt like stealing, or simply living in the North. Continuing the student drinks trend, I journeyed back to my fresher days and ordered the classic student drink: a snakebite. For the uninitiated, a snakebite combines a half pint of lager with a half pint of cider, topped off with a squirt of blackcurrant cordial. Despite rumours to the contrary, snakebites are not illegal in the UK though you'll only really be served one in a bar that caters to students. Whether the combination of beer and cider gets you drunker I have no idea, but at a pound a pint it was worth trying out, at least for old time's sake.

We took our plastic pound pints up to the roof terrace to join the throngs of students with no lectures tomorrow morning (or at least no lectures they planned on attending). It was there that I had one of those moments when you realise you're getting old. Looking around at the hairless and unwrinkled faces of Bangor's students, I couldn't help but feel a little annoyed at the fact that here they were, studying on student loans paid for by my taxes (let's be honest, very few students are ever going to fully pay off their £27,000 three year tuition loans) and drinking while they could be studying, preparing themselves for the adult world once they graduated. It shocked me that the thought even entered my head, but it's been six years since I graduated and, well, I'm not one of them anymore. Perhaps it was jealousy. Here they were surrounded by friends, drinking in a bar on a Monday night, having a great time by the looks of things. Would I want to go back to uni though? Looking around, I couldn't find anything to convince me that this was a better lifestyle really. They all looked so young, so innocent, and really, despite the fact that they're students, so uneducated. Not through lack of traditional education, but through lack of life experience. I supposed that these were mainly first years and so they are eighteen years old and through the three years of university they'll get a fair share of life experience, but really, coming from my experience, university doesn't really prepare you for the realities of the working world. These guys were all going to wake up in three years' time to the shock that they need to work, and work hard, to get what they want out of life. I wasn't convinced that any of them, swigging their pound pints and lighting their roll-ups, were really aware of that.

I awoke the next day without the inevitable hangover that those students would be enduring, though with the smell of tobacco in my clothes and an ulcer from the ridiculous amounts of sugar I must have drunk from the Fat Frog. I guess you can't expect to survive pound pints unscathed. It was a chillier day outside by the looks of things, in contrast to the beautiful sunshine of the previous day. Ben and I had a quick breakfast in the student halls kitchen (still no washing up liquid) and then jumped in the car and sped off across the Menai Strait to Beaumaris.

'Beautiful marsh' may sound like an oxymoron, but that is exactly where Beaumaris Castle is located. Looking out across the northern entrance to the Menai Strait between mainland Wales and Anglesey, Beaumaris is considered the most technically perfect castle in the UK with James of St George employing the 'walls within walls' concept again to great effect, but it's also known as the 'greatest castle never built' according to the sandwich board just inside the entrance. More correctly, Beaumaris is the greatest castle never finished. Due to Edward I running out of money, building work was stopped thirty five years after it was started and the castle was never completed as per its ambitious design. James of St George had grander plans than the king could afford, with his remit being to design the most perfect castle known to man. With a flat area of land serving as his blank canvas, he could build practically anything with no natural features to take into consideration like at Harlech. As a result, Beaumaris appears more like a palace than a fortification, perhaps because its high walls were never completed to their intended height so it appears dainty rather than mighty in comparison to the other three castles. Still, it came with the full complement of defensive devices like the murder holes in the gate-passage and the portcullis, though the moat doesn't completely wrap the building nowadays, having been partially filled, and seems more of a water feature than a defense mechanism. With its children's play area and crazy golf next to it, it seems more like a kiddy-size castle than a stronghold designed to protect those within.

Ben and I were the first to enter the castle that day

and for a time we were the only souls around. It was rather wonderful having the castle to ourselves. We climbed up to walkway running along the walls, surveying the views of the misty hills of Snowdonia and the strait, and venturing inside the narrow corridors and bare rooms of the castle. We discovered that James of St George certainly accounted for the comforts of guests and those who would inhabit the castle, allowing for no less than thirty two toilets. The perfect castle comes with plenty of choices over where to do your business, I suppose. James also wanted symmetry, and the castle is perfect because of it. An octagon shaped outer wall surrounding the square inner building with round towers jutting out like jewels in a crown. It looks perfect from every angle, despite its unfinished and half ruined state. Again, without the roofs and the floors, it's hard to imagine that anyone once lived here, or that it was in any way comfortable. Indeed, because of its unfinished state and its inadequacy for preventing attacks, it was never really lived in much. Owain Glyndŵr took it during the revolt against English rule at the start of the 1400s but it was retaken by the Royalists and then changed hands a few times between the Bulkeley family and Parliament while continuing to fall into disrepair and having its stones and lead repurposed for other projects. It was used as a subject for artists in the 1800s, being part of Lord Thomas Bulkeley's estate, and that seems to have set the tone for its purpose ever since. It's a beautiful castle set in beautiful surroundings. That, and it's the perfect place for a game of hide and seek, with its endless passageways which disorientate you because they all look so similar - the danger of symmetry I suppose. Ben and I didn't have time for a game before a bus load of school kids arrived and set about running through the passageways in their own games of chase. We escaped them by hiding away in the exhibits which gave us the chance to explore the chapel and watch a short film which divulged the history of the castle in a circular cabin. Suitably educated, we tried out a few of the hands-on exhibits that allow you to appreciate the masonry and carpentry work undertaken by the builders in the 1300s, though Ben managed to snap the head off a plastic axe by standing on it and we swiftly left the exhibits before anyone caught us.

Once you've walked around the walls and passageways, taken in the views and inspected the moss making itself at home in the walls, there's not a great deal else to do at Beaumaris. With the school kids running around like prisoners on day release, we hastened for the exit and went in search of caffeine which was duly supplied by the delightful Over House Bistro which was doing a roaring trade in hot drinks on this cold and windy morning. Not quite time for lunch, we decided to take Little Car up to Penmon Point, the very easternmost part of Anglesey, and check out the views of the offshore lighthouse and Puffin Island. Penmon Point is accessed by a private road and as such we had to pay a toll of £3 to a fellow sat on a chair in the cold. I wondered if this charge would deter other tourists (it certainly deterred whoever did StreetView for Google Maps as the images stop just short of the toll booth) but there were a fair few other visitors in the carpark when we arrived, parking right on the edge of the land, just above the beach, with wonderful views of the black and white striped lighthouse standing lonely amongst the crashing waves. Ben and I enjoyed a fun game of 'Stone Shooting' a variant of Clay Pigeon Shooting, where one of us would launch a stone up into the air from behind the other person who would then attempt to hit the flying stone by throwing a stone of their own. We must have spent a good thirty minutes trying in vain to make two stones connect in the air, but after many, many attempts we called it a day with just a few near hits recorded. At least we hadn't hit each other, unlike one holiday as a child that I can recall during which I threw a stone into the back of my older cousin's head with all the consequences that you can imagine ensuing.

Arms aching from competitively trying to throw stones into the sea as far as we could, we drove back to Bangor and tried out a ramen restaurant in the centre of town. After living in Japan a few years ago, I'm now hesitant about eating Japanese food outside of Japan as many so-called Japanese restaurants don't have Japanese owners and often don't match the quality of food that I enjoyed in Japan. Noodle One on Bangor's high street is an exception though, with a steaming tasty bowl of udon noodle presented in front of me that cured the rumbling stomach induced by running round castle ramparts and chucking stones into the sea that morning. We slurped up and then headed out onto the road again, this time to the fourth and final castle on the UNESCO list: Conwy.

As it was Ben's favourite we had decided to save it until last, though it was built just before Beaumaris and was finished within six years. It's much more similar to Caernarfon Castle with a walled city and a rectangular enclosure style and has had a fairly similar history to the other castles, being involved in battles between Welsh revolters like Madog ap Llywelyn and Owain Glyndŵr and English kings, and suffering from lack of maintenance in the centuries that followed. While he used force a few years later to unsuccessfully attempt to take Caernarfon castle, Owain Glyndŵr used a sneakier tactic to take Conwy out of English hands. Two of his supporters, rumoured to be his cousins, pretended to be carpenters and somehow talked their way past the guards at the gates of Conwy Castle while the garrison were in the chapel on Good Friday. The Welsh rebels took control of the castle and the walled town and held on to it for three months before negotiating a surrender with the king. Now that's the way to do it!
Like Caernarfon, it too was garrisoned by Royalists in

the English Civil War and was afterwards saved from slighting but suffered dereliction and stripping of its resources in the 17th century. Today, like all four castles, it's just the stone shell that remains, but one can get a clear idea of the power and strength of the fortification from its dizzyingly high towers and the grand remains of halls within the walls of the castle. Walking along the tops of the walls, Ben and I could see out to the Irish Sea and watch cars, pedestrians and trains cross to the otherside of the River Conwy along the three individual bridges, Telford's gorgeous suspension bridge, Stephenson's tubular railway bridge, and someone's unimaginative 1950s concrete stone and metal lump of a road bridge. In many ways, it's only fair and fitting that trains and pedestrians get to cross on architectural gems and cars are consigned to the mundane modern offering. Of course though, the blandest bridge is also the busiest so I suppose what it lacks in beauty it makes up for in functionality. In truth, it's really not that bad. It even features, pride of place, on the front cover of the tourist leaflet. It's just not up there with the Telford or a Stephenson creation, that's all.

As well as the three bridges to Caernarfon's one, it's the trains that make Conwy so distinguishable as the rail line runs below the outer wall of the castle, squeezing the rocky promontory that Conwy castle is built upon, making you feel, just like at Harlech, that you are a figure on a model railway exhibit. Perhaps it's the unassuming entrance to Conwy Castle, crossing over the modern day moat of the traffic lights, but the inside is spectacular, arguably the most complex and complete of the four. A path winds its way through the centre of the outer ward with all the necessary parts of a castle like a Great Hall, the kitchens and the chapel shooting off from it and then you walk on into the inner ward which, though roofless now, would once have housed the royals and the elite. Ben and I made our way into the Chapel Tower to take a look at a curious feature rarely found in medieval castles. The chapel is small with beautiful stained glass windows installed in 2012 and up a small flight of steps from it is the 'watching tower' from where the king would sit by himself with a slit view of the altar. Why King Edward wanted his own private, yet restricted, view of the services is open to speculation, but conveniently there is a latrine should he have needed to switch thrones mid-service. Ben imitated using the facilities to their intended purpose, though as much as he would have wanted the acclaim of shitting where a king of England once did his business too, the facilities were, as with all the castles, simply holes in the stonework nowadays. Though he did spend the Christmas of 1294 here at Conwy while the castle was under siege from Welsh revolters, Edward actually spent very little time at this castle, just three months or so. This was not for lack of comfort though, for the accomodation would have been at that time rather opulent and with grand fireplaces and windows, as well as luxurious furniture and fine art wall decorations. It's hard to imagine now with the bare, dingy walls and the immense amount of moss growing out from the stones, but at one time the walls would have been painted and the rooms would have been warm and toasty. Nowadays, the wind was piercing through every nook and cranny it could find and I'd have had to be persuaded hard to spend a night on the cold, hard floors.

Conwy's castle is complemented by the three quarters of a mile long wall that circles the old town where once the English lived, ready to form a militia if the town suddenly came under attack from the nearby Welsh. The wall is in remarkable health considering its age and it can still be walked along to inspect the tight streets of the old town and the more spacious houses outside the walls. Twenty one towers interrupt the wall, even where it rises steeply over the crest of a hill, and traffic waits, usually patiently, to enter and depart through the turreted gates. Ben and I walked a part of it, peering into the locals' gardens and being careful to not trip over the cobbles. We ended up at the quay where Ben had promised a visit to something rather special, though for him it wouldn't be much of a comfortable stay. The smallest house in Great Britain, measuring just 182 cm across and 304 cm back with a height of 310 cm, is a former fisherman's house that was an infill between cottages, though just the cottage to its right remains. Nowadays it's a unique tourist attraction with visitors passing behind a curtain for a pound to take a peek at the tiny living area on the lower floor and climb the stairs to the miniscule bedroom above.

All 195 cm of Ben managed to bend down and enter without too much difficulty, though his head comfortably touched the ceiling and he wouldn't have had much fun in the kiddy size bed. Inside an audio guide detailed the history of the house and its occupants and we could inspect the various accoutrements of a Victorian household, a stove for boiling water, a place to sit, a table with some sort of dried brain decoration on it. There were a few articles on the walls, including the newspaper clippings from the funeral of the previous owner, who was a journalist and author well known for standing outside the house in traditional Welsh costume to attract custom. Nowadays you can still find someone in full costume, flowery bonnet and red shawl, outside the house dealing with the tens of thousands of tourists from around the world who come to marvel at the fact that someone, and even couples sometimes, used to live in a space the same size as most people's pantries. As you might expect from the smallest house in the country, not a great deal of time is needed to tour around the house, we waited longer in the queue outside, but it is unique and of reasonable interest if you're in the area. I'd far rather spend a night in the tiny bed upstairs than in the King's bedchamber in the castle along the quay.

Of course neither bedroom was an option, Airbnb hasn't stretched that far yet. Ben and I returned to our actual accommodation and readied ourselves for another night on the tiles of Bangor. We started in the student union bar again which soon got commandeered by a huge group of pirates from the Mountain Walking society (really just teenage students sipping rum on the rocks and wincing) and then moved on to another student bar named Varsity that obliged with a Snakebite (worryingly, I was starting to get the taste for them back) before finishing off the night with another hike up Bitch Hill (up which we saw a number of young pirates struggling). With Liverpool in the morning, we bade each other the earliest goodnight of the trip and separated into our respective rooms.

Back in my room, I wondered if Ben had enjoyed the trip, difficult it was to tell due to his stoic demeanour. The trip had been enhanced by having him along with me, as travel almost always is bettered by being joined by the right companion, and having him as my chauffeur, driving me, Miss Daisy, certainly assisted me greatly. On the drive back, he had even admitted that possibly he could be persuaded into joining me on other trips to World Heritage sites. We'd see about that, I supposed. I might have to return to the hills of Snowdonia after all. Listening to the radio in the morning, there had been an item on a possible new World Heritage site in Wales, the slate landscape of Gwynedd. Wales may have a fourth site in a few years time as the nomination takes a few years to be decided upon. It would be another boost to this region of the UK, having another world-renowned heritage site drawing more tourists to one of the traditionally more deprived areas of the country. As we drove along the North Wales Expressway, east out of the country, we passed countless examples of buildings and houses with slate roofs, likely mined out of the

Bethesda Nantile belt that stretches out just to the south of Bangor. Slate roofed the 19th century world and Welsh slate can be found all over the country and in many countries abroad with its reputation as one of the best quality slates to be found. It's another feather in the cap for this region along with its castles and, should the bid be successful, ensure that Wales's natural and historical beauty be protected.

UK UNESCO World Heritage Site #8 of 28

Liverpool – Maritime Mercantile City (2004)

A dock in danger

Name the two former World Heritage Sites which were struck off the list because their heritage was compromised by modern development. Any guesses? No? Well, they are Oman's Arabian Oryx Sanctuary (delisted due to 90% of the site being turned into an oil field) and Germany's Dresden Elbe Valley (delisted because of the controversial construction of the Waldschlösschen Bridge). Liverpool, at the time of writing, could well be the third to join the blacklist. It was added in 2004 but plans to regenerate 150 acres of dockland by building apartments and a cruise terminal in 2012 meant that UNESCO placed it on its World Heritage In Danger list. Since then, the city has teetered on the edge of losing its precious UNESCO status and despite the developer of the Liverpool Waters project, Peel, declaring that there is no likelihood of the original plan ever going ahead now, the threat still remains. The general sense is that

Liverpool cares very little about its World Heritage status, concentrating on economic growth and job creation without realising what role heritage can play in helping with this. Although the mayor and various city politicians have expressed their desire to remain on the list and a raft of measures have been proposed to ensure skyscrapers don't dominate the historic waterfront, Liverpool remains on the endangered list and redevelopment plans promising billions of pounds of investment look ever more tempting.

Time will tell if the city gives in to the will of developers or if heritage is put first, but with no time to waste, Ben and I hopped into Little Car and sped off back to England. We zoomed past Conwy, where we'd stopped off to see the castle the previous day, and before we knew it we were heading up the Mersey through ports and industrial lands towards Birkenhead. We'd decided that driving into central Liverpool and having to find parking wouldn't be the best idea so we parked up at Woodside Pier and caught the ferry across the Mersey to Pier Head. Running against the clock we managed to commit only one wrong turn at the many roundabouts and junctions leading us to the water's edge. I jumped out of the car to get ferry tickets while Ben ran to the pay and display machine. We made it onto the ferry just on time, joining the gaggle of other tourists climbing abroad for a ride on one of the most famous ferry crossings in the world.

Just to let you know that you are on a ferry crossing the Mersey, the ferry operators blast out the haunting vocals of Gerry Marsden's 1964 hit 'Ferry Cross the Mersey', a song you will have reverberating around your head for the rest of the time you spend by the water in Liverpool. It's a beautiful homage to Liverpool, a city where people 'don't care what your name is boy / we'll never turn you away'. On a chilly, overcast morning, travelling on grey water to a grey city, Liverpool didn't seem so inviting as the song suggested, but the explosion of colour from our dazzle camouflaged boat made us feel that we were from a coloured world travelling to a black and white existence. Dazzle camouflage is a remarkable idea. Rather than hiding from enemy boats, inventor Normal Wilkinson had the idea that using bright colours and geometric shapes could mislead the enemy and cause them to take up poor firing positions. It was used a lot in WW1 and a bit in WW2, though its effectiveness is still debated. Nowadays, the only effect of dazzle is to make the tour boats that cross the Mersey look like a children's play area. Still, it's far better than the standard white colour you get on other ferries. At least the tour companies on the other side could see us coming.

As we bobbed around on the Mersey we came into clearer sight of the Three Graces that make Liverpool's skyline one of the most recognisable in the world. Standing tallest to the left is the Liver Building with its mythical liver birds facing opposite directions, supposedly, as the commentary onboard was telling us, to protect the city's citizens and the sailors coming into port. There are though a few cheekier theories, based on the male liver bird looking towards the city for a pub and the female liver bird looking out to sea to spot any handsome sailors, that exist and are probably more popularly told by Liverpudlians.
In the middle of the three stands the palatial Cunard Building which was home to the eponymous shipping company until the 1960s, and nowadays hosts the British Music Experience. Third, furthest to the right, is the Edwardian Baroque style Port of Liverpool Building, noticeable for its central dome. All three are spectacular in their own right, but together they create a formidable threesome that summarise Liverpool's incredible architecture. With more Georgian buildings than Bath and more than 2000 listed buildings, Liverpool is an architect's dream. Many of these

structures are included in the UNESCO World Heritage listing, but they are under threat from taller, modern buildings which obstruct the skyline. The view is perfect from the ferry, but walking around the city, the views of these stone marvels are often blocked by sleek glassy towers.

Rocking up at Pier Head, we wriggled our way off the boat ahead of the grannies and pushchair families and dived into the Fab Four cafe to grab coffees for the road. Pier Head is home to The Beatles Experience and there are statues of the four of them outside, surrounded day and night by fans almost expecting them to move and start performing one of their hits. Ben and I had just seen the Fab Four over the previous two days (also non-moving, but a fair bit older) so we moved onto the first set of docks that are part of this World Heritage site that stretches around 3 miles north to south. Coffee cups adorned with the heads of four, floppy-haired Scousers in our chilly hands, we sped off on foot to Stanley Dock, the only inland dock built in Liverpool and the northernmost part of the World Heritage site.

To get there you have to pass through Princes Dock, an area with smart though lifeless apartment blocks, before merging onto Waterloo Road which Ben so eloquently described as 'a right shithole'. In fairness, he wasn't too far wrong. There was more litter than paving stones on the pavement and high walls with painful-looking spiked gates on both sides. We walked along quickly, hoping to get to Stanley Dock, take a picture and turn around to get back to Pier Head. In truth, there wasn't a great deal to lok at once we arrived. There's no access to the docks of course and so it was only by peeping through a corrugated iron gate that we were able to see Stanley Dock and appreciate its size next to the gargantuan red-bricked Tobacco Warehouse, in itself well worth the walk as it's a monumental structure (the largest of its kind in the world) that testifies to the industry that must have been going on many years ago. A burger van was parked by the road serving construction workers of building sites nearby, but it was clear that this area of the city had been abandoned for a while. A waterfront that must have been thriving at one time, now eerily quiet and a little daunting. Something that a little revdelopment could solve, I'm sorry to say.

Next up were the Albert Docks, and thanks to redevelopment these live in stark contrast to Stanley Docks. With Liverpool's main museums in the area, the dock has shopping, food, plush apartments and more coffee outlets than you can shake an instant coffee stirrer at. We had a time and a place to be though so we sped through the commercial crap and arrived at the Maritime Museum in time for the start of the Old Docks tour. It's a free walking tour led by guides at the Maritime Museum and it has become something of a hot ticket, judging by the museum's insistence that we book in advance. Ben and I had managed to snag the last two places when I phoned that morning.

We were made to wait a little for it too. The man on the end of the line when I had booked the tour had said that it met in the foyer of the Maritime Museum ten minutes before the start time of 12.00 and that was where we appeared to be stood now at 12.01 thinking to ourselves 'are we in the wrong place?' There were a few other hopeful tour goers also apparently wondering the same, but in typical British fashion we didn't dare suppose that the other was waiting for the same thing so stayed quiet, ready to jump into action should a wave of once waiting pensioners start hurrying towards a door. It worked a lot like this when there didn't use to be those snazzy electronic departure boards on station platforms. You'd have to judge the appearance of those also waiting to determine whether you too were also meant to be waiting on that particular platform or whether your train had suddenly jumped platforms. Sneaking glances at tickets held in hands, eavesdropping into conversations to see if any clues could be divulged: it used to be hard work. Of course, you could just go round asking fellow passengers if they too were waiting for the 12.45 to Guildford, but they might start a conversation with you and, with at least an hour on the same train together, that just could not be risked. As such, Ben and I paced slowly around the foyer, waiting for a booming voice to announce themselves as the tour leader for the Old Docks tour.

Thankfully it wasn't too much of a wait in the end. In fairness, Gary, our guide, had just returned from showing a group of visually impaired people around the docks (hence his tardiness) and so we all looked down and shuffled our feet in embarrassment that we'd been mumbling and grumbling about five minutes added on to our days. After a brief introduction to what we were going to be seeing on the tour, Gary led us out of the foyer where he delivered a tongue-in-cheek safety briefing about crossing roads and made us wait for the green man to show before we crossed the six-laned Strand Street that nowadays divides the city from its docks. I'm pleased to report that we all made it across.

Now we were on the other side, we could see the full extent of the development of Liverpool City centre known as Liverpool One. Basically, it's one of those places that kicks off their 'One BIG festive street party' in mid-November, and since it was mid-October every available advertising space was occupied by six food posters reminding me of this. It's a monster of a compex. Restaurant chains everywhere, a cinema, hotels, bars, an adventure golf course, and pretty much every UK clothing store chain you can name covered by five close shopping districts. It dominates a huge area of Liverpool's retail space, located where water once lapped against the sides of docks. There are reminders of this all around if you know what you are looking for. William Hutchinson's remarkable sea level measurements, recorded at every high water for almost thirty years in the 1700s, are inscribed on the pavement. A line through the shopping centre gardens we were now standing in demonstrates where the water used to rise to, where we were standing right now would once have been water. Where shoppers were now walking along carrying their brown paper Primark bags, there would have been a natural tidal pool running off the Mersey. It was that tidal pool that was partially filled and locked in from the river with quay walls to create the Old Dock, billed by our guide as the reason why present-day Liverpool is the way it is today. Without this dock, Liverpool may not exist and with that all that Liverpool has produced and invented. The city even takes its name from this pool, 'liver' meaning 'muddy' or 'thick' in Old English and it was the genius usage of this pool that enabled Thomas Steere to create the world's first 'wet' dock and thus set Liverpool on course for untold riches and a place in world history. As Gary our guide stated *'the importance of this dock cannot be underestimated'*.

Practically salivating with the thought of seeing this marvel, we all followed Gary to an entrance to an underground car park next to Bill's, a British cafe chain that can be found in dozens of locations around the UK. He gathered us round and then motioned at us to follow him into the car park foyer. Bemused, we followed him through sets of doors, past other doors that lead to the backs of the shops in the shopping centre with exotic locations like 'yellow zone', bare brick and silver insulation over the piping. Before we walked in, Gary reminded us all to keep cameras and other loose items close. *'No throwing your wives or husbands into the dock, please. We won't be able to get them out again, though that may tempt you even*

further'. We chuckled. I preemptively warned Ben that throwing me into the dock would not be in any way funny.
'What about your notebook?'
'Don't you flipping dare.'

The final door led us down some steps and into the covered area that houses the north-east portion of the Old Dock. Walkways lead you into the dock, allowing you to stand above it and appreciate the brickwork that looks holed and knobbly today, but kept the water in with a special lime mortar that was a forerunner of cement. Old Dock was the only dock to be made of bricks, all others in Liverpool following it were constructed using stone, and it is said that the bricks were pilfered from Liverpool Castle which was demolished in 1726. Though it was monstrously expensive to build, the dock paid for itself within three months, establishing Liverpool as a metropolis of world trade. Most significantly, it quickly usurped other ports as goods could be unloaded within 36 hours, as opposed to the normal unloading time of two weeks. This had the catalyst effect of local businesses catering to sailors who now had only 36 hours in which to pursue their carnal pleasures and thus the area around the docks became a, let's say lively, area in the 1700s.

Guide Gary gave us a detailed explanation of how the Old Dock came to be preserved in this way, below shoppers and their cars. It's all down to the benevolence of the former Duke of Westminster, Gerald Grosvenor, who owned the Grosvenor Group that redeveloped Liverpool's city centre while the city was European Capital of Culture. He was adamant that the Old Dock be preserved and opened up to the public so that people could see a slice of Liverpool's history below their Ugg boots and Converse. Though it requires being part of this tour, and involves a trip through shop back entrances, at least Liverpool's development has not totally destroyed the city's history. It's worth remembering that below all the modern products of trade and globalisation lies a key part of the story of world trade and the Global Village that we live in today. Although the Old Dock was cutting edge technology in its day, it lasted only a hundred years or so before becoming obsolete due to the increase in size of the ships that were being used to carry goods around the world. Ships tend to increase in size while docks stay the same so once 1000 ton ships started being used, Old Dock was no longer suitable and other docks in Liverpool replaced it. As such, Old Dock was mostly used by the local populace as a sewage depository, much to the ire of the local archaeology students who were enlisted to help excavate the dock centuries later. In 1826 Old Dock was closed, filled in, and had a new custom house built on top of it. The Custom House was the most impressive building in Liverpool until the Three Graces came along, but it was heavily bombed during the Blitz in May 1941 and was deemed irreparable despite local pleas to restore it. The site lay vacant for many decades until the Liverpool One development rejuvenated the area and we have what you can see today. While the shops, restaurants and indoor golf facilities of Liverpool One were being built, archaeologists were working to uncover the walls of Old Dock. It's amazing to think that while the future of Liverpool was being constructed, Liverpool's past was being revealed with every layer that archaeologists dug down. Every brick and stone in the wall was cleaned and discarded items from local Liverpudlians were found amongst the remains of sewage including ropes, coins and pottery. Today, only one twentieth of the dock is able to be seen, the rest lies under the development of modern day Liverpool, but it's one twentieth that has revealed a lot about the past lives of Liverpudlians and about the achievement of building the world's first 'wet' dock with only the previous experience of building canals to guide them.

Well worth preserving amongst the glut of modern day conveniences, I feel.

Gary's explanation was fascinating, so much so in fact that while we were all listening, a clatter and a crash sounded from the bottom of the Old Dock. Peering over the edge, we could see a walking stick lying on the excavated floor, under the walkway that we were all standing on. One of the gentlemen on our tour had been concentrating so much on Gary's words that he had let his walking stick fall in the gap between the floor and the side of the walkway. We all recalled the specific warning that Gary had given us before we walked in. In many ways, in typical British schadenfreude style, we had all wanted to see this happen, and we were now all waiting with baited breath to see what would happen next. There was no quick fix, but Gary could get the guys at Liverpool One to go down and fetch it. Still, a few people got their cameras out, dangled them over the edge, and took a picture of the walking stick's misfortune. As a nation, we love bad things happening to other people - it's the basis of the popularity behind many reality shows and our strain of comedy in the UK. We revel in other people's strokes of bad luck.

After the talk we were free to wander around the walkways, being extra careful of our possessions of course, and then exit the way we had come in. Ben and I were pushed for time, but I wanted to ask Gary about the very real possibility of Liverpool losing its World Heritage status. In essence, Gary wasn't too hopeful. Landmarks owned by foreign investors, desire and necessity for economic development, the lack of public awareness on issues of conservation and heritage related to World Heritage status. UNESCO has allowed Liverpool to keep its status for the time being, but it still has the city on its danger list. The city council and Historic England have proposed a skyline policy for new buildings so that developments do not rise above the heritage buildings in Liverpool's historic centre and on its waterfront. However, enticing proposals from developers keep being produced and the city council will have to make some tough decisions in the future as to which direction they want the city to go in. What's more important: heritage or modern development?

Of course, heritage is a relatively new concept. Those in the 1700s would have had few qualms about pulling down old buildings or building new ones in the shade of more historic sites. They would have chosen investment hands down. Up to forty or fifty years ago, humans didn't really care too much about heritage. Now in the age of mass tourism it's become important to preserve historical buildings, but, as the construction of the Customs House over Old Dock in the 1800s shows, it's never been much of a concern before.

Thankfully though, at the very least there is a slice of truly remarkable heritage open to the public under a shopping centre, preserving the very thing that made Liverpool great in the first place and the planted the seeds for every other future development to follow. As Gary stressed multiple times, it's doubtful that Liverpool, and everything that the city has produced, would exist now without the ingenuity of the Old Dock. It can't be underestimated.

UK UNESCO World Heritage Site #9 of 28

Blenheim Palace (1987)

How the other half live

Maintaining friendships is such hard work, isn't it? Think about all those classmates from school, all those people you met while at university or in your previous jobs. The guys you travelled with or met at random events. How many of them do you still make a point of catching up with nowadays? Beyond seeing their posts on Instagram, do you actually still keep in contact with them? I have to admit, being 27 now and it being a few years since I was at university let alone school, that I almost never talk to the people I used to regard as my closest friends. Matters of time, distance, and fewer and fewer things in common except for shared memories add to the surety that I may never speak to the vast majority of my 'friends' ever again. I try not to spend a lot of time on social media, but once in a blue moon I'll scroll through and see where people are at. New haircuts, different jobs, the same old changes. People moving on with their lives.

There are a few old friends that I manage to maintain some degree of contact with though. During my summers at university I would go out to Connecticut in the United States and work as a swimming instructor and lifeguard at a summer camp in the Berkshire Hills. It was there that I met a great deal of people my age from around the world and struck up the kinds of friendships that you believe, and are told, are going to last a lifetime. Alas, inevitably many friendships don't stand up to the test of time and distance, but a few have and once a year, in the Autumn, I meet up with a couple of friends from the very first of four summers I spent in Connecticut. Stevo and Sabrina were on the same day-off as me in the first summer and so we spent all our precious free time together. Having only two days off every two weeks meant that we used to make the most of our free time so we ended up having quite a few crazy nights out, despite being well under the drinking age for the States. The summer camp would drive us out into civilisation and drop us in a rather run down town called Torrington where we would book into the Yankee Pedlar Hotel in the centre and set about drinking as much as we possibly could while neglecting other day-off responsibilities such as laundry and calling home. The Yankee Pedlar, reportedly haunted and sadly no longer operating, had a bar called Bogey's attached to it and it was here that we imbibed copious amounts of 'lemonade', as we told the kids. There was one particularly infamous evening when the kindly barmaid allowed us free reign upon her bar, pouring invented cocktails for our delectation and treating us to more alcohol than we could ever hope of paying for. It was the stuff of legend, almost as unbelievable as the stories about the ghost of Alice Conley, the former owner who died in room 353. In remembrance, our yearly gatherings are known as 'Bogey's', though they generally involve a lot less alcohol and rolling around hotel lobbies nowadays. This evening being a Friday night after a long week at work, Stevo in project management and Sabrina in PR (gosh, how they've grown up!), we settled for pizzas and beers around a few boardgames, falling slowly asleep to a horror film that was actually based on, and set in, the very Yankee Pedlar Hotel that we used to stay in (The Innkeepers, in case you were wondering). A year is enough time for life to change significantly enough to have sufficient news for an evening. Stevo had gone freelance, Sabrina had split up with her boyfriend, I'd moved to Bournemouth - those changes, plus the usual round-up of mutual friends' news provided the chat for the evening. It's good to have these yearly moments, kind of like New Year's Eve, to give you perspective on the year gone and to remember more youthful times long ago. It makes the world a little less lonely to see old friends and reminisce. Even if times have changed so much that none of us could keep our eyelids open past midnight.

Next morning, Stevo kindly woke up to give me a lift down to the train station. I think I've got to the point with my friends where they don't question or query my travels. Getting up at 7am on a Saturday to go and see a palace isn't that strange to me, but perhaps it is to some. We said a heartfelt goodbye at the station, hoping that it would be less than a year before we work out a time to see each other again. It's a cliche but life is so busy that fitting in visits to distant friends takes a lot of commitment and time organisation. There just aren't enough weekends to fit in everybody.

Swindon and Oxford are close by, rivals in football, and just a jump between each other on the map, but getting from one to the other necessitates a change of Didcot Parkway, which is just as romantic a stop as you can imagine. Still the connection was less than ten minutes so my grumbling was limited. As the Didcot Parkway train to Oxford is really just a shuttle between the two, the info boards at Didcot Parkway were showing a train terminating and not the next outward journey. Fair enough then that a man walking tentatively onto the train enquired to one of the passengers sat down whether this was indeed the train to Oxford that he presumed it was. The passenger, a young lady with an American accent, answered that she didn't know whether this was the train to Oxford to which the man, with stifled British sarcasm replied, *'so you're sitting on a train but you don't know where it's going?'* They stood there in silence for a moment, she not knowing how to respond to his question, and he caught between needing to know something and having chosen an idiot to ask. Eventually there was an announcement to the platform that the train standing at platform 4 was indeed the service to Oxford and the man sat down and everyone felt more comfortable, but still, it begged the question why the lady didn't know where she was going. Most requests for information to the public are often met with 'I don't know' these days. Perhaps it's people's fear that giving the wrong information will lead to them getting castigated by the enquirer, perhaps it's simply that people just want to avoid interaction with anyone on public transport. Or perhaps it's just that people randomly get on trains without knowing where they are going, just hoping it's going somewhere near their destination. I have no idea how other people spend their Saturdays, but it's true that people get kicks out of some weird train stuff.

No disrespect to Oxford rail station, but I'm sure I'm not the only one who arrives into Oxford expecting to alight at a grand, neo-Gothic building with statues and gargoyles on the walls, faint memories of British Rail and the good old days of rail travel. Given the city's academic reputation and the glorious architecture the university buildings enjoy, it's always a little surprising to roll into what is really not a bad station (compared to some eyesores) but is so run of the mill that it could be anywhere. It doesn't feel befitting because Oxford isn't just anywhere, it's Oxford. Home of the world's oldest English-speaking university and a whole host of world-renowned museums and libraries like the Ashmolean and the Bodleian. A list of world-impacting alumni as tall as its spires exemplifies how special Oxford is, and you'd imagine that each of them at some point had to use a train at some point to get from Oxford to London or elsewhere. Perhaps the station is deliberately understated in an attempt to impress visitors with the architecture once they get into the city (or perhaps it was just lack of imagination in 1970s architecture), but I for one would love a grander entrance to this most-storied of cities.

I was sadly only in Oxford to hop from the train to the bus and within no time I was sat on the 500 service's top deck (at the front, of course. I do love the feeling of seeing overhanging branches smash against the window) and we were heading out of the city centre towards Woodstock. Blenheim's out in the Oxfordshire countryside, past London Oxford airport (a whole 75 miles from Trafalgar Square, but hey, put London in the name, why not). As you draw closer signs advertising palace events appear and as it was early November, the Christmas adverts were out in full force. I was heartened to learn that I was a week too early for 'Christmas at the Palace' (it's as if I deliberately tried to avoid coach upon coach load of dawdling tourists), but as it was a Saturday I was certain that I'd encounter crowds nevertheless. Blenheim attracts around 900,000 tourists a year though it still places outside of the top 40 attractions in the UK, probably due to its £27 entrance charge. Still, close to a million visitors at £27 quid a pop ain't a bad little income for the Duke of Marlborough, now is it? Beats putting it on Airbnb anyway.

Visitors who arrive by bus like myself receive a generous 30% reduction on their ticket, but as I was the only person to get off the bus at the palace (indeed I was the only person on the service for much of the way) it's not clear how many visitors choose to leave their car at home. As I walked through the lavish gates and up the driveway towards the palace it was clear that perhaps most people drive. To pay, I had to wait behind a car to be served at a drive-through hut by the car parks. Once the car in front had been served I had to drive myself forward (resisting the temptation to wind down an imaginary windscreen) to pay my entrance. Noticing my lack of vehicular locomotion, the clerk asked me if I had, by chance, come on the bus. I wanted to reply with a good dose of sarcasm, but I was also quite keen to receive the 30% discount and so I confirmed his suspicion without moving my eyebrows at all and collected my ticket and a map. From the hut I still had a longish stroll up the straight driveway, but there were no cars behind me so I pootled along and enjoyed the morning sun working its bright rays on the dewy lawns. The Italian gentleman at the drive-through had kindly pointed out that I could upgrade my humble ticket to an annual pass for free when inside the palace and so, seeing the booths free as I entered, I did so. With my picture and oh so valuable spam email address taken down (little do they know that I haven't checked that inbox for at least a decade), I was now the proud holder of a little ID card that would grant me access all year round. Not bad at all, Blenheim. At the very least it's a nice souvenir. Waving my card willy nilly around the place as I passed through the checkpoints *('you do know that I am an annual pass holder, don't you?')*, I walked into the Great Courtyard and was met by the sight to my left hand side that makes every visitor forget they are walking and cause a hand to slip into their pocket to grab their camera phone.

It's simply spectacular. Vast columns and steps to your left create an intimidating entrance to those approaching from the grassy lawns that stretch down across a bridge and then up to the distant Victory Monument far away to your right. The grandeur is striking, especially at 10am when the morning sun is gracing the courtyard and just a couple of other tourists are milling around. The state rooms were still getting dressed so we had to wait a little before the great front doors were pushed apart. When they did open, I rushed in a split second ahead of a 30 strong Chinese tour group and got an audio tour device. You find these in place of real tours at many tourist attractions nowadays. Headphones and a mobile phone-like device for selecting the audio number as you walk around. I supposed that the device I'd been handed had actually once been a mobile for it had, for no explicit reason, cameras at the front and the back of the device, much the same way a smartphone would. Why Blenheim has audio tour guide devices with cameras I wasn't able to ask the assistant as soon a wave of tourists crashed over the audio guide desk and I was swept into the palace entrance.

It's rather disorientating being in the centre of the grand hall, you spin around in all directions trying to take it all in, but you simply don't have enough scope in your eyesight to do it justice. I'd started up the audio guide and was learning about the portraits hanging above a balcony adorned with flags when I received a tap on the shoulder from one of the staff.

'Excuse me sir, but you need to wear your bag on your front'.

'On my front?'

'Yes, sir. So that you don't accidentally knock anything over'.

I looked around the room. Every other tourist had their bags hanging over their front. They looked ridiculous. I fought the burning urge to argue against the rules and reason with the gentleman that while he may fear that the careless tourist could potentially upset a standing vase or brush against a picture frame with their tortoise shell, I for one would adopt practices of the utmost caution and could assure him that no accidents would occur with me. However, considering his impeccable uniform, trimmed white beard and plummy voice, I thought better of it and so I adopted my best posh accent to match up to his and enquired as to whether there happened to be a luggage depository where one could relieve oneself of the burden of shouldering one's bag (and any potential responsibility for knocking over a glass cabinet). He told me I'd have to go all the way back to the visitor's centre where I'd be able to avail of a locker. I gave him a haughty thank you and strode back out of the hall to drop my bag off. Well, honestly.

In truth, it was a really good call to leave my bag in the secret stack of lockers by the visitor centre loos and I walked back up the steps into the entrance hall unburdened and feeling rather smug as I looked around at every other tourist carrying their bag on their front and looking like right dunces.

So, where was I? Ah yes. Spread across the high ceiling of the hall, Sir James Thornhill's painting of the first Duke presenting his battle plans for Blindheim to Brittania takes some neck craning to gaze up at, but the audio guide does the hard work for you by showing pictures of the ceiling as it goes through the description. It appears a bundle of figures all lazing on each other's laps until you look closely and follow the description of the audio. I'm not sure it's a totally accurate depiction of what went down at Blindheim, but it sure looks fun with angels and half-naked women floating around. My kind of battle.
Blenheim is an English corruption of the German site where the first Duke inflicted a famous defeat upon the French and it was for this 1704 victory that Queen Anne granted him so royal land upon which to build a

place he could call home. Of course, given a load of land and millions of pounds, we would all build the biggest house possible and General John Churchill went all out. Sir John Vanburgh was the architect enlisted and he set about creating the grandest palace with *'beauty, magnificence, and duration'*. There's no doubt that his aims were achieved, but the building wasn't without its complications. Funds dried up when the Duchess fell out with Queen Anne (not the thing to do when they're paying for your house) and she also had some disagreements with Vanburgh that meant cabinet-maker John Moore took over supervision to Blenheim's completion. Like all things on this grand scale, it took more time and more money than expected, and the Duke didn't live long enough to see its completion. If he had survived, I'm sure the Great Hall would have impressed him. Light travels through the upper windows on parallel sides of the 20 metre high tower casting an ethereal glow on the Romanesque statues that stand on the ledges high above the Christmas trees laden with baubles and lights. These trees were ever-present throughout the state rooms, making the rooms seem homely, if a little bit too much like a high-end department store.

The audio guide took me through the various coloured staterooms with their various leisurely purposes, each with their own stories and oddities. Tapestries and ornate frames hang from the walls, mirrors glimmer behind you and interesting objects like grandfather clocks and silvery ornaments lie just out of reach of passing hands. The ropes discourage you from crossing, but of course there's nothing to stop you from stepping over them and taking a quick nap on the long sofa. Nothing except the wandering, hawk-eyed wardens of course. They would jump on you before you even set a foot down on the wrong side of the ropes. That is if they are not engaged in conversation with each other about Doctor Who. The marvellous thing about headphone audio guides, and the fact that every tourist is wearing a pair, is that one may get the illusion that they cannot be overheard. However, by keeping the headphones on, but the audio off, you can tune into conversations without the conversants knowing that they are being eavesdropped upon. Even standing right next to them they'll happily natter at full volume about their horrendous hangover, Sandra in Accounts' recent break-up, the boss' pervy comments and other such matters you probably shouldn't have to bear overhearing as a paying customer. However, stand right next to them with a notebook and start scribbling, they soon realise. And then silence, with a tinge of embarrassment in the air, ensues once more.

The disadvantage of headphones of course is that they don't block out everything, not the foamy eared type they give out at Blenheim anyway. Should a tour group with a real life tour guide enter the room, you'll get the audio guide drowned out by German or French or any other language emanating from the booming voice of the guide.

From red to green you then pass into the saloon or rather 'the room where the Duke and his family eat Christmas lunch'. It's quite a place to dine, though perhaps a little intimidating with figures from four continents gazing down at you from the high walls. They were painted in 3D by Laguerre with the European figures looking rather dowdy, the Asians and Arabs exotic though expressionless, while the Duke is displayed grandly on the ceiling holding aloft the sword of victory. A modest man, clearly.

Walking round the corner you come across a few more state rooms, very regal, a little over decorated for my taste, and then you enter the long library. Filled from top to bottom with volumes of encyclopedias and other such unopened doorstops (10,000 no less), the long library also serves as the home for the organ, one of the largest in the UK and a superb work of pipes, though possibly not the most conducive accompaniment to reading. Still, you can imagine a young Winston Churchill slipping comfortably into a long reading session, surrounded by knowledge, only to be interrupted by the shrill shrieks of the organ that a professional organist, I supposed, was currently treating the whole library to. During the war the room served as accommodation and a school for displaced children and, as with so many of the rooms at Blenheim, the library has served multiple purposes and the palace has been much more than just a home for the Marlboroughs. MI5 was based there during the Second World War; though the director and a few senior officers stayed in London, their building on St James' Street camouflaged wonderfully by a 'To Let' sign. You know that house round the corner from you that's been 'To Let' for the past year now. Yep, it's full of secret agents. Just letting you know.

Of course, Blenheim is also famous for its association with Churchill and to round off the tour, the audio guide leads you into the Churchill Exhibition, a tribute to 'the greatest Briton' and perhaps a pilgrimage site for some. You can enter the perfectly normal room where he was born, complete with locks of his childhood hair hanging from the backboard, slightly ironic as we only ever see pictures of him now with a distinct lack of hair. If famous birthplaces are your type of thing then great, but it's really just a room with a few pics of the great man when he was a long time out of nappies and more into running the country than round the estate. The following exhibition was an appropriate tribute to Churchill. Listening to his speeches on the interactive video displays, you get the idea loud and clear that he was someone well-respected and listened to. It's that firm tone of voice that makes you believe the war will be won, even seventy years later. In these days of political turmoil in Britain, it wouldn't half be nice to hear his resolute and powerful vocal tones from the benches of the House of Commons to reassure us that everything's going to be alright.

The sun had been streaming through the windows of the state rooms while I'd been walking around, but as soon as I stepped outside, rain started to bucket down, forcing dawdling tourists in the Great Courtyard to jog towards the dry inlets. I planned to balance the morning indoors with an afternoon exploring the grounds but the weather had chosen to spite me by doing the absolute opposite to what I desired. What was I to do?

Screw it, that's what.

I had limited time at the palace despite the annual pass resting in my breast pocket and I wasn't going to let a little rain stop me. As I ventured out though towards the Grand Bridge, it became clear to me that this was more than a little downpour. I had my Poundland umbrella to raise above my head, at least keeping my hair and face dry, but with its broken and bent supports it limply dripped large drops of rain onto my bag and down my back. The rain was slanted, attacking me from the front, so I used the umbrella as a shield, sacrificing the view ahead of me. Somehow, blindly walking with just a metre's view in front of me, I managed to make it over the bridge and not into the river.

My aim was Victory Monument, situated at the peak of a slope that rolls regally down to the bridge. It offers superlative views of the palace, with the monument lining up directly with the gates of the palace. I stopped myself multiple times from turning round to admire the view halfway up the slope, knowing that 'the finest view in England', according to Churchill's father, would be all the more spectacular if I could resist turning around before the top of the slope. Well, it wasn't easy, but I succeeded. I believe I even avoided treading in any sheep poo in the process, probably as a result of looking where I was going instead of admiring the view. As I approached the top, miraculously the clouds parted, the sprinkler system turned off, I put down my umbrella and I followed my shadow up to the hulk of a monument, dedicated by the Duke to the Duke (himself) and to his own modest abode. Then, I caved in.

I turned 180 degrees and my eyes rested upon the undeniably pleasant view of verdant green arrowing down to a stone bridge and then soaring up to meet the grandest of buildings. Symmetrical beauty in all its glory. Rain clouds hung over the palace, but the grass was bathed in sunlight, making the palace seem darkly imposing, just the way it was intended. Although it's really only the sheep and the tourists who see it from this angle, it was built to intimidate visitors. I'd noticed that morning that if you look up as you walk between its stone pillars (outer pillars square, inner pillars cylindrical) you see eyes painted on the canopy ceiling staring down at you. A baroque CCTV. The Duke is watching you.

Once you've drunk in the view, and eaten your packed lunch as I did, there's not much else to do but walk back down the slope, avoiding the sheep shit landmines as you go, and obliging young couples by kindly snapping a quick photo of them posing in front of the view. I'm always the photographer. I genuinely believe people seek me out to take a photo of them, even forming queues to have me snap them posing arm-in-arm with their beau. It's the same with directions - I can't go anywhere without being asked how to get somewhere. I honestly get asked to take photos of people multiple times during visits to tourist places, though thankfully it's lessened with the advent of selfie sticks. Of course, I'm unfailingly obliging, I don't mind really, but why always me? And do you realise how it makes the lone traveller feel to be asked to take a picture of a swooning couple or a gregarious group? I try not to let it hurt too hard, I love being able to explore places without being under the demands of others, but it does sometimes cause pangs of loneliness. Even more so when they offer to return the favour and I think to myself, what the hell's the point? Why would I want a picture of myself blocking the view behind me? If you need to prove that you visited somewhere by taking a picture of your head obscuring the very thing that you have travelled to see, then, well, I don't know what to say. You just travel for different reasons than I do.

As I passed back over Grand Bridge, I spotted a couple that had taken the whole 'we were here' photo a step further. They had an actual professional photographer (or at least a very willing friend) snapping them as they pretended to walk, talk and smile naturally over the bridge. The photographer called out directions as they walked. *'Smile more'*, *'hold hands'*, *'keep walking'*. The man's smart suit jacket was soaking wet (so romantic) but they continued walking backwards and forwards over the bridge, replaying the same poses, stopping normal pedestrians from crossing their path and ruining their pictures. So, and I know this is pathetic but still, I walked from side to side across their path with my bright green waterproof bag on my back. Only a few times mind, but still, it served them right.

The rain started up again so I made my way indoors and enquired at the visitor's information desk about a Main State Room guided tour they were advertising, this time with an actual human being. I thought it might provide an interesting contrast to the audio guide tour, but the man on the desk actively dissuaded me from joining it. The human guided tours would actually be entirely withdrawn by the end of the year and really, as I had already done the audio guide tour, there was no reason for me to waste my time walking around the state rooms again. I couldn't help but agree with him that the technology was easier, cheaper, and more accessible than having a human guide. It seems a shame perhaps, but that's the way it's going. Considering the numbers of tourists that Blenheim has to cater for, it makes perfect sense to give each visitor a device with two inexplicable cameras instead of grouping them with a human who would have to be multilingual and paid accordingly. Instead, I followed his alternative recommendation to check out the Pleasure Gardens and amuse myself with the maze and various other attractions. Apart from the maze and the little train that runs to the Pleasure Gardens, there wasn't much open in terms of attractions. Understandably, most of the Gardens had closed for the winter. The maze had the added challenge of large puddles to contend with but it was still accessible if you were willing to practise your long jump technique and, despite taking a lot less than the 25 minutes estimated by the sign at the entrance, it was a fun diversion. It's the world's second-largest symbolic maze (viewed from above the design makes out various articles of war) and takes six gardeners a week to prune, then another week to find their way out. After touring the palace with its one way systems and signs pointing you everywhere, it's quite a release of freedom to be able to make your own choice whether to go right or left.

I ventured into other attractions like the Butterfly House, the Lavender Garden and the 'Blenheim Bygones' exhibition (really just a collection of the gardeners' old tools, if you're into 1950s lawnmowers), but my legs were tiring and concentration was starting to lag. It was a sure sign that perhaps it was time to start looking at buses back to Oxford when I responded to one couple's question of whether the 'Blenheim Bygones' exhibition was worth going into with *'Yes, there's plenty of hoes to see'* to which the wife promptly turned her husband around and marched him away. Time to go, Greg...

Before I left though I had just enough time to squeeze in the Water Terraces, South Lawn and the Italian gardens. All stunning and worth more time than I had to give to them. The South Lawn in particular has some interesting features. Beyond the ha-ha wall (a name I love as much as the concept of not interrupting sweeping views with walls, but hiding them in a ditch instead), the tower of St Martin's church in the neighbouring village of Bladon can be seen. Churchill is buried here, adhering to his wishes to lie in rest in view of one of his favourite places. Just as with birth places, I struggle to see the interest in going to see where someone famous is buried, but I suppose Churchill's choice of burial ground affirms his love for Blenheim and legitimises further the palace's marketing of Churchill as 'our Greatest Briton'. It's a massive bonus for them, especially when trying to attract tourists through the palace gates. Blenheim was saved only by the funds of the 9th Duke's marriage to Consuelo Vanderbilt, the heiress of the American railroad billionaires, towards the end of the 19th century and it is kept going today by the thousands of tourists who choose Blenheim over visiting the many, many other stately homes scattered throughout England. Blenheim, in turn, benefits the local community hugely with thousands of jobs linked to the palace's activities and millions of pounds generated for the local economy and charities supported by the palace. Blenheim is a terrific example of mass tourism done sustainably with benefits for local people while maintaining valuable heritage. Reflecting on it back in Oxford over a pint of Old Hooky in the Eagle and the Child pub (famously frequented by Lewis Carroll and JRR Tolkien amongst other literary elites), I realised that Blenheim was one of the UK's World Heritage sites that could do just as well with the WHS as without it. It's deservedly packed with tourists year-round. It's full of events, fun things to do (you can even drive a golf buggy around, for a price) and, even when it's pissing with rain, must provide a wonderful place for the good people of Woodstock to walk their dog. A few lucky Woodstockians even have a view of the lake and grounds from their bedroom windows. Really, despite being built for just one man, Blenheim is now for everyone (I can feel a marketing slogan coming on), open to all who come to have their day as a Duke or Duchess (there, I couldn't help myself).

Now, if John Vanburgh could come back to life and sort out Oxford Rail station...

UK UNESCO World Heritage Site #10 of 28

Canterbury Cathedral, St Augustine's Abbey, and St Martin's Church (1988)

Gold, frankincense and myrrh, cathedral, abbey, church.

'*Well, people used to do this by horse*', I thought to myself. That was back in the medieval ages though, not now in the first few days of 2019. Traditional New Year greetings to train users in the UK comes in the form of rail replacement buses. To get to my final destination of Canterbury from Bournemouth I'd have to take a bus to Southampton Airport and then take a further four trains into London and back out. In fact, maybe I'd prefer the horse, just as the pilgrims who used to venture across the south of England to this storied city did years ago. Only thing was, I didn't have a horse and, well, I did have a discounted yet still vastly overpriced ticket to Canterbury. Bus, train and whatever else UK public transport would throw at me, it would have to do.

At least I had the correct ticket for my destination. My conscience was pricked while overhearing a conversation between the ticket office staff at Southampton Airport Parkway and a young travelling couple.
'Two returns to Stratford, please'.
'Upon-Avon?', the ticket office lady zipped back, catching the couple off guard.
'Err… yeah'. It was an instant reply. The sort that you give when you haven't actually heard or understood the question but give anyway because it's easier than getting the question repeated.
'Ok, that's £146.90'.
The couple paid, took their tickets and scuttled off muttering to each other about how expensive trains to London are nowadays. Still, whether they enjoyed the Olympic Park or not, I'm sure the ticket error worked itself out sooner rather than later. I do hope so anyway.

Britain does have quite a number of doppelganger town names, so being specific as to which Stratford, Ashford, or Gillingham you want to go to can be necessary. Newport is by far the most copied name for a town or city in the UK with at least nine places taking the name. Wales' third largest city is probably the most well-known, along with Newport on the Isle of Wight, but nine Newports is nothing compared to the forty two that can be found across the United States from Florida to Washington. At least Newport in Wales and Newport Isle of Wight are near water. Newport, Oklahoma barely has a stream running through it, let alone cargo ships and ferries necessitating a new port. Many places in North America and Oceania take their names from British towns and villages, the most notable being New York, and so there are plenty of placename doppelgangers when comparing the UK with its friends in the US, Canada, Australia and New Zealand. Canterburys can be found in all four countries. Towns in Connecticut and New Hampshire, a region in New Zealand, suburbs of Sydney and Melbourne, and a small village in New Brunswick, Canada. Not to mention all the roads, schools, surnames, universities and ships that take the name too.

I was pretty sure though my ticket was for Canterbury, UK. After a slew of trains I was finally on the final leg of my outbound journey. The carriage was silent until Rainham when a loud, screechy voice boarded with the simply unbeatable opening statement.
'And then I realised I'd forgotten the condoms!'
This was to be a conversation I just had to eavesdrop on. Fortunately, it wasn't hard. There were villagers in Timbuktu who had to turn their TV sets up. Despite the seering volume levels, I was actually seriously impressed by the teenage girl's ability to tell her friend, and inadvertently the rest of the carriage, about her recent happenings. She nattered at a rapidity that I could barely keep up with, let alone attempt myself and she, full credit to her GCSE English teacher for this, remarkably used all the conventions of a gripping story teller. The build up of events preluding the big reveal dramatically relayed with pauses for suspense and intonation so varied I was hanging on to every word. The content wasn't exactly Shakespearean, more Chaucerian in many ways, but the way she

talked about the guy she'd met who had then taken her into a drug's den was genuinely gripping and I mean it with all sincerity. Storytelling could be seen today as a lost art. We seem a long way from Chaucer's pilgrims recounting tales to each other as they journeyed along the route the train was taking me. Perhaps though not so much has changed. There's still the same thirst for bawdy tales.
It certainly beat overhearing the elderly couple in front of me who would respond to every futile question asked by the other with '*ey?*', causing an exasperated repeat of the question and a terse answer. Their lives seemed as colourless as the Kent countryside we were passing through, the 'Garden of England' dead in the bleak midwinter.

The train afforded landscape views of Canterbury's skyline as Canterbury East slid into view, the spire of the cathedral pointing far above the rooftops. One of two rail stations in the city, the other being Canterbury West, these pair are, for the geographically conscious among us, the most confusing in the British Isles. If you consult a map you can see clearly that Canterbury East is located to the south of the city and directly north of it is Canterbury West which lies north of the city. They should really be called Canterbury South and Canterbury North respectively. England is a weird country as it is but really, when you have two rail stations in a city, one to the north and one to the south, you don't call them East and West, do you? Welcome to England: the weirdest country on Earth.

One thing they have done correctly, and rather excellently in my opinion, is link Canterbury East to the city. You roll out of the station, over a footbridge and instantly you're within the city walls and it's a straight shot to the cathedral. Just follow the spire. It couldn't be simpler.
I zoomed along Castle Street to the cathedral and a mere ten minutes after alighting I was booked onto the

midday tour of the cathedral, leaflet in hand and a yellow sticker on my breast, feeling rather like I'd landed on my feet.

A small group of us yellow stickered tourists gathered at the foot of a 'tour starts here' sign and at 12 on the dot our guide, Hilary, was asking us where we were from and warmly welcoming us to the cathedral. Twelve on the dot also meant one of the canons requesting a pause within the cathedral while the hourly prayers were offered. We stopped to join in the Lord's prayer, a hum rising up into the heavens of the cathedral's heights, and then the tour resumed. Noticing our curious inspections of the roof during the prayers, Hilary explained the renovation work which was going on in the nave. Unfortunately for us tourists, though certainly a blessing for the ancient cathedral, the nave's ceiling was having work done to it and so a maze of scaffolding and wooden planks blocked the view of the soaring heights of the nave ceiling that reach eighty feet (24 metres). I suppose even heaven needs renovating sometimes.

The cathedral is undergoing a huge period of renovation, something I suppose will always need doing for when they complete it however many years from now, they'll probably have to start renovating it all over again. It seems an eternal struggle to keep many of England's historic buildings standing. Canterbury Cathedral costs £18,000 a day to maintain and run, a fact that was mentioned at almost every turn, but at least goes some way to explaining why they charge £12.50 entry and slap a £5 charge on a volunteer-led tour. Quite a few online reviews of the cathedral I'd read before visiting had lambasted the place for having the nerve to charge entry to a place of worship. I disagreed with them before, and even more so after visiting the cathedral. The cathedral receives no funding from any other source and the ticket can be upgraded to an annual pass for free. Services, of course, are also free. Of course, they could just ask for donations, but how many visitors would it take to donate £18,000 each and every day? A lot more than 18,000, that's for sure.

At the time I visited they were sorting out the nave ceiling and roof and also had exterior scaffolding around some of the towers to replace the lead tiles and work on the stone that has been crumbling away. The cathedral also had a new visitor centre on its way with community spaces included while paths around the cathedral had been dug up, leaving large gaps surrounded by barriers. All necessary work that may spoil a few photo opportunities, but is ultimately being done to ensure the vitality of the cathedral for centuries to come.

In the nave, an art installation, one of quite a number around the cathedral, tried to make up for the lack of a ceiling. The scaffolding had a hundred glass vases shaped like tear drops hanging from it formed in the shape of what was apparently meant to be a ship. 'Nave' coming from the Latin 'navis' meaning ship, the shape seemed appropriate, if not easy to misinterpret from where I was standing.

Hilary led us from the nave to what is arguably the highlight of the cathedral, the main hall (known as The Martyrdom) was where Canterbury's most beloved celebrity was brutally assassinated in 1170. Thomas Becket was a good friend of King Henry II, so much so that he was made Archbishop of Canterbury in 1161 by the King in an attempt to gain more control over the unruly church. Becket took his role very seriously and his allegiances to his friend the king and his role in the church were strained over clerical privilege, so much so that he spent six years exiled in France. Upon his return, tensions flared up again and Henry audible frustrations were actioned by four knights who took the king's words rather too literally and smashed Becket's skull open on the very spot where we were now stood. We gulped collectively as Hilary relayed the bloody details of Becket's end, but really his death was just the start of his legacy that endures today. Pilgrims started to come from all over the land in the hope of a miracle, buoyed by the stories of the martyr Becket's blood curing leprosy, paralysis and even death. As one of our tour group quipped *'the NHS could do with some of Becket's blood!'* Some of the seven hundred or so miracles attributed to Becket are pictured in the Miracle Windows in Trinity Chapel, functional works of art that describe so clearly what life would have been like in the 12th century and how revered St Thomas of Canterbury really was. Of course, it was Becket that inspired pilgrimages across the country, including those of Chaucer's characters. Really it's him Canterbury has to thank for putting the city so firmly on the map.

Along with the stained-glass windows, Hilary also described in detail the cathedral's other beauties. Staring upwards, it's impossible to keep your mouth from opening in amazement at the kaleidoscopic ceilings, the fan vaulting - only found in England - spreading out from the pillars in contrast with the French fiel vaulting which acts like branches to support the vast ceiling. Indeed, Canterbury Cathedral is like a forest of stone. The pillars as tree trunks, the vaulting as branches, and the windows as gaps in the trees casting crepuscular rays down to the forest floor where the church congregation sit on wooden chairs, staring up in awe at the splendour of creation. It's an interior that instantly inspires the admirer to think of a world beyond that of which they know. The very purpose, I suppose, of any cathedral.

The tour finished up at the Bossanyi windows, the eponymous artist, who suffered as a Hungarian Jew during both world wars, created these two glass-stained windows in 1960 so they bring a modern touch to an art form that we consider so ancient, and they serve as a representation of salvation and peace in the modern age. Hilary engaged us in a game of 'spot the swastika' while looking at 'Salvation' as in amongst its many symbols there is a tiny swastika painted in reference to the terrors of WWII. While literally full of history with plaques, tombs, and memorials scattered liberally throughout, the cathedral has its modern touches too. The problems and woes of the people, the uncertainty and need for calm, are still present today as much as they were in the past, as Hilary reminded us upon ending the tour. She told us all that it requires a place like Canterbury Cathedral to extract you from the pains of daily life and to enhance your humanity by reminding you of where you stand in the world. Canterbury Cathedral is the history of England in stone, French stone admittedly, but still, nonetheless, the cathedral stands as a reminder that whatever we and our country endure, some things remain a constant. I retraced the steps of the tour once we had disbanded, taking time to admire the Crypt and the Cloisters. Then it was time to visit a different church of significantly smaller proportions but of no less importance.

St Martin's is a little way out of the city walls, hidden off a main road and surrounded by suburbia. You couldn't find a less incongruous location for the oldest English-speaking church in the world, but here amongst people's houses and cars it is. The graveyard, dotted with mossy headstones, provides a spiritual oasis around the petite stone building. Walking up to it you feel yourself slipping into the past and by the time you step gingerly through the doorway guarded by a creaking oak door you feel you have arrived in the sixth century when a disused Roman church was renovated by Queen Bertha of Kent. You almost expect the man who gently welcomes you in to be speaking in Old English, but instead he clearly and briefly explains what there is to see and hands you a laminated guide to borrow as you tour the tiny church. Despite its size, there is plenty to note.

Most notably from a historical perspective there are clear remains of the old Roman walls which still form part of the apse between the altar and the congregation. The wall, unpainted and rough, probably dates from the fourth century, though Christians are known to have existed in Britain before 200AD. The Romans left in 410AD, their rule occupied by the Anglo-Saxons who were around when St Augustine's monks rebuilt and extended the church in their mission to convert the pagan King Ethelbert and his people to Christianity. The font, located to the right of the entrance and surrounded by beautiful mosaic tiles is Norman, but Ethelbert was probably baptised here in 597AD. Ethelbert, now known as St Ethelbert due to his role in converting the Anglo-Saxons to Christianity, was the first English king to convert and so can be attributed with helping to turn the whole country into the Christian nation it is today.

Away from kings, the church also accommodated those at the less-fortunate end of life. To the left of the entrance is the squint, an angled hole in the wall from where lepers would peer in at mass being celebrated in medieval times. This sign of care for the poor and downtrodden echos the actions of the church's namesake, St Martin. A glass-stained window a few rows up from the squint shows Martin upon a horse as a young Roman soldier slicing his cloak in half to share it with a beggar. He later became Bishop of Tours from where Queen Bertha would hail around two centuries later. The links in history of the occupations of Britain and the Christian conversion of its people are so clearly intertwined in this quaint, modest little church. St Martin's shows that you don't have to be mighty and powerful like Canterbury Cathedral to have had an impact upon the history and culture of a country. I departed with small donation in exchange for a paper copy of the laminated information sheet and a gentle thank you to the guardian of the church, and walked back down the graveyard path to the twenty first century for a cappuccino.

I found such nourishment at a cafe called Canteen (which was actually a cafe, though I did return my cup to the kitchen wondering which format, canteen or cafe, they preferred) and then sped on to Evensong. A daily service of hymns and a few readings, it's held in the Quire, the part of the cathedral where the choir (quire and choir really do show how confusing English spelling is, they're homophones) sit in those beautiful oak benches with lanterns illuminating their song sheets. I'd arrived a bit too close to the start of the service to get a seat on the benches with the choir, but I made do with a normal seat closer to the altar.

Entering into a new church for a service always makes me feel like an impostor, even though I attended Catholic mass every Sunday during my childhood. Catholic and Anglican services and prayers do differ and so you have to be careful not to be caught out while in the other denomination. I was reading the words in the guide very carefully. Others may not feel like this, but I've found that churches always make you feel welcome, happy to have visitors who have no idea when to sit or stand or which book to be singing from. The impostor syndrome evaporates but there's still a lot of etiquette to remember. The sign of the cross, the amens, the genuflecting. I did think that leaving halfway through is generally frowned upon though a few did depart during the service to my surprise. It was only 45 minutes and not much apart from listening to the beautiful echoes rebounding off the pillars and walls was required. It was, in truth, very peaceful and calming, the perfect antidote to a busy day, like a hot bath to soak into surrounded by bubbles. Some found it very comforting indeed. I observed a big, bald man across the way from me slipping uncontrollably into a nap, stirring only with jerks of his head and dribbling slightly. Church can have that effect on some. For me it was just pleasant to see the cathedral being used for its purpose. It is so many things: archives, burial grounds, memorials to war victims and that's just in the cathedral. Within the walled precincts there are houses, a school, offices and much more. However, fundamentally, it is a church with one very clear purpose: a space to give Christians a place to praise God. It was wonderful in action. As good as going on a tour of a famous place is, be that a football stadium, a theatre or a cathedral, it's always best to see it being used, to see it in action. Canterbury is very much a living, working cathedral with multiple services everyday of the year. That would be my advice, go to a service and see it being used for purpose. If nothing else, the choirs, now mixed-gender since 2014, are divine to listen to.

With the hymns floating around my mind, I walked out of the precincts for the final time that day and found my accommodation for the night in a place called Kipp's. The kind French receptionist showed me to a single room that would make a matchbox seem like a royal suite but perhaps it only felt that way because it was packed with everything I could ever possibly need for a one night stay. For less than £30, I had a TV, sink, tea and coffee set and a bed comfier than my own at home. I tried to swing a cat, failed, and then fell fast asleep snug, wonderfully warm, and still with the echoes of the Evensong choir swirling around my mind.

The morning brought more treasures to head out and see. Canterbury is not only well-known because of its religious sites, but also because of the pilgrimages taken to them. The most famous of these pilgrimages didn't actually happen, but Chaucer's Canterbury Tales have become representative of the journeys that real pilgrims made and the way that they whiled away the days spent on horseback. Though the tales, told by a wide variety of pilgrims, don't involve Canterbury or even much religion for that matter, Chaucer's imaginary tales of lust, woe and revenge are inextricably linked to the city. One of the city's main draws for tourists, and a break from the plethora of religious sites, is the Canterbury Tales interactive experience. I wasn't too sure what to expect but as it promised interactive retellings of five of the tales that I'd been forced to read for English Literature A Level, I was interested to see if I recalled much if anything. We'd done Chaucer's tales for a whole term, our teacher Mrs Brown reading them out in Middle English while we pretended to be able to read along before translating them for us word for word. Just providing a translated copy and getting us to read it at home would have sufficed but Mrs Brown had twelve weeks to fill so we worked slowly on the language of each tale, trying in vain to understand it. Though it's a classic of the English language, the book that catapulted English into literary fields, it isn't the most readable of texts. I was therefore keen to see how the interactive experience would attempt to make the tales comprehensible.

I was greeted by a teenager on the front desk dressed in a brown cloak and unable to make eye contact. He in turn introduced myself and the rest of my fellow tourists-cum-pilgrims to Alice, our tour guide through the experience and, I supposed, a drama student or, at the very worst, an actress very short on work. In fairness, she was engaging, enthralling us with the story despite the fact that she tells the same script to groups of tourists five times a day five days a week. She began by introducing us to the five characters we'd be hearing stories from: the Knight, the Miller, the Wife of Bath, the Nun's priest, and the Pardoner. Then we were led from the 'Tabard Inn' in 'Southwark' to Canterbury along more or less the same route that the train had taken me the previous day through Rochester, Sittingbourne and other Medway river towns. Within our party there were two Germans who probably understood Alice better than us Brits when she performed a sample of Chaucer's English. It's a curious, bubbling mix that pricks the ears at a few modern Germanic parts of English, but for the most part is unintelligible. Chaucer's characters would, had they been real, spoken a lilt similar to this. The surroundings also added a commendable dab of authenticity to the experience. I forgot I was in the centre of modern Canterbury with the waxworks, house fronts and even the smell of manure wafting around the stables combining to transport me back in time.

For ease of dealing with tour groups in other languages I supposed, Alice was replaced by an audio guide for the five tales, but she still led us through the exhibits, the moving parts of the sets and projections out of the windows performing more or less in sync with the audio guide. We started with the Knight recounting a battle between two related knights fighting over a girl, then moving on from love to lust through the streets of Medieval England we were treated to the low comedy of the Miller's Tale, complete with an arse being stuck out of the window for Absolon to kiss. Next up, the Wife of Bath's tale showed women's positions in society, with a knight accused of rape on a quest to discover what women most desire leading him to accept a woman's sovereignty. The Nun's Priest's tale tells an old fable about gullibility and the pitfalls of pride with animals, a cock and a fox, the main characters, cue the farmyard scene with waxy sheep and thatched houses. Finally, the tour ended rather appropriately with the Pardoner's tale which tells of three young men who venture out to kill Death but actually end up killing each other. That tale rounded off fifty rather enjoyable minutes during which I realised that I'd forgotten more or less all the key points of the Canterbury Tales (sorry, Mrs Brown…), but I still get to keep my A grade in A Level English Literature. Makes you wonder

sometimes what the point of school is.
All too soon we were back in 2019, via the gift shop of course, and I had to take a second to reacquaint myself with the sound of cars and the shiny shop fronts. I still had one part of the World Heritage site to visit, St Augustine's Abbey, and so I walked out of the city walls and presented myself at a smart museum welcome desk to start another journey back in time, this one even earlier in parts than the 14th century.

In many ways Canterbury is the tale of two churches. While the cathedral stands proud and all efforts are consumed in keeping it that way, St Augustine's Abbey has experienced an ungraceful decline to the ruins that it is today. Once one of the most impressive abbeys in Europe, it was taken apart upon the orders of Henry VIII during the Dissolution of the Monasteries. Various repurposes have failed to leave it in a better condition than knee high foundations and bits of wall. The only way to see it all in its former glory is to don a pair of the Virtual Reality goggles in the visitor centre and wave your head around as you watch the graphic images of a fine complex of chapels, cloisters and towers. I'd never experienced VR before, but I was pretty impressed. Although graphics, I could feel my legs wanting to start walking as I floated through the nave of the abbey. God knows what it would have looked like to other visitors in the museum so thankfully I was the only one around on a drizzly Sunday afternoon. After the virtual reality came the real reality, accompanied by a very informative audio guide. A few others were outside, stepping over and around the ruins but no one else was clasping a device to their ear like me. A young couple walking a dog (or, I wondered, was the dog walking them?) stood behind me at one of the fourteen info boards, the girlfriend asking her boyfriend *'Shall we educate ourselves or just walk Bracken?'* The boyfriend grunted and they moved on. It seemed strange to me that they'd paid almost £7 each to just walk their dog on the grass, but I guess it's £14 extra for English Heritage to keep on preserving places like St Augustine's. It takes all types.

The other couple taking a Sunday stroll around the abbey had a baby with them whom they left alone to play on the grass while they snapped photos with their smartphones. Baby in the chapel. Baby in the kitchens. Baby by the stones. A wonderful collection of snaps I had no doubt that they'd be sharing with the world and his dog via the internet. They too, I supposed, had also paid £7 each, or at least had an English Heritage membership. St Augustine's Abbey was clearly in no fit state to be of use anymore other than as a heritage site, but people were still making use of it, albeit for recreational rather than religious uses.

After Henry VIII claimed the abbey for the Crown, part of it became a royal residence whose future guests included Queen Elizabeth I, but much of it was dismantled and the materials sold for use elsewhere. Various noblemen held the keys over the 17th and 18th centuries until the Alfred Beer and Company brewery took over the site and started to hold festivals and parties in the grounds to the disapproval of some of the more puritanical types in Canterbury. One of these, the Kent MP Alexander Beresford Hope, was so shocked that he bought the grounds and restored the faith to St Augustine's by starting a missionary college where churchmen were taught how to spread Christianity in Britain's colonies. In that way, St Augustine's Abbey completed a full circle. Augustine had come to Britain to spread Christianity and over 1200 years later his abbey was being used to spread Christianity from the old world to the new world. As Augustine's Abbey was a place of teaching and learning, and as a school was founded on the site when Henry VIII dissolved the monastery, the present school that stands adjacent to the heritage site is credited with being the oldest continuously operating school in the world. The King's School, no prizes for guessing which king it's named after, is also the oldest charity in the UK. While the monks are long gone from the site, there is still learning going on within the grounds of the former abbey, although some would rather walk their dog and watch it shit on the grass.

I returned my audio guide to the desk, spurning the opportunity to have another go on the VR headset, and then walked back into the centre of Canterbury. As it was the Epiphany, there was a carol service being held in the cathedral and, not being one to miss the opportunity to sing carols with the rude bits included, I hastened there and found a spot in the nave under the enormous glass bottles. Alas, there was no 'We three kings' or 'While shepherds washed their socks' (sorry, watched their flocks, my mistake) but once again there was that soul-reviving calm and tranquility within the grand pillars and gothic sculptures. The candles flickered, the Christmas tree glittered and the choir sent me slumbering deep into the recesses of my mind. I thought of how wonderful it would be if every city in the UK were like Canterbury with its quaint cafes, spots of remarkable world heritage scattered here and there, and its calm, almost sacred atmosphere. A genteel city, the type of city that perhaps tourists imagine to exist all over England before they visit. I thought back to the hordes of French students around the town and the Americans on my tour of the cathedral the previous day. They were here only to visit London and Canterbury. Nothing more of little old England. Their expectations of England, what they would have read about the country in their guidebooks and on websites, would, I'm sure, have been met. For the quintessential English experience, I'm not sure many places do it better than Canterbury. Then, as Matthew chapter two was being read, I thought about the three wise men of Canterbury, the magnificent magi who bear the gifts of the city. The cathedral is clearly gold, the standout gift with its precious value. It caused, and still causes, men and women from across the country and the globe to set out from home to find it. St Augustine's Abbey and St Martin's church are the myrrh and frankincense, no less important as gifts and certainly important in history, but rather unknown by the general population and more modest because of it. Despite their lack of splendour compared to gold, they are valuable in themselves for their unique scent and their use in religious services within the Christian Church.

Gold, frankincense and myrrh; cathedral, abbey and church. Canterbury is blessed with gifts.

UK UNESCO World Heritage Site #11 of 28

Maritime Greenwich (1997)

The home of time

I spotted Glenn at the foot of the stairs, crouched slightly low as if he were about to start a mid-distance race.

'Next train's in a minute. Let's run.'

Before even a 'hello', we were running along the bridge at Clapham Junction.

'I needed some exercise after sitting on that train for two hours'.
'Come on. They close the doors thirty seconds early now'.

We swerved left and tip-tapped down the stairs at a speed Fred Astaire would have been proud of. The 09.13 was still there. The board said 09.12.17. The doors were beeping. We leapt into the train, startling the passengers sat waiting patiently for the train to depart. The doors slid closed and we took a collective sigh of relief. We'd saved ourselves six minutes.

Time is of the essence in London. The pace of life in the city is faster than just about anywhere else on earth. Trains and tubes zip by, black cabs and red double deckers swerve into the curbs and the people, the Londoners, walk as if they're being chased. It's frenetic. Time is counted in seconds rather than minutes here and every second counts.

London, or more specifically Greenwich, is the home of time. It was here that the world chose to put the Prime Meridian, longitude at 0 degrees, which dictates where you, I, and everybody else on earth is in terms of distance east or west from the line. Effectively the Meridian Line is the vertical brother of the equator, allowing ships and sailors to know their exact position anywhere on the world's oceans. It is immeasurably important and, for this reason, makes Greenwich an inarguable UNESCO World Heritage site. But Greenwich isn't just famous for time. As the home of the Royal Navy's colleges for well over a hundred years until 1998, it has also had an unquantifiable influence upon Britain's maritime history and therefore much of the world's history during the 19th and 20th centuries. Located on the southern banks of the

Thames to the east of central London, its history now faces London's present head on. Glenn and I, after arriving into Greenwich on the top deck of one of those iconic double deckers, started our day by taking the hike up to the Royal Observatory. Once at the top we grabbed coffees and then stood at the viewpoint to take in one of the great vistas of London.

'It's not even a tenth of New York's skyline, is it?'

We were looking down Greenwich Park and across the river to Canary Wharf, London's CBD. Glenn's point was pretty valid. London, until recently, has never been much of a skyscraper city due to height restrictions lasting until the 1960s and current rules about not blocking sight lines of famous monuments. Apart from Canary Wharf, a few buildings in The City and Southwark's The Shard, London doesn't even come close to its neighbours across the pond, though conversely it has more skyscrapers and people than any other city in Europe, and the trend is set to continue. In amongst the grey sticks that reach up into the grey sky, there are plenty of cranes. London has thirteen skyscrapers currently under construction and dozens more are planned to transform the skyline. There are still strict regulations to preserve protected views, but London's future is very much up in the grey clouds that hang over the city. Canary Wharf provides a very contrasting background to the English Baroque style Old Royal Naval College with the sumptuous Queen's House a white jewel amongst the light grey colonnades and domed towers. The red-bricked Greenwich Power Station to the right of the college adds a third architectural style into the mix, completing the physical timeline of architectural styles London has experienced in the last four hundred years. For my money, I'd rather have the oldest of the styles, the English Baroque over the plainer, more modern two.

We downed our coffees and proceeded inside the

Royal Observatory complex. £13.50 gained us entry to Flamsteed House, the Great Equatorial telescope and, of course, the Meridian Line. The line is a rather arbitrary concept. Just within the gates of the complex, there's a strobe light running along the pavement with the coordinates of various world cities listed alongside it. It's about ten metres long, just enough for forty Chinese teenagers to be pushed into formation by their tour leader for the obligatory photo on the line. They stood there, one foot in the west, one foot in the east, waiting, expecting something magical to occur.

Of course, nothing happened. The idea of a meridian line is pure human invention. It doesn't really matter where the line is, just that there is a line at all. Also, the line exists north and south of the ten metres demarcated at Greenwich. It runs through Greenwich Park, through London's 2012 Olympic park, Cambridge, western France, eastern Spain, five countries in west Africa and Antarctica, but you don't see any of those places charging thirteen quid for the privilege of standing on the invisible line. The line intersects the equator in the Gulf of Guinea, 611km south of Ghana, 1078km west of Gabon, but it's Greenwich where it's recognised the most. The crowds straddling a strobe light taking selfies of their feet don't know it, but the line they think is so special wasn't the original meridian line at Greenwich and it isn't the current meridian line either. The first Greenwich meridian was established in 1750 a few metres to the west of where the tourists line up today. It stayed there, marked only by a stone pillar for 101 years when George Airy, 7th Astronomer Royal, had a new telescope installed and chose to move the meridian line, indeed the entire understanding of eastern and western hemispheres, a little to the east to suit himself. Talk about moving heaven and earth, but that's what you can do with an invisible arbitrary line. Again, it's not where it exists, it's the fact that it does exist that's important, though try telling the French that. They weren't too happy that London was chosen by the delegates at the International Meridian Conference in 1884. Anyway, it's all by the by now. Since 1984, the IRM (International Reference Meridian) agreed by every country to be the true meridian is located 102.5 metres to the east of the historic Prime Meridian of the world that everyone who pays their £13.50 believes is the dividing line between the hemispheres. Indeed, because of the earth's crust, it moves by 2.5cm every year. The Royal Observatory at Greenwich are pretty coy on informing people about this for obvious reasons. If you really do want to have a foot in each hemisphere you need to be standing legs wide open under one of the trees in Greenwich Park. It's hard to believe, but doing so would make you look even more of a prat than the people queueing to selfie themselves on the strobe light.

That said, the entry fee does give you much more than just standing on a line that isn't what it claims to be. Glenn and I shrugged our shoulders and got on with touring the museums. Glenn, fresh from a summer at the World Cup in Russia, had been showing off his cyrillic reading skills by reading out the Russian translated signs in the welcome centre.

'билетная касса', he slowly read out loud.
'Ticket office'.
'That's what I said'.
'So you've been brushing up your Russian, have you?'
'Oh you know, comes easily to me'.

It served him right that I went off to get us a couple of audio guides I had his programmed to Russian. He wasn't best pleased.
'But I thought you spoke fluent Russian, mate!'

With Glenn's Russian guide babbling away (he put it to his ear and everything), we entered Flamsteed House to get a feel for life back in the 1600s. For forty years, John Flamsteed woke up at various points during the night to observe the stars, all in the endeavour to improve Britain's star charts for King Charles II and Britain's captains. Nowadays it's possible to go up to the Octagon Room, designed by Sir Christopher Wren, from where the astronomer royals would have spent the nights watching the skies. These days London is one of the most light polluted cities in the world and so any attempt to observe the stars now would be fruitless. It's only as recent as 2018 that it has been possible again due to modern telescope filters that can tune out air and light pollution to observe the galaxies. Before 2018, the Royal Observatory hadn't actually been able to observe anything for more than half a century. It's a story that repeats itself around the world. Research conducted in 2016 estimated that a third of the world, and much of Europe, could not see through the light pollution to view the Milky Way. We've lost our ability to look up to the sky and see hundreds of thousands of bright stars twinkling back at us, the odd one shooting off across the sky. It's a sad truth that observatories are trying to get round to ensure the next generation of star gazers. For many young people in our cities, stars don't exist.

We moved through the exhibits sandwiched between camera-happy tourists. There is a wealth of information to take in. The info boards plus the audio guide shower you with facts and statistics. Inspecting the charts and contraptions that tell time and location for sailors, it was very difficult for mere mortals like Glenn and I to understand. Even in this age of technology and information, working out the maths and the science behind the inventions and discoveries made by men such as Flamsteed, his peer Edmond Halley, and the clockmaker John Harrison is frankly beyond my intelligence. I was particularly swept off my feet by Harrison. A Yorkshireman, he was a self-taught clockmaker before the age of Youtube DIY videos who invented the chronometer and therefore solved the problem of calculating longitude at sea. In these days of satnavs and Google Maps that might not seem like much, but think about it a second and you realise how much anyone at sea, now and back then, owes to his genius. In the 18th century, long-distance voyages were incredibly risky, not least because ships were unable to position themselves globally and therefore avoid being shipwrecked. The British government offered a prize of £20,000 (well over a million today) to the person who could accurately measure longitude at sea. Harrison dedicated himself to the cause. The equivalent of today's man tinkering in his garden shed, he made various marine timekeepers tested by the navy until he reached his fourth prototype, H4, that was incorporated into a pocket watch that won him the government's reward, though it appears Parliament reneged on their deal and he was only awarded half the amount. This timepiece was used by famed captains such as Bligh and Cook, ultimately helping Britain to achieve dominance over the seas and found the empire that dominated the 19th century. Looking at his clocks, H1 to H4, displayed in a line in the museum, you can't help but marvel at them. The intricate workings, springs, nuts, bolts - all the components that combine to make a machine that's not just useful, but beautiful too. Really, Harrison was just a bloke tinkering about, like so many of the people who changed the world to form the one we live in today. It's simply remarkable.

Walking out of 'clock porn land' into the open, I asked Glenn what the time was as, rather ironically, none of the clocks in the museum were set to the correct time.

'Well, the battery has caused the quartz crystal to

oscillate at a precise frequency to generate electric pulses from the circuit driving the stepping motor that turns the hands to inform me that it's 11.28am'.

I thanked him and we proceeded out of the observatory complex. A quick whip round the Queen's House to balance our new found scientific knowledge with some art appreciation and then lunch over a few pints to, you know, let the knowledge sink in nice and comfy.
Greenwich had around eighty pubs back in its heyday when the Royal Navy college was training up sailors for missions abroad and the astronomers needed a break from their calculations. It was a hub for sailors, then scientists and now for students as the University of Greenwich has taken up much of the Old Royal Naval College buildings. Finding a pub wasn't difficult. We settled into one and got stuck into the ale. After a few we checked our timepieces (thanks again John Harrison et al) and decided that with the hour hand at one and the 13.30 tour of the ORNC starting in the Visitor Centre a few minutes walk away we had time for another pint. It's always the third that gets me. We drank up and ran out the door to meet David, our guide of Greenwich's centrepiece for the free forty five minute tour.

Now a forty five minute tour doesn't seem long, but that's only if you and your mate aren't busting for a piss. David led us serenely out of the Visitor Centre to the Cutty Sark, the last remaining tea clipper now a museum and the statue of Sir Walter Raleigh. We also happened upon the birthplace of one Henry VIII, nowadays just a plaque on the ground where the Tudor palace of Greenwich once stood. His birthplace is overlooked by a statue of King George II, or rather it would be if the statue were not covered up over winter to protect the marble. It looked rather like King George had been put in a bodybag by anarchists to be thrown into the nearby Thames. When he's not covered up, he has a fine view of the river and Canary Wharf beyond it, but we continued up through the college green to the Royal Naval College itself.

UNESCO rather grandly states that Maritime Greenwich is the 'finest and most dramatically sited architectural and landscape ensemble in the British Isles'. David, shivering slightly with pride, called it the 'the finest architecture in the world'. Neither of them are far wrong. Standing in the middle of College Way which runs through the site, you can see the genius of Sir Christopher Wren's design, the symmetry of large dome towers on either side with colonnades running behind them up to the perfectly petite Queen's House, behind which rolling green peeps out and the Royal Observatory appears daintily out of the tops of the ancient trees. Wren was so honoured to be chosen as the one to design Greenwich Hospital, as it was designated back in the late seventeenth century, that he waived any fee. It was a hospital for retired seamen, in the hospitality sense of the word, commissioned by Queen Mary II after she witnessed the injured state of sailors returning from the Battle of La Hougue in 1692. Just like the men's efforts on the waters of the English Channel, its style was planned to be grand. The wide avenue leading down to the river from the Queen's House had to be maintained and so the Hospital was built on either side, like a guard of honour, creating the masterpiece that we see today.

Not only was the building grand on the outside, it was also lavishly decorated within. David led us into the hospital's chapel of St Peter and St Paul which was started by Wren but not completed before his death. After a devastating fire it was redesigned and rebuilt by James 'Athenian' Stuart, but the truly incredible contribution is that of master plasterer John Papworth. We walked up the steps to enter through the oak door of the chapel, pausing briefly to hear about the memorials in the chapel vestibule, and were met by a sumptuous ceiling. Sky blue and gold, the delicate plaster is shaped into octagonal and square patterns, getting smaller as they approach the centre of the ceiling which is adorned with intricate central ornaments shaped like a bouquet of leaves. The plaster, carved rather than moulded, has a practical purpose as well as an aesthetic one, aiding the excellent acoustics in the chapel which is still used for services today. The Samuel Green organ at the back of the chapel has pale gold pipes to match the golden decorations, though the pipes, David knowingly informed us, are purely decorative. Though decorative too, the rope design of the black and white marble floor harks to the chapel's maritime connections. You can only speculate, but the sailor's must have felt an incredible sense of awe while attending services here, having seen only the dark insides of the ships and the grey, polluted ports of the world throughout the rest of their lives.

While the chapel is a fine work of art, the crowning glory of the Old Royal Naval Colleges is the Painted Hall, likened to the Sistine Chapel in Rome with vast painted ceilings and walls. Sir James Thornhill dedicated nineteen years to his masterpiece which encompasses forty thousand square feet of allegorical and historical figures telling the stories of Britain's scientific, political and naval achievements. Alas, I had to make do with pictures off the internet as two years' worth of renovations still had a couple more months to run before the hall would be reopened to the public. It's a common theme amongst almost all of Britain's heritage that some parts are closed for renovation, but on the bright side, at least it gives reason to return.

In recompense, the growing numbers on David's tour (we seemed to sweep general visitors to the chapel along with us as we left) made their way to a less impressive, but perhaps more appropriate facility for the old sailors to occupy their remaining days with. Glenn and I were increasingly in need of a place to relieve ourselves as we walked at the front of the group to the Victorian skittles alley.

'Do you reckon they'd notice if I just nipped behind that colonnade there?'
'Probably mate'.
'Damn, I really need a piss'.
'Me too. It's only meant to be a 45 minute tour though'.

We soldiered on. Down the steps to the skittles alley we both eyed up a female loo. The male equivalent didn't seem to be around anywhere. We were both thinking the same thing. Resisting the growing temptation we entered the skittles alley and learnt from David about how students at the Royal Naval College would come down here for hours of skittles. The site closed as a hospital in 1869, but was reopened four years later as a training establishment for the Royal Navy. The young students must have whiled away a fair few hours down in the alley as the lanes, skittles and the bowling balls looked like they'd taken a fair bit of use. Their wearied appearance could also be down to the tourists on tours like ours who are given a go to send a ball down the lane. One such member of our group, an elderly gentleman with his wife and family, was cajoled into giving a demonstration, buoyed by his qualifications as a keen bowler that his smarmy wife couldn't help to mention. He picked up the lignum vitae ball, stumbling a little with the surprising weight of it and sent it rolling down the lane where it curved and rolled into the gutter.

'I forgot to mention the uneven surface!', David admitted, chuckling along to himself as he had done so endearingly with all of his little jokes.

The bowls champion had another go and this time

managed to get a few skittles to fall down. Of course, he then had to walk down the long hallway to pick them up again, a job that discouraged anyone else from having a go for fear of bowling a strike and having to make the solemn walk down the lane to put the toys back in their place.

The whole room was an insight into the lives of those who studied here at Greenwich, learning from the masters of the sea at the time when Britannia ruled the waves. It was the university of the Navy for many of Britain's captains who sailed around the world during the days of empire, but also trained foreign commanders and admirals who took what they learned at Greenwich to their native navies. Nowadays some of the buildings are filled with students from the University of Greenwich whose campus is within the World Heritage site so the atmosphere of learning continues, as does the number of pubs within the local area.

It was the pub Glenn and I had to blame for our desperate state at this moment. We filed out of the skittles alley with the group, Glenn dallying at the back of the group and then leaving my side as we passed by the women's toilets. I didn't realise he'd sneaked off until I looked around as the group and I walked out of the building. As luck would have it there was a toilet, a male toilet, just by the exit door and so I diverted quickly from the group, nipped inside, and enjoyed the facilities safe in the knowledge that I for one wouldn't be startling any ladies.

I caught up with the group on College Way where they were taking in the domed towers again. Glenn rejoined me a minute later as David was telling us about the details of the two domed towers.

'There was a men's, you know'.
'Whatever'.

Similar to the dome of St Paul's Cathedral, Wren's most famous work, the two towers have clock faces, though the tower to the right as you face the Queen's House does not tell the time, but rather the points of a compass with a marker linked to a weather vane on the roof. It is, according to David, the only vertical compass in the world, not that it was built for that prestigious status though of course. Looking towards the Old Royal Naval College from their boats on the Thames the sailors would have been able to tell at a glance which way the wind was blowing. You'd just have to hope that you didn't miss it while making your way up or down the Thames, not that Greenwich is easy to miss. From the water, the 'Canaletto' view, named after the Venetian painter who created the famous depiction of Greenwich from the other side of the river, is unmissable. Nowadays it's as simple as walking under the river through a pedestrian tunnel to get to the Isle of Dogs (so named as Charles II used to keep his yapping pups there) to take in the view of Greenwich in all its glory. It's certainly an improvement on the view of the dull grey office blocks of Canary Wharf from the Greenwich side of the river.

The tour finished up back at the Visitor Centre and by that time Glenn and I had forgotten all about our ordeal and were thirsty for another pint of ale. We went for a quick beer in the Old Brewery, acknowledging that it's what the old pensioners would have done given their three pints a day ration. This brewery was built in 1717 to supply the hospital (got to keep the old boys happy), but closed when the old sailors were replaced by the naval students. It's now a fancy gastropub, but was close enough for us to down a pint, before we rounded off our visit to Greenwich with the National Maritime Museum.

It was lucky we did too. The museum was literally heaving with toddlers and kids. We wondered whether we'd walked into a kindergarten by mistake. Prams parked in all corners, screams and shouts echoing in the open space and weary parents slumped in cafe chairs clutching coffee cups with a glazed look in their eyes. Thankfully this was mainly just the entrance area and the mezzanine floor, and once we wandered into one of the many galleries, peace and studious learning resumed. With a maritime history as vast and detailed as Britain's I can imagine it's impossible to select what should be shown in the National Maritime Museum, but there was a bit of everything with galleries focused on the trade of the East India trading company, on courageous captains like Nelson and an exhibition on Britain's next attempt to win the America's Cup, the pinnacle of race sailing. The windsport is unrecognisable from the seatrade and ocean wars that preceded it, but the science is essentially the same. Get the wind in your sails and you'll be victorious. As part of an island nation, Britons have sailed all over the world, to fight, to colonise, to trade, to discover new places and cultures, and nowadays to be the best. With no part of the United Kingdom more than seventy miles from the sea, you could say that the sea is integral to the nation, and certainly it was key to Britain's dominance in the 18th and 19th centuries. The great captains and admirals like Nelson, Cook, Drake, Raleigh and many others are lauded and remembered as heroes of the nation, but it can't be forgotten that they were joined on their voyages by hundreds of simple sailors, seamen who spent their lives on the waves in the worst of conditions and were rewarded with only gruel and beer. These men were the locals of Greenwich and other ports and seafaring parts of the country who were drafted, sometimes involuntarily, into working on the warships, tradeships and colliers that wrote so much of the history of the last five hundred years.

It was these men that I was thinking about when Glenn and I made our way by bus to South Bermondsey and to the New Den for the cup tie between Millwall and Everton. As football fanatics the both of us, it was inconceivable that Glenn and I would meet up and not go to see a game. We would go to watch our local non-league team every Saturday while I was a teenager and now we arrange to go to games every so often, sometimes just random non-league games with a small stand and railing round the pitch differentiating it from park football and other times a professional game around the London area. Glenn's adopted professional side, Millwall, have a dreadful reputation of hooliganism and are regarded as a step back to the dark days of English football in the 1980s when fighting on the terraces between gangs was commonplace. Going to their stadium, the New Den, is always an experience, and always one that you hope will not end in a knife to your throat. In a slightly sadistic way, it's great fun. The atmosphere, always electric, is something not found very much in football nowadays as VIP hospitality suites serving prawn sandwiches to sponsors and their guests has taken over. There's no possibility of getting a prawn sandwich at the New Den. You get a burger, accept the risk of food poisoning, and eat it before it gets punched out of your hands.

As we took our place in the stand that Glenn had promised was home to the most drugged up, psychopathic, vermin-like supporters *('Don't look at your ticket. Don't look anyone in the eye. Don't expect to sit down')*, it dawned on me that these gentlemen, roaring their team on while holding a fag or spliff in one hand and a packet of coke in the other, were the very men that would have found themselves on the boats heading out of Greenwich and to the far corners of the world. They would have been the dogsbodies working on the boats, helping to sail them as to their captain's orders by changing the sails and scrubbing the decks. They would have been the other people on these boats captained by the great British heroes like Nelson and Cook. It would have been them on the voyages of discovery gaping in awe at the naked beauties of the South Pacific islands or loading the cannons to fire cannonball after cannonball at foreign enemy ships. But here they were nowadays, with no other excitement in their life other than watching an FA Cup fourth round tie and taking as many legal and illegal stimulants as possible. Just to get that buzz. Just to escape the mundanity of life.

I spent the goalless first half wondering about the lives and the fate of men like those I was surrounded by. Certainly being on a boat fighting the French or looking out for new lands couldn't have been easy, but I pondered whether it was preferable to fighting cops outside a football stadium and shouting abuse at millionaire footballers. It highlighted for me the way that the world has changed and with it our lives. Although, thanks to the idea of preserving heritage, we still have the grand buildings and the revolutionary machines to marvel at, we live very different lives to the people of the past centuries, the people who used those buildings with reason and those machines with a purpose. Nowadays their only purpose is to remind us of where we came from, what the past was like. We shuffle round the buildings on guided tours and gaze at the machines in glass cabinets, but we don't get the joy of using them, of discovering new things through them. The only new things to discover are the old things of the past that we haven't learned about yet.

As it happened, there was a fair bit of buzz at the final whistle. Millwall, the underdogs, defeated the Premier League boys to cause a cup upset by scoring in the final minute. The fanatics went crazy, hugging, punching the air, screaming their lungs out. Glenn and I left them to it. We caught the first train out of the nearby rail station and reflected on a real day of two halves. First Maritime Greenwich, the grand monument to Britain's maritime heritage and the home of so much world-changing innovation as well as endeavour and the pursuit of knowledge. Then, the New Den; almost a polar opposite. Britain as it is today. The pursuit of thrills, escaping the 9 to 5. The same men, but vastly different environments. Still Greenwich, but after all the discovery has been done. As we waited on the station platform for the train back to Clapham, I noticed an anchor tattooed onto the bare arm of one of the Millwall fans, a crude sketch filled in with deep purple ink. The link to the sea is still profound.

UK UNESCO World Heritage Site #12 of 28

Palace of Westminster and Westminster Abbey including Saint Margaret's Church (1987)

A palace for a parliament, an abbey for a nation.

What did you want to be when you were a child? Though always susceptible to change, children can have fairly solid ideas of what job they want to do when they grow up. Doctors, teachers, firemen, actresses, footballers. Often kids want to follow their parents and often they aim high: the boss of a company, world champion, even Prime Minister. That's what my little sister, Anna-Maria, always said she wanted to be. Whenever aunts or grandparents would enquire about what us three kids wanted to be in the future, my brother and I would mumble something about famous sportstars or actors, but my sister would always outrightly declare that she wanted to be Prime Minister of the UK, or, failing that, Queen. It didn't surprise us, nor did anyone ever tell her she couldn't dream that high. Growing up with a brother either side of her, she had to be pretty strong and determined to survive, I suppose. With no sisters of her own, nor any female cousins until her teenage years, she must have looked up to my mother and her three sisters.

Alas, Anna-Maria hasn't realised her childhood ambition of being the UK's third female Prime Minister (yet, anyway) but she does work in central London for a government agency. She has the high-flying career I guess she saw herself in when she was asked that question all those years ago. Still, not being PM doesn't stop you from entering Parliament, at least as a tourist anyway. As such she'd kindly agreed to join me for a tour of the UNESCO World Heritage listed Palace of Westminster where the UK's two house system of governance has been housed since the 1200s.

While A-M harboured ambitions of being in the government, I'm sure that my parents and grandparents would have loved Ben and I to be employed in surroundings similar to the other half of Westminster's World Heritage site. Growing up in a Catholic family, it was mentioned more than a few times with expective glances that the Church was short of priests and it was up to us boys to step up and serve. It was never really likely though. Sorry Mum. Ben and I now work in education just as our mum did, so I suppose she inspired us in different ways.
Westminster Abbey has been Anglican since the 16th century so wouldn't have ended up there anyway (unless we had really rebelled!) It was the first stop on my Holy Trinity of Westminster World Heritage sites for the day. I arrived into London Waterloo, Parliament peeping out from across the river between skyscraper developments as the train eased into Britain's busiest rail station. I zipped along Westminster Bridge, the walk across the river that I and many others must have done a thousand times though it still never gets

old. It still gives you that 'I'm in London' feeling, even on an overcast day and with the Elizabeth Tower (Big Ben) and other parts of the Palace of Westminster covered in grey scaffolding. The amount of rubbish rolling around in the breeze and the occasional waft of urine also gave me that recognisable London sensation. As great as London has become, it's still disgusting in parts.

I rounded the Palace and entered Westminster Abbey behind it. The architecture of the Palace was inspired by that of the Abbey, the two deliberately blending Gothic styles to match each other. The Abbey is several hundred years older, but has far less scaffolding around it. I sped through the entry gate, security nonchalantly gazing into my bag, and booked myself onto the guided tour starting in twenty minutes' time. There is of course the option to use the audio guide, but for an extra fiver you can upgrade, if you will, to a human and, though only available for English speakers, it's money well spent in my opinion. A group of around twenty five of us gathered around the corner from the entrance and were met by one of the vergers, John, who gracefully guided us around, his vestments sweeping along in his wake, and his mellifluous voice describing the history of the Abbey. We started at the northern entrance to the Abbey with the Coronation Chair. Every monarch who is coronated at the Abbey, that's all but two of them since 1066, takes their seat in King Edward's rather battered old chair. It's hidden just to the right of the monarch's entrance and has had the buttocks of thirty eight monarchs-to-be placed upon it, though given its wizened state it looks like every person who has ever entered Westminster Abbey has had a go. Graffiti etched into wood would also suggest that it's been well-loved, though in fairness it is around 700 years old. Truth be told, it looks very uncomfortable with its straight back. I'm sure most monarchs were keen to get off it after sitting through their hours-long coronations.

John span around and led us over the floor monument to Sir Winston Churchill, placed centrally at the entrance. Ever the humourist, Churchill turned down the offer of being buried at the Abbey stating that he'd spent his life being walked over and so didn't want the trend to continue after death. A few metres up the aisle the tomb of the Unknown Soldier is bordered by poppies, partly in significance of those flowers which grew in Flanders fields where so many unknown soldiers fell and partly to prevent people from walking over the tomb, it being the only one in the whole abbey to have this privilege. The Abbey is covered like a tattoo addict with monuments and memorials to the great and the good of the country. Augustus Pugin, who designed the interior of the Palace of Westminster, hated the memorials displayed in the interior of the Westminster Abbey calling them 'incongruous and detestable'; the sheer amount and variety of them covering almost every square inch of wall and floor space. William Morris said that they were 'the most hideous specimens of the false art in the world'. Personally, I have to disagree. They're a distracting fascination, making you walk into the backs of other visitors as you try to read as many as possible while you shuffle past. They're incredibly special too. The tomb of the Unknown Soldier was the first to recognise the unknown war dead, and has since been copied throughout the world. We paused for a moment to consider the sacrifices made by millions in the fight for peace and then John led us up the aisle into the quire, gliding through the headphone-toting tourists with us stumbling in his graceful wake. We were treated to a perk of the human-led tour in the quire, being allowed exclusive access to the seats upon which the choir lead the hymns, their sheets illuminated by the red lamps shades. This is one of the most ornately decorated areas of a building dripping with elaborate statues, plaques and lavish colours. Gold and royal blue dominate. Everywhere you look there is something of significance. I took a seat in the back row of the quire, a few places away from the Queen's own seat, indicated with the royal crest. These seats were where many important people were sat during events such as the Queen's coronation in 1953 and Prince William's wedding in 2011. The Queen has her own seat in the abbey as the abbey technically is hers. It comes under the rather peculiar title of a Royal Peculiar, meaning that it's under the jurisdiction of the monarch rather than the archbishop.

Walking up from the quire to the altar, we paused to look down at the floor in front of the altar. It's one of Westminster's greatest treasures despite its faded, uneven state. The Cosmati pavement is 750 years old, stones of different shapes and sizes laid in mesmerising patterns upon a base of Purbeck marble. Few people aside from Royals getting married or clergy officiating those ceremonies ever stand on it now, but now it can be viewed and immensely appreciated from the heights of the triforium with the recent opening of the Queen's Diamond Jubilee Galleries.

On the hunt for more treasures, John led us past a guarding verger up the stairs to a platform surrounded by tombs. Closed to the rest of the rabble (that extra fiver for a human tour was paying off), the St Edward shrine is the very heart of the Abbey. We sat down amongst the stone tombs that contain the remains of kings and queens of England from centuries ago. John granted us time to wander in this special space freely, pointing out the missing mosaic pieces that pilgrims to St Edward's shrine would nick as a lucky souvenir. St Edward was once King Edward and is known commonly as Edward the Confessor; the last king of the House of Wessex whose death was followed by William the Conqueror's accession in 1066. Edward was moved to this central shrine by

Henry III and is surrounded by 5 kings and 4 queens, as we were too while circling the 10 foot tall rectangular shrine admiring the pockmarked decoration and the sheer weight of history around us. Although now all that really remains in the tombs is rotting corpses, once those corpses were the kings and queens we all read about in history books, the figures that make up the long list of Britain's royal past. You can care as little or as much as you want about it, but if you do think about who these entombed cadavers once were, it is truly staggering that you're standing right next to them.

The Verger-guard opened up the rope again to let us out and we continued a few more steps into the Lady Chapel at the very back of the Abbey. Built from 1502-17, it's about as regal a place as you'll ever see with banners and Knight's helmets decorating the sides. The knights are part of the Order of the Bath, which sounds like a nightly activity for parents with young children, but is actually an order of chivalry founded by George I and nowadays consisting of ex-Army chiefs, high-ranking civil servants and other old blokes. The interesting aspect of the knights is their carved and painted crests displayed around the room. Looking around, you see the traditional heads of lions, unicorns and dragons, but also a few curious ones including a naked woman's top half and a devil dog with pitchfork. A few items you wouldn't initially expect to see in the most important church in the country. The name, (you were wondering, weren't you?), comes from part of the knights' initiation which involved bathing. Nowadays the ritual has been cut down to just a sword on the shoulder, the knights being trusted to look after their own hygiene these days.

Now gravely in danger of death by history dates, John worked our way back round along the other side of the abbey to Poet's Corner for the last stop of the tour.

The trend for the burial and memorialising of writers started with Chaucer who is buried here and today it's probably the part tourists most wish they could take photos of. Only they can't, under strict supervision of various well-positioned vergers. Just about every celebrated British author up to Philip Larkin is presented here, regardless of their views on religion. Shakespeare, Tennyson, Byron, Auden, Hardy, Betjeman, Eliot; the litany is simply staggering. It means that the abbey is also a who's who of British culture. With Scientist's Corner as well, it's a true shrine to the ingenuity and imagination of the British. It's easy to be blasé about the place, but Westminster Abbey is drenched in history, significance, and culture. If there were one place to show off Britain's history and culture to a tourist, perhaps the Abbey would be it. It is, as one observer put it, the Valhalla of Britain. And it's not just inside either. Stepping out into the cloisters, more memorials and plaques are displayed on walls and floors. People from Edmond Halley to an 18th century plumber at the Abbey in the same space. That's rather extraordinary. If the memorials weren't enough, by the entrance to the Chapter House is Britain's oldest door, a tiny wooden entry illuminated by a spotlight and signed. I mean, does Westminster Abbey really need any more claims to fame?

The Chapter House is a large round space with stained-glass windows displaying various momentous events that have shaped its history. Once the meeting place for the monks, it was used as the House of Commons from the 14th century to 1547 when the House moved to its present location in the Palace of Westminster. I was circling the room thoughtfully when I felt a few buzzes in my pocket and realised that my time at the Abbey was almost up. It was Anna-Maria. She was waiting for me at the Cromwell entrance to the Palace. It was almost time for our tour. I dragged myself away, passing through the obligatory gift shop as I exited. Bowled over by the history of Westminster Abbey, I took a deep breath and then headed off to the Palace of Westminster for more history; moving from religion to politics but still with a very strong royal theme going on.

A-M and I managed to meet up in the midst of Tourist Central and we started the understandably far stricter security process to enter the seat of power of the UK. *'What time's our flight again?'* I joked with A-M as we deposited our valuables, belts, watches, coats, bags, dignity and any jokes about politicians into airport-style tubs that were fed through a scanner. Sod's law that my bag flashed up and I had to explain why I was bringing a selection of whiteboard markers in the Houses of Parliament to a dour young security guard. The tools of a teacher. I could have quipped that I was coming in to teach the MPs a lesson, but the security guards didn't look like the types that do jokes. As it was, my bag was fine and we were able to join our tour on time.

Again, I had opted for the human-led tour instead of the audio guide. It's just nicer not to wander around like a zombie with headphones on and a device in hand. Our guide, Rowena, welcomed us inside the cavernous Westminster Hall and we started the tour by walking briskly through the whole building to the opposite end.

'Blimey, this tour is going pretty fast'.
'Yeah, it might be nice to stop and hear about some of the history'.

We zoomed through various rooms to begin in the Royal Court where we could start our exploration of possibly London's most recognisable building. It had been the main home of the Royal Family from 1016 and served a dual purpose with Parliament from the 13th century, however a fire during the reign of Henry

VIII meant that the royals moved out and the politicians were given the building for the two houses of parliament. Through various redesigns the royal palace began to accommodate the parliament better but the politicians still struggled for space so perhaps it was almost a relief when in 1834 a fire swept through much of the building. Parliament needed a new place to meet and, despite being offered Buckingham Palace by William IV, they chose to set a competition to build a new Palace of Westminster on the same traditional site. It took thirty years for Charles Barry's winning design to be realised (by which time he was long dead) but eventually the building we see today was completed and Britain had a new icon set alongside the River Thames, a vast Gothic facade with a 170 foot tall tower planted by Westminster Bridge. At the top of this tower possibly the most recognisable clock in the world is displayed; the last work of Augustus Pugin, also the designer of the palace's interiors, who then descended into madness and was committed to Royal Bethlem Hospital, commonly known as Bedlam.

Pugin's work before his sorry demise into lunacy is breathtaking. The palace has possibly the grandest interior I've ever walked through. We were now in the Royal Gallery, battle scenes from Agincourt and Waterloo looked dull surrounded by the sheer amount of gold leaf, shiny mahogany and intricate carvings. Rowena explained that occasionally Ministers of Parliament (MPs) sit in this room to work together and discuss matters of politics. With the chandeliers and glass stained windows, it must feel a world away from the 21st century reality of a country. I couldn't help but feel that this may present a problem. The Palace of Westminster is seen quite understandably as the ivory tower from which MPs make life-changing decisions without quite realising the consequences. How can these MPs, a tenth of whom went to the same £32,000 a year private school, really empathise with the people of the UK and their issues when they are surrounded by such opulence? How could you really consider deeply the relative poverty that 20% of Britons live in when you're sat in a beautiful dark oak chair surrounded by frescoes and portraits of dead royals? How can MPs even imagine real life in such a fantastical environment?

It made me think of a few stories I'd been reading a few days before about the UK Parliament moving out of London into a modern building somewhere more central in the country like Manchester. It's a compelling argument that has rumbled along for years. Primarily the move would restore balance to the Union, aid the Northern England economy, and could also take advantage of high real-estate prices in London. It would also mean that the six billion pounds being spent on repairing and restoring the Palace of Westminster could be saved. Due to the restoration, MPs are being forced to have a dry-run and see what parliament outside of the Palace of Westminster feels like from around 2025 while works to restore the palace continue. They won't be going far though with most offices and the two houses moving only a stone's throw away.

Walking through the rooms there was the occasional bit of scaffolding with Westminster Hall, where we'd started the tour, the most obvious example. All of the Elizabeth Tower containing Big Ben is covered and many other exterior parts are similarly being worked on. Other World Heritage sites in the UK I'd been to previously had been getting a makeover too, and others had been restored over recent years, but the sheer scale and cost of repairing the Palace of Westminster made me think how far and how much you should go to keep a building. Of course, the place is not just heritage, it's also heavily used by politicians and tourists alike. It's also an icon of the country, a symbol of democracy across the world. However, when it's that amount of taxpayers money being used to restore a building that relatively isn't that old (1840) and isn't actually fit for current purpose (there are only 427 seats for the 650 MPs in the House of Commons), you can see the argument for moving the seat of power in the country elsewhere, and out of London would bring benefits to other parts of the country. Honestly, I was torn in two minds. Talking it over the next day with my middle-aged parents who have lived in the South all their lives, they were shocked that I even suggested such a thing as moving the seat of power away from London and repurposing the Palace. I suppose that would be most Southerners' reaction. It's London. It's always been there. Changing it would be heresy.

Rowena indulged us with many stories behind the sculptures and paintings as we made our way towards the House of Lords. Just before you enter the House where the wise and wealthy of Britain consider bills and keep the government in check, a huge statue of Queen Victoria, instantly recognisable, is planted against the wall next to the door which leads to the House. Women have only been able to be MPs since 1918, and have only been allowed in the House of Lords since 1958. Nowadays women represent about a quarter of the peers, but in Victoria's time she would have been the only female in the House. No wonder she wanted an intimidating statue of herself to face the Lords as they passed into chamber. Rowena told us how she'd insisted on various beautifying features to her statue, but at 2.5 metres tall and with Justice and Mercy by her side the statue would have achieved its purpose.

Women are also represented on the wall around the Prince's Chamber where we were stood but they happen to be the rather unlucky wives of Henry VIII. They met their fates because of Henry's desire to separate from the Catholic Church, but decades later, under the reign of the anti-Catholic James I, a band of men led by the infamous Guy Fawkes stored gunpowder under the very floor we were stood on in the hope of blasting the king out of his seat and the Protestants out of the country. The King would have been visiting the House of Lords for the annual State Opening of Parliament and would have been sat on the other side of the wall from where Queen Victoria is now. Now in the House of Lords, Rowena pointed out the Sovereign's Throne, a jewel-encrusted, red velvet seat to plump a royal bottom that was obviously modelled on Coronation Chair I'd seen earlier in Westminster Abbey. Apparently Michael Jackson once offered to buy it but was flatly refused, being told, as Rowena quoted, to 'beat it'. We walked round and up into the red leather benches, standing rather than sitting as none of us had inherited a peerage or descended from nobles. Being of noble blood was once the only way to enter the House until reforms gave us the modern-day system of peerages being nominated by the Prime Minister and approved by the Queen.

Nowadays the Lords come from various walks of life, and, some say, are more representative of the country than the elected House of Commons. The percentages of ethnic minorities and women are around the same in both Houses, but the three main parties are represented more equally, the third largest group actually being the crossbenchers who don't represent any political party. Since the House of Lords Act in 1999, the right of the 750 or so Hereditary Peers to sit in the House of Lords has been abolished and 90 of the 92 Hereditary Lords who sit in the Lords Chamber today have to be elected by other members of the House. There are a lot of myths and assumptions about the House of Lords and Rowena was quick to dispel them, highlighting that it was the Lords who were crucial in passing recent key legislation. In many ways, they are more qualified to give their opinion on particular topics than the MPs. Some of the well-known peers include Tanni Grey-Thompson, Britain's most successful female Paralympian, and Alan Sugar, one of the UK's most recognisable businessmen; both experts in their fields of sport and business respectively and therefore probably the right people to ask when consulting government plans on these topics. It makes far more sense than having career politicians who have never been a doctor or a teacher filling roles like Health Secretary or Education Secretary. Surely it's better to have someone who knows something about these sectors in charge rather than a smart suit with a degree in spin and smarminess.

Anna-Maria and I swapped thoughts on this as we passed through the Peers House lobby and Peers Corridor to Central Hall, the heart of the Palace from which life spreads to all parts of the parliament. Neither of us had really known what the House of Lords was or what it did before Rowena's myth-blasting talk. I was racking my brain to think of a time, if any, when we'd been taught about it at school, but nothing came to mind. Ask most Brits and I'm sure not many would be able to give an accurate description of how their system of governance works. It's as complicated as it is historic. Added to that is voter apathy. A third of eligible voters in the UK did not vote at all in the General Election in 2017. There's a perception of politicians as pure evil, they're all as bad as each other. In turn there's a lot of anger directed towards them and to Westminster itself. While the Palace of Westminster may represent a world-famous building and the seat of democracy for some, it means omnipotence and overarching control for others. Many do not feel that their views are represented by the MPs sitting in the House of Commons. MPs dwell in constituencies, 650 parts of the UK divided into around 80,000 inhabitants which is also, interestingly enough, the salary for an MP in pounds per year. So, a pound a person for the MPs who work in the Palace from Monday to Thursday, returning to their constituencies on Fridays to hold 'surgeries' where they meet their local populace. Representing 80,000 people may have seemed small to the American gentleman on our tour (*'Oh, that's tiny!'*)', but there are few other jobs that require one person to represent the views of so many. Even comparing it to running a company, there are few companies in the UK that have over 80,000 employees. Of course, MPs will never meet most of their constituents and some will not have been voted in by the majority of their representees, but still, my dismissive view of MPs hard work was melting. That was until we continued through into the House of Commons.

You might have expected the House of Lords to be opulent and, appropriately for its name, it is. But the House of Commons, the house of normal people who want to better their nation as a whole by representing the people in their part of the country, is just as gold-adorned, wood-sculpted, and pompously-decorated as the House of Lords. It's also, like most things you see on TV, even smaller than expected. Compared to the cavernous parliaments around the world that are always set up in a circle or semi-circle, the House of Commons is intimate like a boxing ring, just as Winston Churchill reportedly preferred it. You can see everyone, and everyone can see you. There are no hiding places in a room that small.

Rowena led us up into the backbenches (though not the very back bench as security wanted it clear just in case of, well, something) and we gazed around the room we had all seen a million times on the news before. It's rather like being on a film set. You've seen it so often on TV that it's hard to believe that it really exists. The turtle green seats, the dark wood panelling, the large desk in the centre with its despatch boxes facing each other. The politicians who stand at these despatch boxes, the characters of the soap opera Britain has been playing out of the last few years, seem made up too. Bushy-haired Theresa May stands there fiercely delivering her speeches while across from her Jeremy Corbyn sits smiling wryly, surrounded by his fellow MPs slouching back on those green leather benches. The MPs, jostling with the Speaker in his high chair, bob up and down when a new speaker starts and there are the murmurs, the shrieks, the jeers, the boos, the outbursts from the benches. Watching any Prime Minister's Questions debate is often like watching a TV drama, the witty remarks almost seem rehearsed. Being there, standing on those very benches, feels surreal. I almost had to ask A-M to pinch me.

The UK Parliament is a strange beast, appropriate really for what I feel is the weirdest country in the world. The House of Commons has only 427 seats for 650 MPs and they don't like people sitting on their laps so prayer cards are used to decide who gets a seat. First order of the day is a Christian prayer and backbenchers who attend Prayers are able to complete a prayer card with their name and insert it into a slot on their seat to guarantee a seat for the day. It's the only way to ensure you have a seat, and thus a potential say in any debate. No prayer equals no seat equals no say! The only way to get a say is to rise from your seat and catch the eye of the Speaker, hence the reason why MPs bob up and down so much during debates.

Then there's the voting. In major votes that are close, MPs leave their seats and run like cattle into the voting lobbies either side of the chamber to register whether they are an 'aye' or a 'no'. Bells are rung in nearby pubs to notify MPs that a vote is taking place. Once the herds have been counted, the vote result is then passed to the Speaker who announces it.

The Speaker is also the subject of much tradition. Once elected, he is physically dragged to the Speaker's Chair by MPs, a tradition stemming from a past role of the Speaker which was to report the opinions of the Commons to the King. They say don't shoot the messenger, but seven Speakers were beheaded between the 13th and 15th centuries. Not a job for the faint-hearted.

Neither is being a politician, in the past or the present. Fortunately there are some measures in place to avoid confrontation. There are red lines in front of the facing front benches that MPs may not step over. The lines are exactly two sword lengths apart to keep quarrels verbal rather than physical and MPs still have a sword hook in their cloakrooms. The rather ridiculous traditions were met with gentle chuckles from the audience on our tour, but I suppose that once they served a purpose. Like many things in the UK, once they were needed, but now not, though we often, for posterity's sake I suppose, still keep the traditions. One tradition of not letting the public sit on the benches seemed flexible though. A security guard in the chamber motioned to the elderly gentleman in front of me that he could sit down for a rest, a lovely gesture that Rowena claimed was the first time she'd ever known it to happen. Walking out of the House of Commons back towards Westminster Hall, the son speculated whether his father had possibly just made history as the first non-elected member of the public to ever sit in the House of Commons. Who knows, perhaps we had just witnessed a moment in history.

That's the rather funny thing about traditions. Once they're broken, I suppose we realise that they weren't really needed anyway, and we were just doing it that way because that's the way it had always been done. We often have rules for rules' sake, and the UK Parliament is a good example of that. Things could, and arguably should change, but any break with tradition is often seen as a negative. Those were the arguments behind rejecting women's rights to vote, but rightly, just over a hundred years ago, the tradition was changed and the country benefited. Rowena rounded off our talk by pointing up at the modern artwork above the entrance to St Stephen's Hall that commemorates the long campaign that led to women's suffrage. Mary Branson's 'New Dawn' consists of 168 glass discs arranged in a circle under a ceiling arch that change colour throughout the day, much like a permanent sunrise above the main entrance into the heart of the parliament. It's a sign that the UK Parliament can change, hope for the future, and a strong message of equality. Despite its antiquated ways, there are signs that change for the better is possible.

All the walking around Parliament had left A-M and I rather hungry so we repaired to the Jubilee Cafe within the Palace for a bite to eat. The amount of gluten-free and vegan options was another sign of Parliament moving with the times, though the curious prices of the food and drink were yet another demonstration of how strange the UK's government really is. I'd never seen prices like it anywhere. Sandwiches started at £3.78, the tomato soup was £5.12 and a pot of tea was £2.02. Whether it was for amusement's sake or a chance for tourists to actually spend their one and two pences instead of chucking them in the hotel bin, we had no idea but it was beguiling to say the least. We also popped into the adjoining gift shop which was selling encaustic tiles dug up from the floors of the Palace for £200 a pop. Fair enough if people are stupid enough to buy them, but I've never known any country to literally be selling off physical parts of its own heritage, and its government building for that matter, to tourists. Is that where the UK is now? Selling the floor tiles to overseas visitors. Still, at least at £200 for a 10x10cm tile, it wasn't selling itself short. A-M and I wondered how many tiles you would need to sell to make £6 billion.

There was just enough time to pop into St Margaret's Church, the place of worship for MPs and part of the World Heritage Site, before we went to see the Abbey in action during 3pm Evensong. St Margaret's is a quaint church, like a mini-Westminster Abbey with an organ and a small quire, and rows of traditional style wooden pews. It's beautiful without the need to be grand and impressive like its neighbour. It was built by the Benedictine monks at the Abbey so that the public could go to church without disturbing the monks in the abbey. Nowadays it's used for public worship undisturbed by the tourists in the abbey so the roles have reversed. That said, it has a few claims to fame of its own. Writers Samuel Pepys and John Milton were married here, as was Winston Churchill. William Caxton, who brought the printing press to British shores, and the explorer Walter Raleigh are both buried at St Margaret's. Though not covered in plaques like the abbey, there are a few tablets dedicated to the persons above around the church.

Back to the Abbey for me, and a first time visit for A-M, just in time for Evensong led by the Westminster Abbey Choir who are still all-male, unlike at Canterbury Cathedral. We were sat right by the Cosmati floor, able to sit back and listen to the choral echoes bounce off the stonework and fill the central crossing. Though the central crossing lacks a spire (plans have been put forward in recent times to build one) it still reaches a height of 140 feet and is wonderful for gazing up into the heavens as the readings and hymns wash over your ears. Outside the chaos of central London continues, but within a building set in the middle of one of the world's busiest cities you can find an enormous and surprising degree of peace. As at Canterbury, experiencing the building in action surpasses any tour that you could ever join. It gave me time to appreciate the fine architecture and decoration of a building that is iconic throughout the country and the world. Looking around yourself, you realise the weight of history that surrounds you. All the kings and queens who have been coronated on the very steps I was sat next to. All the royal weddings held on the same black and white patterned floor my feet were now resting on. It's the opulence, the gold and the rich mahogany, that give the abbey its stature and its importance, a church fit for a king. I suppose that's the purpose of the rich surroundings of the Palace of Westminster too. Though the lavish decorations may alienate MPs from their constituents, it must remind them that they are in a place where every important decision has been made for centuries, where wars have been declared, where social programs have been created, and where politicians have stood up for the rights of their people and the good of their country. Hopefully being surrounded by such history allows MPs to learn from history, think of the consequences, and make the right decisions. If MPs were surrounded by bland modernity with its meaningless designs and decoration in a brand-spanking new Houses of Parliament somewhere up north, would they really feel the weight of previous generations and sense the duty that history gives you? Without the Houses of Parliament at Westminster, wouldn't the UK lose a crucial facet of its identity? Or is Britain so full of history that it can barely take a step forward? Are we so lost in past glories that we can't look ahead to the needs of the future? It's up to the politicians who sit in the benches that A-M and I stood in front of to decide where the UK goes from here. How much of its tradition should it shed without losing the colour from its richly-decorated skin?

UK UNESCO World Heritage Site #13 of 28

Royal Botanic Gardens, Kew (2003)

Spring bloom at Kew

As I stepped out at Kew Gardens Station I could see instantly why the trains were being delayed. Debris from fierce winds blowing through the capital was leaving twigs and leaves scattered across the station forecourt. It billowed and howled at any loose object, tipping coffee shop chairs over and almost whisking people off their feet. Kew Gardens, the UNESCO World Heritage site I'd planned to see, had considered closing for the day, such was the ferocity of the gales.

Fortunately my wind-affected journey was not to be in

vain and my appropriately named friend Anila, her name the same as the Hindu God of Wind, was waiting for me inside the entrance cafe with a coffee to shake me out of my chill. It was rather warming to see her. We hadn't seen each other since the summer, she with a busy job in the capital that was taking over her life.

'How's London life?', I asked, receiving the same tube nightmare and 12 hour day with barely time to breathe story I'd heard from every other friend who now calls London home.

'But it's amazing, y'know. Living in London. So many things to see and do and eat. Just so diverse'.

I shrugged. Despite being a Londoner, I can see more reasons not to live in London than to live there. The stress, the crime, the pollution. I don't need to live in London for work, so why put up with it? That's what I tell myself anyway whenever I catch myself lusting at social media pictures of friends in swanky bars with fancy cocktails or coffees or waiting, tickets in hand, to enter a West End show or an O2 gig.

I suppose that those who do settle in London do so for places like Kew Gardens. The world's largest botanic gardens was created in 1759 when two royal parks were amalgamated to provide a place for the public to come and appreciate nature, and a place for Britain to show off the floral treasures it had stumbled upon while on the great voyages of discovery. Covering over 300 acres and holding 14,000 trees, it is a monumental heritage item, not just of the UK's nature, but of the world's. It may be located in the UK but really it contains the entire globe, with the sections of the famed Victorian glasshouses divided into countries and continents. As such, it's rightly popular with tourists from around the world, and this day in particular with Colombians due to the month long

Colombian orchid exhibition that was about to end. With 2.5 million visitors a year, and this Spring Sunday a sunny if not incredibly blustery day, I was surprised that Anila had managed to snag us two of the fifteen spaces on the 11am introduction tour led by one of Kew's knowledgeable volunteer guides. We downed our coffees and met our guide, Janet, at the tour desk where we had to meet the other tourists. Except there weren't any other tourists. No one else had signed up for the tour. Slightly embarrassed but feeling rather privileged, Anila and I had a private tour as not one of the other thousands of tourists had wanted to join the free tour that Kew kindly provides.

Their loss. Perhaps it's the land train with audio commentary that people prefer (it was packed when it rolled past us in the afternoon) or simply people visit Kew just to have a walk around and gaze lazily at the tree tags that give the plant's Latin name and little else. Perhaps it's because people don't expect there to be much of a story behind trees, but, as Janet happily enlightened us, there is a wealth of background to the extraordinarily varied and deliberately planned tree collection at Kew.

Now, I must profess some ignorance. I can barely tell one tree from another, let alone identify plants or flowers. Of course, I can point out an oak from a sycamore, or a daffodil from a rose, but much more than that and I'm hopelessly lacking in knowledge. I'd love to know the name of every tree and plant I pass, even more so to know its properties and uses. I remember walking around a natural reserve in Montreal with a guy who'd studied Botany and happened to be staying at the same couchsurfing house as me. As we walked he pointed out every single plant and listed its medicinal properties, blowing away my brain with useful and fascinating knowledge. Janet was of the same ilk. Diminutive, she barely had to duck to get under the low hanging branches, but a tower of knowledge, Janet talked passionately about what we were passing by as we walked to our first stop, the Temple of Bellona: a petite four-columned shelter sticking out of the woods that allowed us brief respite from the bitterly cold wind. Even up close it was impossible to tell that it's made of wood not stone, but, as soon as you rap your knuckles against it you can sense the soft wood behind the thick white paint.

Bemused, we ventured back out like penguins into an Antarctic storm and took in the Pagoda vista. Kew is as much about the space between the trees as it is about the trees themselves. There are various darting vistas crossing the 300 acres like strobe lights cutting across a green dance floor, and they provide an opportunity for the trees to create guards of honour from one building to the next. This particular vista has English oaks lined up to present the Chinese-style octagonal tower that William Chambers built in 1762, just a few years after the park opened. We gazed down it for a while then turned our backs to walk to the Palm House. Slightly younger and much larger than its counterpart in Belfast, Kew's Palm House is an extraordinary marriage of iron and glass, iconic as the world's most important structure of its type and home to many endangered species of tropical plants. Letting the moulding iron doors close behind you as you step inside, your first sensation is the welcoming humidity hug that smothers you, banishing the chill that you left behind you outside. In a mere few steps we'd travelled from brutally cold London to the Amazon rainforest, and boy was I glad to be inside!

Janet was keen to point out the banana plants from which a few bunches of mini bananas hung and we were able to spot many other familiar food items as we walked around. Plants aren't just for nourishment though. Janet also pointed out the Madagascar periwinkle which is an ornamental plant and, with its pink petals, is a rather beautiful one at that. However, it's also used in cancer treatment. Indeed, one of its derived compounds, Vincristine, has raised the survival rate in childhood leukaemia from 10% to 90%. Despite its miraculous properties, the periwinkle has had to overcome the threat of extinction from deforestation. It could be reasonably supposed that had it not been found to have these properties, it would have died with its secrets intact. Fortunately, it was found before extinction and is easy to cultivate, nowadays being found around the world. It's just one of many examples of how incredibly important plants are for humans and how much respect we should be giving our natural world. How many more miracle plants are out there? We won't know if they become extinct before we find them.

I suppose it takes places like Kew to educate us to the wonders of our world and the Palm House is a wonderful school in which to learn. The only time I'd previously visited was in fact a school trip, though I remembered very little spare the excited frenzy caused when Jack Campfield spotted marijuana and coca leaves growing in an exhibit. We crowded round to stare at the green leaves until a teacher shooed us along and we spent the rest of the time running around disturbing other visitors and dropping litter everywhere. It was fair to say that my second visit was teaching me more than the first.

Not being preoccupied by a game of 'It', I now noticed the genius design of Decimus Burton and Richard Turner which allows the palms to stretch out with 19 metres of height to grow into helped by the fact that remarkably there's barely a support pylon in place. You don't ever feel restricted in the Palm House, it's an open space that, with your eyes barely closed, you could well believe is in one of the great rainforests of the world. The Palm House was completely dismantled, restored and rebuilt in 1988. It's still showing its age slightly, especially when compared with the twice as large Temperate House which spent five years being renovated before reopening in 2018. However, with the pond reflecting its glassy upturned hulls, it's a superlative sight, and deservedly the icon of Kew.

Zipping up after the humidity of the Palm House, Janet led Anila and I out to a more recent addition to Kew's landscape, one that she couldn't stop herself from waxing lyrical about. *'Simply the most amazing bridge'* cuts Kew's major lake in half and is one of the genius examples of architecture that marries nature and man's necessities. Approaching it from the Syon vista it looked as if the bronze uprights that provide the sides of the bridge weren't sufficiently spaced out enough. Indeed a little boy was trying to squeeze himself between them as we walked closer.
Now facing the bridge as we walked round we noticed its serpentine shape and the way the uprights now appeared to provide gapless sides to the snaking granite platform. It's like an optical illusion, the genius being that you can look at the bridge side on and see right through it to the other end of the lake; it doesn't interrupt your view. It also, I supposed, by being a serpentine shape, allows more people to walk along it than a straight bridge. It's one of those things you see and can't help but think 'wow, someone's actually thought about that hard'.
It's so logical, yet unobvious. So many buildings and bridges are ill-thought out. Constructions like the Sackler bridge are so simple yet so full of thought. I joined Janet in the Sackler bridge's fan club. It's not just the natural world that's beautiful, occasionally man can be inspired by nature and create something wonderful too.

We walked over the bridge, pointing out the orange head of a Mandarin duck floating under as we passed over and walked along the grass to the Temperate

House. It is hard to say what the jewel in Kew's crown is, but the Temperate House stakes a good claim. A huge chain of glasshouses with the two small rectangular houses linked to either side of the central large glass house by octagonal conservatories, it's sparkling clean as all new things are. We entered through the southern end and were instantly transported to Africa with all manner of plants, many rare and endangered, endemic to the continent tidily displayed.

'People compare this house to a train station'. Janet was full of surprises, but this one took me aback. Personally, I couldn't see the resemblance. Rather I felt that the Coade stone gives the house the appearance of an ornate statue that you are able to climb inside and explore. It's far more beautiful and cleaner than any train station I've been to. Janet walked as we ducked and dived under the overhanging leaves, taking us into the Americas past the beautiful fuschias *('Which I'm sure you know all about')* and then into Australasia and finally Asia.

Janet left us to it at the end of the Temperate House. We bade farewell to our source of all knowledge and then blindly continued our walk, choosing to head up the spiral staircase to the viewing platform that surrounds the central glasshouse. Now face to face with the palms, we could see the scale of the colours, sizes, shapes and the whole diversity of this microcosm of the natural world.

'It's kind of like a metaphor for London, don't you think? Plants instead of people, but such diversity all in one place and sharing the same environment.'

'Kind of. I mean, London isn't so fairly distributed and I guess plants don't have issues with integration and segregation'.

'Yeah, but it's open to new arrivals, just like London

itself. It has a little of everything from the world'.

'Is London really that welcoming? Is London really open?'

It was something to chew on as we gazed around the Temperate House, the wind howling at the window panes while the sun rays cast light across the flowerbeds, illuminating the scene. You could stay up there for hours, but our stomachs were rumbling after the walking tour and so we ventured out for some sustenance.

Kew has a number of restaurants catering for a variety of tastes though, like all London attractions, not all budgets. We plumped for the Orangery. There wasn't much citrus to be seen, but we did manage to snag a table opposite of pair of loud grannies to enjoy pie and mash and fish cakes. The Orangery is a fine place to dine with smartly dressed staff and a good selection of hot and cold meals, but, again like many tourist attraction food outlets, it resembles feeding time at the zoo when busy. There simply wasn't enough space for the amount of people who wanted to eat, forcing groups to share tables and chairs to be commandeered. That's without mentioning the cacophany of crying babies and the crash of dropped cutlery and glasses. It was rather like an upmarket school canteen. Maybe it would have been better to bring a limp cheese sandwich and munch on it by the Palm House pond as my fellow students and I had done all those years ago on our school trip.
Anila and I ate our rapidly cooling food quickly and then engaged in one of the great debates in British culture. Scones: jam then cream, or cream then jam? We almost fell out over it, though I had to eat humble pie when I compared my cream then jam mess to Anila's jam then cream perfection. Who cares anyway? It all goes to the same place. A bittersweet loss.

Licking the jam and cream off our lips, we braved the cold once again having captured enough warmth within the Orangery to keep us going for a few more hours. We chose to do a lap of the grounds, following the outskirts of the park to the pagoda in the opposite corner. As we walked, we talked about this and that: work, life, mutual acquaintances; the normal catch-up. I don't know about you but I really struggle to hold a conversation and appreciate a walk at the same time. My brain seemingly can't process the two simultaneously. For that reason, I can recall very little of our walk through the rhododendron except for bumping into a Colombian student from school.

'Teacher!'

'How the… Hello! How are you Maria?'

The teacher's curse strikes again.

Waving goodbye to my student, we continued walking and talking, Anila bemused by my celebrity status, until we reached the meeting of Syon vista and Cedar vista at the edge of the River Thames. I simply had to stop and fall silent. The view, even through my teary eyes in the face of the blasting wind, was beyond words. The vistas themselves lend superb views but across the water sits Syon House, the Duke of Northumberland's not so humble abode. Though not part of Kew, it's very much appreciable from its grounds. Turner painted this very view but it's even more striking in real life, a plump fortress like facade topped by a stone lion complemented by vast grounds that would be grand anywhere in the country but even more so when you consider that this is in one of the most expensive cities in the world per square metre. It makes you wonder how on earth this is London. The river is so idyllic, the undergrowth wild, the riverbank unmaintained with the water dragging the fallen branches. It could be the middle of nowhere. It really could.

That is until the roar of yet another A380 reverberates directly above you. I hadn't wanted to mention this, wish I didn't have to write about this at all, but there is one hugely disappointing factor about Kew, one that I'd argue could possibly harm its World Heritage status. Heathrow, Europe's largest airport, lies a few miles to the west and plane after plane, every couple of minutes or so, interrupts the tranquility to come into land. It's impossible to ignore without headphones and then you'd never get the sound of the bird life in Kew's trees. I suppose it's just the price you have to pay for having Kew where it is. It's understandable, a necessary evil, but it doesn't half spoil what is so close to paradise. Anila commented that it's a reminder of the life we live, beauty punctuated by the noisy, polluting reality of the modern world. I am not saying that the planes should be stopped. I've flown into and out of Heathrow many times, as you probably have too, but I wish it didn't have to spoil a place as special as Kew.

Still, you can't let it get you down. Kew is precious. You just to have to try to ignore it. Treat the planes as if they are the annoying people at work who bug you all day long, the ones who never shut up. Just shut them out and focus on what's good. I shan't be mentioning them again.

It does though bring me on to the inevitable topic that surrounds a natural place like Kew: Climate Change. Why does Kew exist? To exhibit and catalogue the flora and fauna of the world. In the past, when famed explorer and botanist Joseph Banks was around, it was to show the world to the general public. Now it serves to show what the world was like before we humans ignored the warning lights and continued to drive full speed towards global warming by consuming the products that we know damage our delicate environment.

Actually, is it so delicate? Really our world is pretty robust. It evolves to survive. Take the Redwoods Janet showed Anila and I on the tour. They have adapted to their fire-prone environment in California to become fire-retardant, their bark regrowing phoenix-like from the ashes. Other trees and plants perform similar acts to persist. Some die out of course, some get ravaged by introduced species or by the changing climate, but others find a way to live on. There is though, I'm sure, a limit. Humans are testing that limit like never before.

Even so, there's extraordinary resilience in the beauty. I suppose too that it is this beauty that ensures survival. Humans, as well as insects, are deeply attracted by the plethora of shades of colour of flowers and plants. We treasure and admire the most beautiful flowers and plants. The great example of this at Kew this particular weekend was the Colombian orchid exhibition. Sold out weeks in advance, queues stretched for over a hundred metres to the Princess of Wales conservatory, visitors in line to witness the displays, the patterns, the shades of bright colours. The queue was there all day long. Buses, the post office, and festival loos maybe, but orchids - I'd never seen people queue for flowers, not even on the morning of Valentine's day. Queues at Kew; it seemed rather appropriate. Bizarre as it was to see, it was rather warming inside to see such dedication to seeing a flower, even if it is just so you can attract Instagram likes. People must have waited over an hour to get inside. The dedication was commendable, but Anila and I found a perfectly easy way to avoid the hours shuffling forward at a rate of inches. We rounded the conservatory and peered in through the windows to see the orchid collection for ourselves. No queueing required when you are displaying something in a glasshouse with a paved walkway around it. Still, I'd have liked a closer look. Maybe there was something i was missing out on as a ticketless tourist. The smell being one of course.

We didn't miss out on Colombia though. Being the world's most biodiverse country by area and home of delicious produce, it was being celebrated with the food and coffee in the cafes and restaurants. Returning to where we started after our lengthy, leg-stretching lap of the park, we ventured into the rather posh 'The Botanical' restaurant and were led to a perfect table for two by the window with the sun blazing across the lake and through our window. It was time for more coffee, the stop giving us a chance to also discuss the finer points of what we had seen now that we were edging towards closing time. I had the important questions lined up.

'Are these flowers real or fake?', I asked Anila, feeling the leaves of the plant on our table.

''Real, I think'.

I nipped my thumbnail into one. Sure enough, the sap informed me that it was real.

'What about those behind you?'

I pointed to the glass case featuring a variety of 30cm tall flowers.

'Fake, I'm afraid.'

'Funny, isn't it? A botanical gardens with fake plants in their restaurants.'

'It's just there for show. Like so much of today's world.'

I thought back to the Madagascar periwinkle. The utility of plants for saving the lives of humans amongst their multiple other uses. Banks and others didn't just collect plants and set up botanical gardens for the beauty of plants, they wanted to exploit their uses. I also thought of Janet's eulogy on trees as we'd passed the redwoods.

'They're sentient beings, they're living just like you and I.'

Now, you could just dismiss Janet as an old hippy, influenced by fairy tales and fantasy books that feature talking trees, but I think she has a valid point. Trees are deeply spiritual, they have been for millenia, and they react to the world around them. They are often described as the lungs of the earth, but it takes a hell of a lot of trees to clear up the crap we pump into the atmosphere. Kew's 14,000 trees are capable of drawing out 6.8 tonnes of carbon dioxide. Seems pretty impressive until you calculate that 6.8 tonnes is equivalent to the emissions of slightly less than 2 cars per year. That could be two visitors to Kew. There are around 37 registered million cars in the UK. There are around 3 billion trees in the UK, 47 for each person, but this goes almost nowhere to replace the amount of CO2 each Briton is responsible for. What would Banks say to our climate change predicament? What would anyone who set up Kew Gardens say? Do something - that's what.

I suppose a positive I could draw from our day at Kew is that despite the planes (damn, I said I wouldn't mention them again!), there is a place in the world that holds the UK's and indeed the world's natural heritage. Kew ought to be a world UNESCO heritage site, not just a UK one. It might be located in London, but it could be located in any temperate country really.

Well, actually, could it? The thing is that, despite living in a densely populated country, Britons have an extraordinary curiosity and love for the great outdoors. Britons are generally passionate gardeners. The popularity of having a garden and of gardening TV and radio shows proves that. Britons travelling off to far parts of the earth to discover and collect nature again shows that the people of this tiny island have a real passion for the natural world. It makes sense that the largest botanical garden is in the UK because Brits are so green-fingered. We are really fascinated by it.

Coming up on the train I'd been listening to a BBC podcast in which the presenter visited a laboratory at Kew. The scientist, of whom there are over 350 working at Kew, showed the presenter a draw measuring one cubed metre that holds 55,000 different plants' DNA. A seedbank. Within that cubed metre in the lab is more diversity than the Amazon rainforest. Humans, I could conclude from my day at Kew, know the importance of nature, both its aesthetic and its medicinal qualities, but we aren't so aware of how our lifestyles are affecting the earth's nature. A fifth of plant species are in danger of becoming extinct, and while we may shed a tear for polar bears and rhinos dwindling in number, I would hazard a guess that virtually no one has felt a pang in their stomach for the loss of our plant species. But we should. Kew is there to provide that pang with a sharp gardening fork to the gut. The Royal Botanical Gardens at Kew are perhaps the UK's most valuable UNESCO World Heritage site.

UK UNESCO World Heritage Site #14 of 28

Derwent Valley Mills (2001)

From tiny streams, great rivers flow.

I'd done it. After one last lesson, one last student's question, one last farewell to colleagues, I was free. It's a strange feeling your last day at work. You realise that everything you do is the last of a long, long series of actions that you have repeated day in, day out for months and years. In actual fact, the eighteen months I'd spent at the academy was the longest I'd ever worked anywhere. That in itself was an achievement. After finishing a job a period of travel typically follows and it was so this time too. After a final beer in the local shared with a couple of colleagues, it was time for an early night before an 05.20 National Express bus up to the Midlands.

Once we'd made our way north out of London I was lost in new territory. I have to admit that I have the typical Southerner disposition that anywhere north of Watford is The North. I kept an eye on Google Maps as we passed through Hertfordshire into Bedfordshire and through various other Shires towards Derbyshire, passing by towns that I'd heard of in the football results but never really thought of as existing. For Southerners like myself, the Midlands and the North of England form a scattered map of cities of towns. Quiz someone from the South where one city is in relation to another and they will typically have no idea. Is Birmingham north of Leicester? How far is Nottingham from Sheffield? And where the hell is Warwick?

I had so much information to take in to dispel my pig ignorance. Where I was heading is considered to be very much the heart of England, and the thin line of water that connects Matlock with Derby (known as the Derwent Valley) was so vital in the Industrial Revolution that had it not existed it is doubtful that there would have been much of an industrial murmur, let alone a revolution. Added to the UNESCO World Heritage List in 2001, the Derwent Valley is home to the world's first factory system. Now, on initial reading, I have to admit that the idea of exploring cotton mills and old factories wasn't much to set my heart racing, but my interest was piqued by how the man central to Derwent's history, Richard Arkwright, went from obscurity and relative poverty to become the richest man in the country. There had to be a story in that, surely.

I got a taste of the monumental contribution that this central corridor of England has made to the country and to the world at the very appropriately named Pride Park stadium on the Saturday afternoon I arrived. The video played just before the players walked out into the Saturday sunshine stirred the emotions somewhat, not that the vociferous crowd needed much encouragement with their team a point off the play-offs. Poet Jamie Thrasivoulou's 'We are Derby' poem etched over dramatic music rhymed through the various reasons to be proud: *'WE. ARE. DERBY. Rail track city, birthplace of the Industrial Revolution, where inventors span cogs to engineer solutions… heritage built on cognizance'.*

It certainly worked. Derby played with pride and thumped Rotherham by six goals to one. The next day I took the first train of the day from the rail track city up the Derwent Valley and set about discovering the heritage built on cognizance. It was a beautiful day, the train skirting along pretty fields and criss-crossing the Derwent river like a needle and thread. The train guard was in high spirits too.

'Ticket sir, why thank you very much, have a wonderful day sir, lovely day for it, simply splendid, enjoy your Sunday, thank you very much'.

This he repeated for everyone on board, in between getting off at the quaint stations we made stops at to inspect the platforms and make sure the flower beds were in good condition. Smartly dressed with his guard's whistle round his neck, it was clear he took real pride and enjoyment in his job, even when he did get carried away chatting nineteen to the dozen to the old couple in front of me and completely forgetting to check their tickets.

I alighted at Matlock Bath and, with time to while away, meandered along the river footpath with the birds in the trees serenading me. You might have thought that the birthplace of an industrial revolution would be burnt, scarred and bereft of all natural beauty, but the Derwent Valley is as beautiful a place as it was revolutionary. The sides of the valley rise steeply, luxury houses perched precariously, and rocks hanging threateningly. I strapped my backpack on tight and started the climb up a rocky staircase arriving at the top to be welcomed by spectacular views down the valley on the one side and rolling green fields and rocky outcrops known as tors on the other. As it was so early that the cable cars that lift tourists from the foot of the valley to its head were motionless, rocking in the breeze. They looked familiar, and indeed they were, as my parents confirmed later that evening that we'd taken a family trip to Matlock when I was about 10. Again, the beauty of fading memories means that repeated experiences can be enjoyed as if they were original.

I descended and followed the river to the first of the mills for the day, Masson Mill. Built by Arkwright (expect to hear lots about him) in 1783, they are the best preserved examples of an Arkwright cotton spinning mill, nowadays dedicated to selling cotton products rather than producing them. The mills now house around 60 different outlets for some of the UK's most renowned clothing brands, creating a shopping village combined with a textile museum and restaurants that draws around 400,000 visitors a year. I'm rather shop-phobic so I wasn't too disappointed to arrive too early to be let in for Sunday browsing time, but I took in the former mill's aesthetic features and its pretty location on the rolling river. Round the river bend I diverted from the A6 road that wraps itself along the river and ventured down Church Walk, a wooded path that affords splendid views of Arkwright's most obvious display of his self-generated wealth. Fabulously rich with the success of his entrepreneurial ideas and his ownership of dozens of mills that stretched up to Aberdeen, it seems logical the Arkwright would splash out on a residence fit for a king. Willersley Castle, turrets and Venetian windows to boot, basks in morning sunshine with a rolling lawn leading to the Derwent river below. Sadly, due to delays caused by a fire during construction, Arkwright never lived to see the castle he deserved finished and it became a hotel after housing evacuees during the Second World War. Arkwright's house was the impressive, though far more modest, residence that sits on a hill overlooking his first mills at Cromford and he is buried under the floor of the village church he built, St Mary's.

Cromford, a village of around 1400 people, owes its existence to Arkwright as he started up his first mill near the confluence of the Bonsall Brook and Cromford Sough and encouraged people from the local area to come and work in his mills and live in the purpose-built houses nearby.
It was a totally revolutionary idea. Phillip, my tour guide for the Cromford Mills, was able to explain Arkwright's genius with an introductory powerpoint presentation inside one of the mill buildings. Six of us sat in complete awe and admiration for the one man who changed everything about how textiles are produced.

To give a brief and rehashed summary of Arkwright's life and achievements it's easier to look at what the world was like before 1771 and after 1771. Before that year, we had the putting-out system which basically means highly-skilled workers producing low quality items slowly in their own cottages. This was the way cotton and wool products from socks to hats were produced back then. Arkwright's idea was simple yet staggeringly inspirational. He changed high-skilled, low quality production into low-skilled, high-quality production with the invention of the water frame and the factory system. Inspired by clockmaker John Kay's spinning machine, Arkwright patented the water frame in 1769 and chose Cromford as the site to provide the water power needed to make yarn stronger and harder than the yarn produced by the 'spinning jenny' which was the technology at the time that used human power rather than hydropower.

Arkwright had the idea, but he needed some human labour to make it work. Unlike the contemporary technology, it didn't require much skill to operate the water frame and therefore he could employ unskilled women and children and have them trained within days to use the machines. 90% of his workforce was women and children which meant that his labour costs were lower as he could get away with paying them less (no equal pay in those days!) In order to maximise production time, Arkwright decided to house his workers as close to the factory as possible. Building homes with a loom in the top room for the skilled men to work on meant that all family members could be employed. The mother and her kids would set off to work when the bell tolled at 6am and would work for 12 hours. They would be paid the modern equivalent of 10 pence a week, a paltry sum in our minds but good wages in those days, especially when consulting the alternatives of working in the mines or no employment at all. Conditions were slightly better too, but Arkwright instigated rules that we would see as somewhat draconian today. If you didn't enter the factory by the time the bell had finished ringing you wouldn't go to work that day and thus lost a day's pay. Even worse, you would have to work the next day for no pay. It seems harsh to us but maximum output was everything for Arkwright, it was the very essence of his revolutionary idea and what set him apart from the competition. He did, however, develop other revolutionary ideas in the form of worker's rights. One pence a day was deducted from salaries as sick pay and this helped to provide for healthcare for the workers, an idea that was pretty much unheard of back in the late 1700s. Overall, he had plenty of interest from people wanting to work for him and he led the way for the factory workstyle we have today. Even more impressively, he made it work and his ideas were copied all over the world.

He was, as Phillip put it, *'Richard Branson and Alan Sugar rolled into one, the ultimate entrepreneur'*. The second part of his genius was to license his intellectual rights so that he could earn from others who wanted to do the same, cutting deals that meant he could also take a proportion of licensee profits. It made him the richest man in the country - not bad for an unschooled Preston lad who had started with just £5 in his pocket.

Arkwright didn't live without controversy though. He lost his patents in 1785 after jealous Lancastrians dragged him through the courts where it was eventually decided that his specifications were not detailed enough (he had deliberately mixed up the details to protect his ideas). Despite losing his monopoly on a fast-growing industry, by that time Arkwright was as wealthy as could be and a year later his pains were lessened by the king granting him a knighthood.

Philip was questioned by one inquisitive man on the tour as to whether he believed Arkwright could be correctly attributed with the inventions associated with him. It's always a question asked of anyone's success - where from and how did they get the idea. It's especially pertinent when considering the story of Derby Silk Mill founder Thomas Lombe who was apparently assassinated by Italian competitors after being 'inspired' by the Italian silk throwing machines in Piedmont. Phillip assured us that Arkwright's reputation and legacy is deserved. He took something that already existed in people's homes and adapted it so that water did the hard work and factories enabled it to be done on an industrial scale. He also developed the factory system that still exists today and pioneered mechanisation that produces the things we enjoy today on a scale that makes them cheap enough to afford and plentiful enough to be had by everyone. For those things alone, the world holds a debt of gratitude to Arkwright and it means the Derwent Valley is rightly protected as a World Heritage site.

Not everyone was a fan of mechanisation back in the late 1700s though, and with the rise of AI and the loss of low-skilled labour jobs in today's world, we could see revolts that Arkwright had to deal with rise to the surface in the near future. In 1779 a large mill at Birkacre in Lancashire was burnt to the ground in anti-machinery riots. Workers who had jobs that were being replaced by machines could see their income and livelihoods threatened and fear turned to anger against Arkwright and his revolutionary, labour-saving ideas. Could we see anti-technology riots in the future? Look around you at the jobs that were once done by humans that are now performed by machines. The classic example is self-service checkouts. 10 supermarket checkouts being serviced by one assistant where ten people would have been working just a decade or so ago. That's nine people's jobs lost. Translate that story to a multitude of other low-skilled and medium-skilled jobs that have been replaced by automation and you see that thousands upon thousands of people will be out of a job. Fundamentally, humans need to work. However much we moan about the 9-5, it's vital to our existence. Without it, and with food and shelter provided for, we would have too much time for the temptations of life to creep up on us and wreck our worlds from the inside out. The more AI and automation take over, the more this situation will occur. Future-proofing is something

that young people consider nowadays when they're thinking of a career. Which job can I do that will not potentially be replaced by a robot in the future?
How future-proof is your job?

Another job that could be under threat is the role of a tour guide. I'd seen at other UK World Heritage sites how human guides had been replaced by audio guides. No matter how advanced technology gets, I'm absolutely sure that you wouldn't be able to make a robot guide as good as Phillip. It doesn't happen with every guide as sometimes they just aren't engaging, but Phillip was so captivating that I found myself at the end of the tour having remembered almost everything he'd said. My brain is often like a sieve with dates and information. It was no surprise that at the end of the tour, after being lavished with praise by the other members of the tour, he revealed that he used to be a teacher. So here's hoping for my own sake that the teacher's job isn't going to be replaced by robots any time soon!

The harnessing of other forms of power like water and electricity doesn't just affect human employment. Horses were once used in cotton mills and so too with pulling narrowboats along canals until they were replaced by other more efficient sources. My next stop, just across the way from the Cromford Mills was the Cromford Canal and a mile or so journey by narrowboat along it to Leawood Pumphouse. Birdswood, as the narrowboat is named by the volunteer organisation that maintain this stretch of the canal, is occasionally still pulled in the traditional way with a horse, but more often an electric motor is used as was the case today.

I purchased a ticket from the ticket office who were pleasantly amused that an unaccompanied young man was interested in taking a form of transport slower than walking pace for the sheer pleasure of it and no girlfriend to woo. I was joined by a couple of families with grandparents and a fair few couples with newborn babies strapped to the mothers' fronts. It was fortunate though really as while the other patrons were concerned with keeping their young'uns from toppling over the side into the canal I was able to glean plenty of information about the canal from the very friendly volunteer guides. I settled into a seat at the front and was given a photo album, a copy of a text about women working on the canal, and a warming cup of tea to keep me occupied while we made preparations for the voyage down the canal. This was accompanied by a safety announcement read by the iconic British actor Brian Blessed, though rather thankfully he abstained from demonstrating his famous vocal chords and simply informed us in the most dulcet of British accents to safely enjoy the nature along the journey. Once off, our guide Val kept me informed about what we were passing while dog walkers overtook us on the footpath with surprising ease. I had never considered that there was a form of transport slower than walking, but canal boats are it. We pootled along at 2mph and in all its slowness it was glorious, enabling us to perfectly appreciate the delicate nature along the shallow, silted canalway.

While I watched the water glide by, I thought back to my childhood and to summer Sundays when my family and I would take part in that age-old tradition of a Sunday family walk and go along the River Wey. Once or twice we went on a narrowboat called Iona which is drawn by either Buddy or Alizee and travels along the Godalming part of the waterway through a few locks. It's remarkably similar to Birdswood, both 'buttys' that once transported goods to and from industrial centres and both operated by riverboat families. The Godalming waterway is significantly wider than the canal in Cromford but the same sights could be seen: ducks carelessly paddling along, trees and reeds infringing on the water, the sunlight shimmering through the trees as we passed seamlessly along.

Like many of the canals that make up a 3000 mile inland water network around Britain, the legions of volunteers have a real task on their hands to keep the canal operational. Cutting back nature, keeping the canal topped up with water and maintaining the narrowboat are just a few of the many tasks that need to be done by volunteers in order to preserve this slice of Britain's heritage. It recalled to me a two-day cycle trip I'd taken along the Canal du Midi between Bordeaux and Toulouse a few years back. It's also UNESCO World Heritage protected but large parts of the canal were overgrown, dry and probably beyond repair unless many millions could be spent on it. It was how much of the Cromford Canal would have been between 1944 when it was abandoned and the 1970s when the Cromford Canal Society was formed.

Although railways killed the canal star in the mid-1850s, rendering them obsolete, a five mile stretch has been resurrected on the Cromford Canal and the Birdswood covers about a mile and a quarter of this before turning around at Leawood Pumphouse. When we arrived at the Pumphouse, in the process of being renovated at the moment, we all got off and went for a little leg-stretcher across the Wigwell Aqueduct to the other side where we reboarded the boat. The aqueduct was designed by William Jessop who also had a hand in the World Heritage listed Pontcysyllte Aqueduct in Wales, but he had to cover his embarrassment of serious cracks appearing shortly after completion by paying for the distinctive iron cramps out of his own pocket. Still, the bridge is a marvel and looks perfectly strong today over two hundred years after its completion.

Back on the boat and speeding (read barely meandering) back to Cromford Wharf, we were given the chance to explore the cabin at the rear of the boat that the riverboat family would have lived in.

'Is that a bed?' I exclaimed as Jackie, our other tour guide, unfolded a cupboard and laid it flat, creating a flat space around 4 foot long.
'Yep, and a mum, dad and around half a dozen kids would have all slept in here'.

The four of us on this mini-tour of the living quarters were taken aback. It would have been extremely cramped. We could barely fit in ourselves and there was a kitchen and storage space needed as well. The kids wouldn't have been schooled, even after the passing of the Education Act, but they would have been kept out of the mines and the factories so in many ways, despite having to practically sleep on mum or dad every night, they were the lucky ones. They were kept out of the factories and had all the fresh air and sunshine that most of the other children at that time could only dream of. Of course they had to work hard on various tasks assigned by their parents, but I can imagine they had at times an idyllic life, in stark contrast to the kids that would have been hounded by Arkwright's factory bells and would have risked having a finger or an arm sliced off by machinery. It's fair to say that kids these days have it fairly easy nowadays, especially those who get ice creams covered in chocolate sauce at 11 in the morning. I thought about that as I remembered the kids I'd seen licking their 99 flakes earlier by the canal. My parents would never have allowed morning ice creams. No way!

Having totally forgotten about lunch due how interesting everything was to explore, I was growing a large appetite, but I had one more place to explore before heading back to Derby. I managed to catch the once every two hours train from Cromford to Belper and got off to explore the last mills of the day.

Jedidiah Strutt had helped Arkwright with Cromford Mill and was keen to get his own slice of the pie. He founded a site in Belper, eight miles down the Derwent from Cromford, and from there he employed local people and started producing cotton. Belper exploded and grew to a town with 10,000 people and eight mills owned by Strutt. The most famous of these is Belper North Mill which towers above the town and provides an intimidating welcome with its six floors of red bricks looming as you approach. It's not the original sadly as Strutt's mill was destroyed by fire seventeen years after it was built. However, its replacement that we see today was quickly rebuilt by his son, William Strutt, and is one of the oldest-surviving examples of an iron-framed 'fire-proof' building in the world. It's neck-aching to walk around as you gaze up at a building whose technology inspired iron-framed buildings around the world and thus enabled the age of the skyscraper that we live in today.

Again, the Derwent Valley shows that it has had far-reaching influence on today's world. Surprising perhaps for such a quaint and unassuming part of the country, a landscape with gentle rolling hills at the foot of the Peak District and a snaking river running through it. It was this landscape though that enabled people like Arkwright and Strutt to put their ideas into reality and shape the world we live in today. It wouldn't have been possible without the river. Whether it's for mills or for canal boats, the use of the Derwent Valley waterways has come to be pivotal in technological progress. Whether it is this technology that comes eventually to usurp human labour and make us all consumers rather than producers will come to be seen in the future (or perhaps we are already in this state), but for now we can appreciate the confluence of nature's power and humanity's ingenuity. It's a trickling stream that has over the centuries flowed into a vast mega-river, engulfing everything we are today. And its course? That awaits to be seen.

UK UNESCO World Heritage Site #15 of 28

Saltaire (2001)

A role to play in Saltaire

I was gazing out of the window as the train glided along past the Leeds and Liverpool Canal when I saw looming in the near distance a monolithic but eloquent building emerge. It rather reminded me of the factory in Charlie and the Chocolate Factory with its giant chimney and its domination of the landscape, but this factory has windows while Dahl's famously didn't and it didn't require a golden ticket to enter.

Salt's Mill may not have required a golden ticket, but it seemed that the costumed guided tour of the model village did. I'd followed the website's advice and

phoned while on the train that morning, but I was told, in the most sympathetic tone, that, due to oversubscription, adding one more onto a group of 49 would not be possible. I thought about pleading with the lady on the other end of the line, but, as British as ever, I said I understood perfectly well and wished them a good day. After hanging up I felt a tinge of disappointment and then the singe of frustration that I hadn't mentioned that I was writing a book.
'*Why didn't I play the book card?*', I interrogated myself. It's something that I was not at all keen on doing, I'd rather nobody knows that I'm writing a book so I don't get preferential treatment or annoying questions, but at that moment playing the 'book card' would have been very useful. Now I was faced with five hours in a small village with not much to structure my time around. I searched for alternatives but there were no other tours running in Saltaire that day. It would have to be an achingly slow walk around the art galleries to fill my time. That, or just standing in the middle of the village waiting for something to happen to me. The issue with writing about these sites, or any destination really, is that you need a story, you need something extraordinary to happen. I wasn't sure where I'd get that in Saltaire.

As it was, I got off the train at Saltaire's small rail station in rather a bad mood. My plans were in tatters, it was cold and grey even for April, and I had next to no idea what Saltaire is, who Titus Salt was, and what on earth this humongous great mill and crushed rows of houses were all doing here in the Yorkshire countryside. It was time for a coffee.

If I have to start somewhere, I may as well start at the mill I thought so I made my way across the roadbridge and entered the vast complex via an inconspicuous entrance round the side. Coffee, coffee, coffee, I was thinking as I scanned the list of creative enterprises all housed nowadays in the former mill and spotted an

item named 'Salt's Diner'. Perfect I thought, as long as they don't put salt in my cappuccino. Walking up the stairs I saw on the first floor an information desk and so thought I'd enquire as to whether they had any tips or literature that could help me. The lady at the desk was very helpful, but she too could only recommend the costumed walking tour and was surprised to hear that it was oversubscribed.
'They must have a coach party, I'm afraid'.

Just my luck I thought, the one day I visit Saltaire is the one day that the tour is booked up. I thought back to other tours I'd been on at other World Heritage sites. Kew Gardens - Anila and I had been the only ones! How good must this tour be if they've got 49 people to wander around a tiny village near Bradford on a chilly, overcast day in early April?

The lady at the information desk could only hand me a leaflet with brief descriptions of a self-guided walking tour. She recommended that I start at the Saltaire History Exhibition on the second floor, conveniently also the floor where the cafe is located. I thanked her and then spotted the lift by the desk about to head upwards. A young lady had just wheeled a trolley piled with boxes of leaflets into it, but there was just enough space for the trolley and the both of us. I slid in sideways.

Having overheard my conversation she asked *'The history exhibition, right?'*
I responded *'Yes, please'.*
She pressed the second floor button for me and then the third floor button for herself. The doors shut and we started moving up. I felt that awkward, seemingly interminable silence that often descends upon two strangers in a confined space. Lifts really do test the nerves of humans. No one likes to be in a room with a stranger. Less so when that room is six foot by six foot. We both inspected the finer points of the confined space, catching each other's eyes in the

mirror opposite.
The lift stopped and the doors opened.
'The history exhibition is through the doors down there and round the corner'.
'Sorry, where?'
We both stepped out of the lift together and she pointed down the corridor.
'Just down there and to the left'.
'Thanks!'
'Have a nice day'. She smiled.
The sound of the lift doors closing caught my attention.
'Your...'
'Ohh..'
She ran back to the lift and tried to pull open the sliding doors but to no avail. The trolley laden with boxes of leaflets was on its way to the third floor without her. She pressed both buttons by the side of the lift again and again in desperation.
I stood there rooted to the spot, trying to think of ways that I could help even though there were none. The number rose from 2 to 3. Still, I stayed standing by the lift, half out of a feeling of duty seeing as it was my fault and she had been trying to help a lost tourist, and half out of curiosity to see whether the trolley would reappear.
The number fell from 3 to 2 and then the lift doors opened. The trolley was, of course, still there.
'Lucky the trolley didn't disappear!', I commented.
'Yeah!' She laughed. *'Thanks!'*
'No worries', I added, even though I had done nothing to deserve the thanks. This is the way though across the UK, you get thanked for hindering people's work, and you don't get thanked when you actually do something helpful. It's a bizarre country.

Anyway, putting my slight embarrassment to one side, I realised that I'd completely forgotten her helpful directions, but I could see that I was now in the midst of a large open space with chairs, tables and, ahh, an espresso bar. Perfect.

With a strong cappuccino in front of me, I sat back and considered my plans for the day. I kept coming back to just rocking up at the tour and forcing my way on to it. As they would be walking outside I could just stand around on the street corner and listen in. Or I could just go up the meeting place, put on my most charming Surrey accent, and hope that they'd buy my plea. I couldn't take no for an answer. Surely, they'd have a small space for me. It couldn't be a problem really, could it?

Downing the coffee, I resolved to try again with the tour. This time I'd play the book card. A young writer coming to their village to learn about its history. How could they refuse me? I practised my gambit in my head and then avoided the lift to take the stairs back down to ground level and out into the village of Saltaire.

The tour was scheduled to meet at 11.45am at Saltaire United Reformed Church, just across the road from the mill. A few mini-buses were parked up at the entrance and people were streaming in. I walked down the long path to the grand entrance to the church and, feeling the weight of today's story on my shoulders, proceeded to enter. The church is as grand on the outside as it is on the inside with beautiful mahogany pews, bold sculptured roof panels, and two gargantuan chandeliers hanging from the ceiling. I wasn't concentrating on the decor though. I approached the lady organising people to take a seat and introduced myself.

'Hi there, I believe we spoke on the phone earlier, but I was wondering if there was any possibility of a last-minute space on the tour for today?'

I delivered it in the most flowing, intonated RP accent I

could muster. Believe me, it often works. Even in Yorkshire. It's not what you say, it's how you say it.

The tour organiser looked at me and then turned to her audience. *'Everyone, this young gentleman would very much like to join us for our tour today. Are you willing to have him along?'*

At that moment, 49 white-haired heads turned around and 98 wizened eyes stared at me. *'Why yes, of course. That would be lovely. Come and sit down, my dear'.*

Relieved, I paid my £5.50 to Maria, our chief tour guide, and took a pew. In return, Maria handed me a bookmark with the biography of a local man, Henry Dooley, on it and warned me with a mischievous grin: *'You might well regret this'.* How naive I was.

Once we were all settled, Maria introduced the three characters of the tour. To give the tour a sense of reality and a good dose of humour, there are three characters played by the three tour guides. We had Matron Sarah Turner who introduced all the horrible diseases lurking in the 'drinking' water of Bradford's slums in the mid-1800s as well as Mrs Pollie Toothill, wife of flighty Sylvester who lived in Victoria Hall, the grand exhibition hall in the centre of the village. These characters in turn brought their husbands up on to the stage, each played by the two elderly gentlemen who I supposed had been roped in to driving the mini-buses on the Richmond Yorkshire Ladies Luncheon Club day trip to Saltaire. They didn't seem that upset that they were being forced into swapping their modern wives for younger, albeit 19th century, models. That left Maria, or Mrs Ellin Dooley as I should say, to introduce herself and show off her other half. Mother to twelve children, *'common as muck'*, and married to, yep you guessed it, me.

So there I am, standing on the altar of Saltaire United Reformed Church arm in arm with my rather older wife and trying to keep smiling as she announces a special surprise for me: a thirteenth Dooley child is on its way. I'm not sure that this was what I was expecting when I arrived into Saltaire, but at least now I had a story. Indeed, I was, for an hour and a half, a part of the story of Saltaire.

Maria (sorry, my loving wife Ellin) led us out of the church and split us into three groups of 17 to be led around the village by a guide. Occasionally she broke character to tell us about the history of the village and that of its founder Titus Salt, but just as often she would retain her persona, dressed in petticoats that covered her frilly bloomers, interacting with local people walking around minding their own business on the streets. She told us how families were attracted to Saltaire from the poverty-stricken slums of Bradford and employed in the mill in a wide manner of low-skilled jobs that enabled cotton textiles to be produced en masse and sold throughout the world and the British Empire. Saltaire was the model for the factory system that utilised its workers to the utmost, but also provided for them with specifically-built housing, bathing houses, a church, shops, an entertainment hall, a dining hall and many other benefits that were innovative at the time. The houses had a water supply, gas lighting, outdoor privies, living and cooking spaces, and multiple bedrooms. They were the modern new-builds of their day and provided something that just could not be found in many other places at the time. Workers at Salt's mill were also cared for in almshouses when they became too elderly to work, a problem that Salt noticed soon enough as the mill workers in his mills lived into their seventies compared to the twenty years' life expectancy that those in central Bradford could hope for. In essence, Salt improved the lives of factory workers immeasurably. Inspired while serving as the mayor of Bradford in 1848, he witnessed the cholera epidemic that was killing off the citizens and chose to move his business away from the town and into a greenfield site. He was rich enough to be able to construct the largest factory in the world at that time and over 800 houses that would provide clean living conditions for his workers. Overall, it is estimated that he spent today's equivalent of £35 million on various measures to ensure a better life for his workers.

That's what the history books and travel guide books say anyway. Titus Salt is routinely portrayed as incredibly generous (evidenced by his lavish feasts for his workers), a tireless philanthropist (he donated to various causes throughout his life), and a moral, abstemious man (he didn't allow pubs in Saltaire and the most beautiful building in the village is the church). However, Maria revealed that she has found him, over the course of forty years of research, to not be as perfect as he is always portrayed. His generosity extending to his workers often translated into profit for him. Workers had to pay rent for their houses of course, and they were charged for meals in the dining room with meat costing more. Maria demonstrated his desire to eke every last penny out of his workers with the story of what he did with bread crumbs. She asked one of my fellow tourists what she typically does with breadcrumbs.

'Well, I feed them to the birds of course'.
'But madam, do you eat the birds?
'Well, no…
'Well, then it's a waste of money!'

Salt would have all the crumbs collected from the dining tables and then sell the crumbs as food for pigs that were then eaten. That was how money-driven he was. He even charged for hospital appointments. Everything was designed to keep him rich. Sure, he paid his workers, but because he owned literally everything in the village, he would always receive the money back.

Everything in Saltaire is also designed to remind you of whose money built it. I hadn't noticed it before, and I doubt I would have noticed the connections without Maria's guidance, but everything has the intertwined 'T' and 'S' on it. Gates, railings, buildings, even the church pews all have the 'S' for Salt snaking around the 'T' for Titus. Maria related the observations of a Polish tourist she'd been guiding a few years previously. The man was an architect and upon entering the church he had started shaking his head in incredulity. He pointed out that there were only two crosses in the whole of the church, while there were over twenty examples of insignia related to Salt, whether that be his intertwined TS, his self-made family coat of arms, or even a bust of his head. This is no church of God, the Polish tourist said, this is the Church of Titus Salt, and it was built for the followers of his religion who treated him like God. 120,000 people turned out for his funeral and he is now buried in a mausoleum to the left of the altar in his church, guarded by a six foot tall marble angel.

The man was utterly obsessed with himself. There's no clearer evidence for that than the name of the village: Saltaire - a compound of Salt and the River Aire than runs through the village. His name, his face, his legacy is everywhere in the village, and I suppose for his workers he was like a god, omnipotent, omnipresent and omniscient.
His omniesence was clear once Maria pointed out something else I wouldn't have noticed by myself. The design of Salt's village is like an army barracks. Rows of buildings with guard towers a level higher at both ends. This was deliberate of course. Salt wanted complete control and he wanted his workers to follow the line. He even constructed watchtowers at the top of the public buildings like the Victoria Hall and his

mill. Ignoring the beautiful brick facades, the colourful round-topped doors and the pretty flower beds of the houses, it looks Orwellian. It looks oppressive. Of course, workers were free to come and go as they pleased, and they did so, but there is something a little eerie about Saltaire and about the way Salt designed it, especially with the hierarchical system of housing that meant better workers were housed higher up the streets that are named after the most prominent people: kings, queens, and Titus Salt himself.

Maria informed me that Charles Dickens once compared Saltaire to a concentration camp. In some ways, he wasn't far wrong. The turrets, the rows of houses, the factory work. Then again, we are looking at Saltaire and factory conditions from a 21st century perspective. Would we really think of Salt as a cruel, egotistical, demi-god if we were working in his mills, earning a decent wage, living longer, avoiding diseases, and fathering thirteen kids with a whole separate room to stick them in? Perhaps not. There's two sides to every story of course, but on the whole Salt seemed to do a lot of good at a time when the British lower-classes were living in the most abhorrent conditions. I thought of him as a megalomaniac. A lady in the group questioned whether he was autistic. Maria declared him as much a philanthropist as Donald Trump. But still, whatever his means, he changed lives for the better.

It can often be this way with celebrated people. Those who are today lauded as the great humans of their times often have dark secrets that are not mentioned or are conveniently forgotten about. Salt has his dark side as much as many others. Think of Michael Jackson who has been repeatedly accused of paedophilia, Winston Churchill who is blamed for deliberately starving millions of Indians, Henry Ford who was a blatant anti-Semitic, and many, many others. Even those who we now talk about in revered tones have their guilty secrets, amongst them Mother Teresa, Mahatma Ghandi and Nelson Mandela. None of them, including Salt I suppose, ever claimed to be perfect, but we often forget about the other side of the story. John Lennon, Martin Luther King and Thomas Jefferson all had issues with extra-marital affairs and strained relationships with those who they were married to. Though there's no suggestion of infidelity, Titus Salt was married to Caroline Whitlam and had a large number of children over the course of their relationship, a number equal to, including stillbirths and miscarriages, more or less a baby every year of their marriage. She was more or less pregnant at every point during their 22 years of marriage. After Salt died, Caroline moved out of Yorkshire and bought a lavish house on Clapham Common in London, relishing the remaining fifteen years of life by spending her dead husband's money. It couldn't have been easy living with a man like Titus Salt for over twenty years.

Although Salt wanted to leave as much of a legacy in terms of children and insignia as he could, after his death his mill started to decline with the sudden death of his son and the introduction of the McKinley tariffs in the US which the Salts tried to counteract by building a factory in Vermont. Their attempts to save the company were in vain and eventually it was taken over by four local businessmen who modernised the mill and started to get it back running at maximum capacity. This they achieved through channelling Salt's philanthropic spirit until the First World War which brought further struggles to the company. From then on the company and the mill changed hands multiple times until 1986 when overseas markets became too competitive, fashions changed, and the machineless mill was put up for sale.

After Salt came Silver, entrepreneur Jonathan Silver

to be exact, and he breathed new life into the empty mill by transforming it into a venue for art, local businesses and leisure. Nowadays, just like at Masson Mill in the Derwent Valley, the former producer of textiles has become a vendor with the presence of clothing and furnishing retailers. Silver, who sadly died from cancer in 1997, knew that the former mill had to make money to survive. It had to be a commercial operation, or nothing. Such is the way for many heritage buildings nowadays as there's often not enough cause, let alone money, to maintain large buildings like Salt's mill just for the sake of heritage. Salt's mill has transformed itself with multiple businesses and offices, while still retaining its glory and integrity, and that is in itself commendable.

The mill was always designed to be a place of work and production, but Salt clearly didn't want it to be ugly. Inspired by his honeymoon to Italy with Caroline, he commissioned his mill to be built in the Italianate style. The similarities of the campanili and belvederi on Salt's mill to those of the Italianate Osborne House on the Isle of Wight are remarkable. The two were built at the same time and it's clear that Salt wanted not just a functional building, but a beautiful one at that; and he was prepared to pay extra for the design features. Maria told us of her recent trip to the duomo in Milan and remarked how she had been struck by the similarity of Simone de Orsenigo's work in the centre of Milan and Henry Lockwood and William Mawson's design for Salt's Mill. It takes a little imagination, but you can recognise the inspiration when looking at the towers and the entrances.

It's possible then that Salt would have very much approved of his mill's current principal use. Silver was a good friend of famed British artist David Hockney, and the mill is home to the largest permanent collection of Hockney's work, in particular the exhibition entitled 'The Arrival of Spring'. It seemed rather appropriate for this Spring day with the sunshine now beginning to peep out from the cover of Yorkshire clouds. The exhibition displays dozens of iPad drawn pictures that chronologise the coming of Spring in the country lanes and fields of Woldgate, East Yorkshire. A selection of the paintings done for each day between the 1st January and 31st May of 2011 is displayed, showing Hockney's remarkable skill with the iPad stylus and the Brushes app which enabled him to achieve an incredible range of shades and colours. It recalled the crude drawings I used to create on the Microsoft software Paint when I was bored at school, but these actually looked like the scenes they were meant to depict and not just random circles and spray paint trails. Drawing on an iPad may not be what we typically associate with fine art, but it works very well and gave Hockney many advantages like the lack of a need to wait for paint to dry and the ability to be shared and reproduced. As such, it's a stunningly novel art form - the perfect accompaniment to Salt's ideals of modern innovation being used for good. I'm sure Titus would have approved, though perhaps he would have had an issue with the free admission policy.

He would also probably have had an issue with a number of the modern businesses that have sprung up near his mill. In particular, the wonderfully named 'Don't Tell Titus' bar is one that clearly would have broken his no alcohol rule. Sipping down a pint of Saltaire Brewery Blonde while enjoying a delicious chicken roast dinner (with Yorkshire pudding, of course), it felt rather satisfying in a naughty way to be breaking one of Titus' rules. While enjoying the plate and pint, I pondered on everything I'd learned in such a short space of time. My five hours were almost up. The train back to Harrogate where I was basing myself was imminent. I thought back to my arrival that morning. I'd arrived knowing next to zero about Saltaire, and the few facts that I did know had all come from the guide book I had with me and a few Wikipedia pages. Now almost 5 hours later I had gleaned plenty of tales of Titus and been rather impressed and intrigued by Salt and his model village thanks to Maria's tour and the Mill's history exhibition. I felt I'd heard both sides of the Titus Salt story. Walking with her after the tour, Maria told me that she'd been ostracised by the Saltaire History Club on account of a dispute that is detailed in full on the history club's website. The website details supposed rules of Saltaire that have no obvious historical evidence and are sold to tourists as keepsakes and were produced by Maria. Without stepping too far into village politics, from my point of view there is space for both the historically accurate and the historically suggestive to coexist. As Salt was a fairly private man and left no written reason for creating Saltaire, and based on the fact that his workers were illiterate, there appears to be quite a large gap in the information that can either be left empty or can be filled by the imagination. I certainly enjoyed Maria's version, even as a live participant.

So, can you play fast and loose with the history of a UNESCO World Heritage site? Well, when you've got a captive audience of 49 pensioners and one slightly bemused young writer, I guess anything goes. Even roping in said young writer to be your husband. It certainly created a story and I returned to Harrogate with plenty to write about.

UK UNESCO World Heritage Site #16 of 28

Studley Royal Park including the Ruins of Fountains Abbey (1986)

The genius of folly

I don't know how they can call Harrogate bus station a bus station. Dingy, polluted, a total lack of any useful information; most bus stations around the country are not the most pleasant of places. Harrogate, I observed, is probably the first city I've ever been to where the bus station is a nicer place to wait for your mode of transport than the train station. By contrast, Harrogate's train station is bland and totally forgettable, but its bus station, with its black-painted Victorian structure, Roman numeral clocks, and plentiful benches that you can actually sit on is a rather agreeable place from which to start a day trip. I had a little time to spare until the 09.05 to Ripon so gazed around the spotless surroundings and witnessed the rather ingenious feat of spitting on your own shoe as you walk performed by a teenage girl in a pink tracksuit. The tracksuit had something shitty like 'Little Miss Perfect' inscribed down the leg, and I smiled as I watched her try to fling the phlegm off her white sports trainers.

Harrogate's buses, the number 36 I was taking in particular, are something to shout about too. I thought it rather helpful that waiting buses displayed the number of minutes until they were to depart, and stepping aboard my bus, I noticed not just the now standard free WiFi and USB plugs, but also a little book exchange library above the luggage rack. A round of applause for the bright soul that pushed that through the planning meetings at whichever company designed the buses. Alas, only a few tatty thrillers and a Jackie Collins romance were available, but still, the idea's a step forward.

I took a seat at the front of the top deck of the bus, the best seat in the house, and therefore disappointed everybody else who walked up the stairs after me. I could sense them looking my way begrudgingly and then resorting to the seat nearest mine behind me so they could spend the journey making horrendous slurping noises and breathing loudly. The lady behind me must have sucked almost half a dozen hard-boiled sweets, smacking her lips together with every suck, by the time we reached the cathedral city of Ripon. Here I had to change buses and, as an extra bonus, I was also treated to a change of century. The 'bus' to

Fountains Abbey was a cross between a single decker and a mini-bus. Twenty five seats, all of them faded and baggy, with years of dirt etched into the floors. It reminded me instantly of the schoolbus to primary school I used to take in the 1990s, Radio 2 blasting out with Terry Wogan's voice chatting over the songs while you were trying to listen to them. The driver, a kind old man wearing a bright yellow visibility jacket, waved away my contactless card with *'that won't work on here son'* and, unsurprised, I paid my £4.40 with a note and received two shillings and sixpence in change.

I was the only passenger. We set off down the country lanes and fifteen minutes outside of Ripon we pulled up at a smart visitor centre.

'Here you are, sir. Return buses are half eleven, twenty to three, and twenty to five. Enjoy your day'.

'Thank you', I replied and stepped off the rickety old bus. The visitor centre was just across the road but looking at my watch I realised it was ten minutes before opening time. To pass the time, I sat in the sun in the centre's courtyard and counted how many references to UNESCO World Heritage status I could see. Fountains Abbey and Studley Royal became a World Heritage site in 1986, meaning that it is a member of the first and oldest group of UK World Heritage sites, but no site I had been to so far had been so keen to point out the fact. The tag line 'A World Heritage Site' is emblazoned all over the place, from the sides of their minibuses to the jackets of their National Trust employees. Other sites might have a sign on a wall somewhere or even a display board to inform visitors that they are indeed in a place on the same par as the Pyramids at Giza and the Taj Mahal, but Studley Royal had gone all out. I was impressed. If you've got World Heritage status, then flaunt it. It's a pain to get and a hell of a task to keep, with no direct

reward at all. Show it off for all it's worth, I say.

The trouble, I suppose, with World Heritage status is that perhaps it can go to the heads of the trustees and hike up the prices. The woman at the ticket counter told me the price of an adult entry in the same way that you would tell a child about a death in the family.

'Ok, so I'm afraid I have to tell you that with gift aid so we can claim funding from the government the ticket price is seventeen pounds and sixty pence, BUT, this all goes towards maintaining and preserving the wonderful buildings and nature we enjoy here and we make sure every penny is spent in the best way'.

I sensed that she'd experienced the incredulous *'HOW MUCH?'* exclamation from many visitors before and was pre-empting my reaction. In fairness, while £17.60 is clearly steep for what is essentially a nice park and some ruins, I was happy enough to pay it. The thing is, though us tourists would love every museum and park to be free, the costs of upkeep are extraordinary. I think it's fair enough that people should be charged to visit heritage sites, including churches and cathedrals. If they just asked for donations, the public, myself included, would never give enough even to cover the most basic costs. The National Trust, of which Studley Royal and Fountains Abbey are a part, has a reputation for ridiculous entry prices and extortionately priced food and drink, but how else are they meant to keep up the conservation? If it's a question of pay over the odds for entry or not have the site at all, I know which one I'd choose.

In actual fact, once you've spent the whole day marvelling at the largest Cistercian ruins in Europe, having every sensation in your body moved by the beauty of Studley Royal, and enjoyed a free walking tour or two, £17.60 seems like pretty decent value for money. I aimed to get as much out of it as possible, and so presented myself at Porter's Lodge at 11am to begin the Abbey and Park free walking tour led by the exceedingly knowledgeable David. Now, considering that there are no information boards around the abbey ruins nor are there many around the park, you might have thought that the free walking tours would be full to bursting with the hundreds that visit every day, keen to learn something about the near 900 year history of Fountains Abbey and the story behind England's most prominent water garden. Well, apparently not. There were just three of us on the once daily tour. That number was doubled though by three young office interns who, I supposed, had been found at a loose end and so charged with making notes on the tour with a view to changing it in the future. I guess, with just three of us on the tour, perhaps the concept needs some rejuvenation. I can't imagine people pay £17.60 just to walk their dog around some nice parkland. Or do they? People are strange.

David kicked off with the background history of the abbey. From what I recall, it's the classic story of an argument breaking out over the best way to live, one party leaving the other, settling in a remote and wild site, and, despite adversity, triumphing. To give you more of the detail, it was dissident Benedictine monks from York who wanted to live an even more austere way of life and so decided to join the Cistercian Order, so named for the origin of the order which was in Cîteaux (in Latin, Cistercium) near Dijon, France. The monks were given land by the Archbishop of York, but it was so remote and open to the elements that they nearly migrated to France. It was the generous gift of farmland by the former Dean of York Minster that saved them and with it the monks were able to establish a farm that held around 20,000 sheep. The sale of wool gave them the funds to build the abbey and they were further helped by donations from wealthy locals who wanted to buy their passage to heaven. By 1224, the abbey was sending its own ships loaded with wool to Flanders and Italy and the monks were becoming rather wealthy. They had built their abbey from the sandstone and limestone found in cliffs down the valley, and it was complete with an infirmary, guest housing, and the 50 metre high tower, built by the last abbot, that still today creates an imposing welcome as you walk up the River Skell.

David showed us within the cloisters, reroofed in the 19th century, and then we walked through the nave to the crossing where the nine altars would have been positioned. The ruins are superb. Complemented by the addition of lush green lawns, they stand tall and still show the immense masonry work and architectural ambition that the monks and their labourers would have had. It's roofless now, allowing scores of blackbirds to sweep through cackling and plants to grow in the cracks, but it doesn't take much to imagine the sheer grandeur of this place totally dedicated to the silent worship of God. It would have been sheer inspiration to the monks who dedicated their entire lives to the order. Their last passage would have been through Death's Door, an archway to the left of the altar that their body would have been carried through before being buried under the grass behind the abbey.

'After you', David politely offered as we passed through Death's Door ourselves and outside of the abbey. We walked round until we were stood upon unmarked monk's graves under the manicured grass. The monks below our feet would have spent their entire lives reading and praying, eating only vegetable soup, and drinking a gallon of beer a day. How they managed to read anything with a gallon of beer in their brains I have no idea. The laybrothers, dressed in brown rather than white and with their hair still on their heads, would have been the farmhands and were allowed two gallons of beer a day, but still, they had to remain silent and pray whenever they heard the abbey's bells chime in the fields. To us in the modern world it seems like a pretty awful life (apart from the beer allowance), but to them I imagine it was probably preferable to other ways of life. They had a successful international business, other abbeys like theirs were cropping up all over the North of England, and they were at peace. That was until Henry VIII and the dissolution of the monasteries in 1539. Where would British history be if it weren't for good old Henry VIII? It always seems to come back to him. Fountains Abbey might even still have its glass windows and lead roof if it wasn't for his desire to divorce. Fountains Abbey was the richest in the country at the time of the dissolution and everything of worth was stripped away. Taking the roof and the windows made sure that it was uninhabitable and therefore the monks wouldn't return. The site was sold to merchant Sir Richard Gresham and from there it began its decline.

The following centuries saw the abbey and its grounds change hands from Gresham to Stephen Proctor (who repurposed stone from the abbey for his house, Fountains Hall) and then to the Messenger family who sold it to one William Aislabie, the person to whom we have to give thanks for the main part of this remarkable UNESCO World Heritage Site.

David led us from the abbey along the lawns that follow the river, rounding a bend indicated by two weeping willows under which swans and a few ducks floated in the meandering river. Small falls in the river keep it flowing under the aptly named Rustic Bridge and through into what can only be described as the perfect consummation of water, grass, trees, follies, and statues of Greek gods. It's simply immaculate. Like the rest of the site, not a blade of grass is out of place. Even on a fairly overcast day with the sun only occasionally peeping out from behind the mighty clouds, the desired effect of inducing the feelings of splendour, luxury, and privilege was working its magic. Not for the first nor the last time that day, I was flabbergasted. Aislabie, without the help of a landscape designer, created a vision of a wide, gentle river flowing past three ponds, the full moon pond in the centre with crescent moon ponds hugging its sides. Across the water, David pointed out the Temple of Piety, a six pillared shelter that would have hosted picnic parties back in the time that Aislabie was using Studley Royal to impress his many guests. It would have impressed each and every one of his guests, as it does every visitor nowadays, and that was its very purpose. With its perfectly shaped ponds, carefully cut trees, and Neptune with his pronged fork on an island in the middle of the water, it would have captured the imagination of Aislabie's guests. Had they had smartphones, I'm sure they would have been quick to upload a selfie of this most instagrammable of settings. Nowadays we have tourist places deliberately designed for the selfie, with a hashtag carefully placed so we know where to go if we want the photo for ourselves, but Studley Park is perhaps a precursor of this. A park deliberately designed with vistas that would give visitors the ultimate view. The wealthy enjoyed a fine landscape to look upon as much as all of us do now. The only change is that we mostly view it from a phone screen.

David ended the tour there and I decided to join the three interns on the free shuttle bus that carries visitors back up the Visitor Centre. On the way I quizzed Rosie, part of the World Heritage team at Studley, about the status of being a UNESCO site gives. She mentioned that few visitors know about the inscription when they come to Studley, hence why there are dedicated people on the team to inform visitors of this. UNESCO give nothing in terms of funding, and their requirements to keep the status are often strict, but still, the status is something to be prized. I suppose it validates the conservation efforts, gives gravitas to any funding applications, and looks pretty impressive on any tourist literature. Studley Park had certainly splashed it about, and hopefully their efforts continue to attract an increasing amount of visitors to this space.

Back up at the top of the site, I warmed up with a coffee and then an estate-grown venison pie. Studley Royal continues to have a deer park within which three types of deer can be seen so at least I could be assured it was local. Wrapping up tight to avoid the cold outside, I ventured out again and headed in the direction of the deer park towards St Mary's Church, one of the many jewels dotted around this 800 acre site. Designed by William Burges in the High Victorian style that he was so known for, it was funded by the unspent ransom for Lady Ripon's brother who was murdered by Greek bandits in 1870. They must have had a fair bit to spend because the church, especially the chancel, is opulent to say the least. It could be any old church from the outside ignoring its distinctive pinnacled spire, but once inside you see the astonishing colours and rich decoration of Burges' work. I donned a pair of slippers over my shoes to walk upon the mosaic floor and gazed up at the roof with its gold-painted images of Christendom and its angel covered, gold-leafed dome. I'm sure the monks over at the abbey wouldn't have liked its rich displays, but they might have been quietly impressed at this alternative display of dedication to a higher being.

There was still so much more to explore and so I let the slope down to the water gardens take me to the largest pond which finally allows the River Skell to resume its wild and random pursuit of progress down the valley. A bridge led me over the cascade and onto the other side of the river that I hadn't been on before. This was the side of the follies. A folly can have many definitions; it can be a small castle, temple, chapel or some other copy of a building, but its fundamental aim is to decorate a landscape and provide content for the conversations of guests as they explore the grounds of their eccentric host. Studley Park has a number of follies. First I walked up a steep fir tree lined path and through the wonderfully dark Serpentine Tunnel to the Octagon Tower, a lookout from which spectacular views can be obtained and cucumber sandwiches daintily nibbled at. Alas, there was no faithful butler ready to offer me sustenance at the top, but the views still exist. You can see everything from the ponds below and the journey of the river through its cascades to the spire of St Mary's church high to the right hand side. The glorious thing is that at this height you are now level with the tops of many of the trees. Visitors here would have obtained that feeling of superiority and control over nature, and would have been able to admire the exact work of Aislabie in creating this demonstration of art using natural surroundings. Not only would they be admiring the gardens, they would also be admiring the genius of John Aislabie. The man was a former Chancellor of the Exchequer who was given £20,000 worth of stock in exchange for promoting the South Sea company which promised but never delivered on exchanging government debt for bonds. Aislabie was disgraced, thrown out of the House of Commons, and was even imprisoned for a time in the Tower of London. Upon being released from the Tower (now a UNESCO World Heritage site itself, of course), he set about making his gardens (now UNESCO listed also) and, I suppose, tried to recover a little of the reputation and status that he had lost.

I wandered back down the same path and walked along the water until I reached the Temple of Piety. Now on this side of the water I could take in the same view the Aislabie and his guests would have enjoyed years ago. I stood shoulder to shoulder with the middle pillars on the edge of the steps to the temple and took in the very same view that Aislabie knew would impress himself and his visitors so much. As it happened, there was no one else around. No one walking along the river, no one taking photos by the bridge, no one walking along the path towards the temple and forcing me to move on if I wanted any peace. It was wonderful.

I stood on the edge of the steps and became John Aislabie. This land, this creation was mine. Here were nature, water and plants, but all bent to my design. I turned my neck as far as I could to my left shoulder and then moved it as slowly as I could to the right, my eyes feasting on the view, gorging themselves on the landscape. All this was mine. All of this beauty, and all of it was beautiful, belonged to me. In my head, I owned Studley Royal.

And then of course I spotted a couple walking towards the temple and the illusion shattered into a thousand tiny pieces. Reality woke me up and so I walked away from the Temple of Piety, having offered my reverence to God's nature, and climbed back up the path to the Octagon to continue my walk along the cliff top.

I wandered without passing a soul along the woodland path that the horse-drawn carriages carrying Aislabie and his guests would have clip-clopped along. It was chilly, the sun barely breaking through the barrier of trees and cloud, but still the path was lit by life. Grey squirrels scampered up trees, pheasants tiptoed around the fallen twigs and leaves, the only sound was that of birds practising their harmonies. It was pure escapism. Just as Aislabie had envisaged.

After a while I came to a curious green hut that faced out to a gap in the trees overlooking the river. It looked something like a shelter or even storage. I approached it, diverting from the path, and walked through the central doorway that opened my eyes to the most gorgeous view you are ever likely to see. It's called Surprise View, designed by Aislabie to be the ultimate vista that would leave his guests bereft of breath and, boy, does it do so. Momentarily, I too forgot to breathe.

Taking a seat on the right hand bench within the open sided hut, I took my notebook from the breast pocket of my jacket and attempted in vain to describe the scene. In simple terms, the view, framed by evergreen shrubs at the bottom and great leafy branches at the sides, presents a horseshoe bend of the tranquil river upon which a few pure white swans are gliding idly. Verdant lawns shape the river, wavily running parallel to the water, until they reach the hollow windows and roofless ruin of gothically grey Fountains Abbey. Behind the abbey, the hills of the Dales caress over one another. I'd never before felt like I was in a painting, but the scene was so still and perfect that it was like entering a work of art.

Then the scene came to life. A gap in the passing clouds caused bright sunlight to race along the lawn and bathe the abbey in a brief halo of light. Geese flew like Red Arrows in formation and blackbirds circled the abbey ruins. The two weeping willows by the river below were shivering in the breeze. Again, sunlight pierced the clouds and sprinted breathlessly up the lawn. In my mind, the violins from 'Arrival of the Birds' were swooping.
Behind me, behind the hut, I heard the approaching footsteps of people. The feet ran up to the doorway and then burst through. Two little boys with brown tufty hair, little backpacks on their backs, stopped suddenly at the edge of the lookout, spellbound.
'Now *this* is a view!', one declared out loud.

Their father hurried in and, seeing me sat on the bench, shushed them gently. Crouching low with his sons he whispered, just loud enough for me to hear, into their ears: *'life moves very fast these days so you should always take the opportunity to stop and think'*. The two boys stood as still as statues and for a few minutes the three of them just gazed out upon Aislabie's ultimate vista together.

Views are worth nothing if not shared. The wonderful thing about living in today's world is that these views that were once only reserved for the wealthy guests of the Aislabies are now open to everyone and anyone to enjoy. We have so much access to the world. Though we can only dream of being John Aislabie and standing at the Temple of Piety and gazing out at the fusion of nature and art we have created, we can still appreciate the very same views that only the privileged few could once afford. Thanks to organisations like UNESCO, the National Trust, and English Heritage - the three groups that Studley Park and Fountains Abbey are a part of - the heritage of England is being preserved and visitors can experience the awegasms that sites like these can produce. Like Rosie had told me earlier, Studley Royal is trying to do more to promote their World Heritage status. Whether that status attracts more visitors I'm not sure, but what it does do is confirm the outstanding universal value of the Studley Park and Fountains Abbey. As UNESCO so wonderfully put it in their first criterion for the site's listing, the site *'owes its originality and striking beauty to the fact that a humanised landscape was created around the largest medieval ruins in the United Kingdom. The use of these features, combined with the planning of the water garden itself, is a true masterpiece of human creative genius'*.
I couldn't agree more. And neither would the father and his sons, and every other one of Aislabie's modern guests who trek up to take in the 'Surprise View' today. It's genius.

UK UNESCO World Heritage Site #17 of 28

Durham Castle and Cathedral (1986)

Made for a miracle

I'd been to Durham only once before, five years ago while cycling from John O'Groats in Northern Scotland to Land's End at the other end of the country. I remembered its bending river, cobbled stone streets, sloping market place, and the towers of the cathedral stretching high into the air at the very top of the peninsular Durham was chosen for. As soon as I'd checked into my Airbnb and dumped my bags, I walked down a footpath to the River Wear and walked along until I found the spot where five years ago I had spent a night wild camping in a tent with my bike locked to a tree. The exact spot was hard to find. So much had changed in the five years since I'd been. The path was now tarmac instead of earth. It had once been closed off with a metal fence a little way along but now the path continued round the river bend. Cyclists and families and couples occupied the path; I was sure there had been no one here when I set up my tent, its lack of use was why I chose the spot. It would be impossible to wild camp there today.

Thinking back to that night, I realised it was the first time I had ever wild camped in such close proximity to a city centre. There's a thin line between wild camping and homelessness, but it's an important one. Of course, I had the option to sleep in a comfy bed in a hotel if I had really wanted. I camped only because I was carrying a tent with me, it was a balmy summer's evening, and Durham has ample amounts of woodland near its centre. But you still get a similar sensation to that of being homeless. It's wandering around with your bags trying to find somewhere quiet and hidden, it's using coffee shop bathrooms in the morning to brush your teeth and wash your groggy face, it's the fear of being caught in the act and feeling the shame of someone who owns a warm, cosy house looking down upon you. I wild camped a few more times on that journey down to Land's End, but couldn't escape that hollow feeling of anxiety when the light begins to fade and you start thinking of where you are going to sleep that night. Even today, when it gets dark while travelling, I have to assure myself that I have a safe place to stay. Homelessness is a really scary thing.

Homelessness is the blight that afflicts almost every

town and city in the UK today. It's always existed I suppose, but the last few years have seen numbers rise exponentially. It's now commonplace, whereas perhaps it wasn't so much before, to see men and women setting up cardboard beds and sleeping bags in shop doorways. I can't claim to have experienced anything like what they are going through, but the times when I have wild camped, like here in Durham, remind me how lucky I am to be able to afford a nice, cosy Airbnb or hotel. It was freezing cold as I walked back from the Half Moon pub around 10pm and I was so thankful I wasn't camping by the river on this trip.

In the morning, bright but still bitterly cold, I walked into the centre of Durham and started my day at the World Heritage site Visitor Centre. A few sites have these, typically the ones that take their UNESCO World Heritage status more seriously than others, and they typically have a few boards on what World Heritage status is, how it is achieved, and other sites on the list around the world. As it was so with Durham's welcome centre which had a few small rooms detailing world heritage (always the Taj Mahal comparison) and a video room with a film rolling between Durham as a living heritage site and a Lego-figure depiction of the history of Durham's founding and how the castle and cathedral came to be. Although it didn't capture everyone's attention (a mother dragging her son away with *'come on, you've seen enough'* after the first two minutes), I enjoyed the Lego figure moving in stop-start fashion in a cathedral built entirely from sand-coloured Lego bricks. The Lego cathedral used in the film is still viewable today and it is, purportedly, the largest ever Lego model built by the general public who donated a pound for each of the 300,000 bricks used. I'd be seeing it the next day so for the moment I was concentrating on Durham's city history and the beginnings of a castle that became the first college of Durham University, the third oldest in the country after Oxbridge.

The founding of Durham is a decent yarn to tell the kids. Once upon a time there was a pious man named Cuthbert who lived on Holy Island, in the far north of east England. He led a religious life as a monk, a hermit, and briefly as a bishop. Years after his death when monks opened his grave to move him to a more important part of the church at Lindisfarne on Holy Island, his body was found to be undecayed and his clothes still fresh. This was interpreted as a miracle and people came from all over to visit the shrine. That was until 793 when Vikings attacked Lindisfarne and the monks fled. The monks wandered with Cuthbert's shrine for many years, spending time in Chester-le-Street and Ripon, until one day, while wandering near present day Durham, the coffin of St Cuthbert wouldn't move despite the efforts of the monks. They realised this may be divine intervention and during a three day period of prayer, a monk by the name of Eadmer saw St Cuthbert in a vision instructing him to take the coffin to a site called Dun Holm. Not knowing where Dun Holm was, the monks came across a milkmaid who said she had lost her cow. *'Where did you lose it?'* the monks must have asked, and to their surprise she said *'well, in Dun Holm'*. The monks followed the milkmaid and came upon a hilly tongue of land wrapped by the waters of the Wear. It was the perfect protected place for monks who had been chased for years by Vikings and Danes. The monks erected a wooden shelter to cover the remains of St Cuthbert and that is where we find Durham Cathedral today.

In the next century it was the Normans who invaded England and they eventually arrived in the North of England. William the Conqueror achieved power through the Harrying of the North, an act that has been likened to genocide, and appointed William Walcher as Bishop of Durham and, in effect, the first of the Prince Bishops. Durham Castle was built as a residence for the Prince Bishops, hugely powerful clergy who were charged by the king to govern the border region with Scotland. In return for loyalty to the monarchy in the South, the Prince Bishops could levy taxes and so become incredibly wealthy. They were, in effect, second only to the king himself in terms of power. Durham Castle is a plaintive display of their riches with its huge windows and fine architecture that was added to over the centuries. Building started in 1072 and by the time it was finished, it was the quintessential early Norman motte and bailey castle. Various parts were added by later Prince Bishops, but now, in its modern role as a university college, it is mostly student accommodation for Durham University students. For that reason it is off-limits for the wandering members of the public like myself who tend to get sucked into pretty places. The only way to get in, without enrolling or being invited to a posh conference event, is to join a tour lasting an hour. I was handed a fancy lanyard by a lady behind the visitor centre desk and told to present myself at the library on Palace Green a little before 11.15. I sat myself down on a sun-blessed wall and waited until quarter past when a flood of other tourists led by a young lady in a 'tour guide' jacket emerged from the library entrance. Together, we passed through the front gate to the castle and grouped around her in the middle of the courtyard where a wooden bailey would once have stood and admired the 360 degree surroundings of Norman architecture while gazing up towards the students' bedroom windows. It's quite the student digs. I spent my first year in a box room in the peculiar 1960s ziggurats of the University of East Anglia and while we used to have quite a few members of the public peeping into our windows too, living in the historic and touristic surrounds of Durham Castle must require some getting used to.

Our guide Raffaella directed our gazes back to her and started with a potted history of the castle with dates and names. I was trying my hardest to listen but all throughout her opening talk the old man next to me was playing with the collection of coins in his pockets, jingling them about noisily without noticing the disturbance he was causing. *'If you've got too much money, I can always relieve you of some'*, I imagined curtly offering to him. Instead I stayed schtum and bore with the distraction. There was a fair number of us on the tour, around forty I headcounted, but fortunately Rafaella was unperturbed as she took us through into the Norman chapel, a dark stone room with interesting sculpture work on the pillars. Pointing them out with a pen torch and laser, Rafaella showed us lions, groups of men, and even a mermaid, though its form with quite the disfigured face was largely up to interpretation. Mermaids make a good, if not totally unexplainable, story though. The chapel was largely forgotten about in the 19th century and was only re-recognised as a historic chapel after it was used by the RAF as an observation post during WW2. Weekly services are still held in there, but mostly the Tunstall Chapel is used. We passed into the castle's more modern and larger chapel (built 1540), named after Cuthbert Tunstall who succeeded Cardinal Wolsey as Bishop of Durham during the reign of Henry VIII. Tunstall was of course a Catholic bishop at the time when the king was going against the Pope to create his own church in order to get a divorce. During the Reformation, Tunstall reluctantly broke with Rome and kept up appearances with Henry, intelligently siding with the powerful monarch while at the same time doing what he could to protect the monks during the Dissolution of the Monasteries. His portrait hangs centrally on the wall of the chapel named after him and, as Rafaella pointed out, he is painted with his fists clenched, presumably to hold and hide the rosary beads in his hands that would signify his allegiance to the Pope. He was a Catholic to the end, spending time in the Tower of London during the reign of Henry's heir Edward VI before Queen Mary restored him as Bishop of Durham.

Tunstall Chapel is used daily and Durham alumni can even get married there. On the way to their wedding, they'd probably pass through the Tunstall gallery, a corridor that connects the chapel to the Great Hall where feasts and celebrations are held. Again the signs of wealth are all apparent with large glass windows letting in plenty of light (an expensive commodity centuries ago), but there are also heritage riches to be seen in the form of the Norman arch. It's a superbly, though fortuitously, preserved elaborate arch that owes its present condition to being put inside and plastered over. With the plaster now removed, the layers of the shapes, patterns and rosettes can be seen.

The Prince Bishops were also ambitious architects and this is seen with the next stop on the tour: the flying staircase, though nowadays known as 'the black staircase' on account of its colour and as necessary supports were added later to the structure just to keep it up, let alone 'flying'. The 17th century staircase is still useable but it noticeably leans downwards from the wall as its oak steps are too heavy to support themselves. It was built more for beauty than for utility, with steps shallow enough to make it look as if a bishop with his long robes on were floating down the stairs. It is adorned with pineapples, though due to their plump nature they could be misinterpreted. Raffaella gave us a chance to guess what they were before informing us that pineapples were a prized fruit a few hundred years ago, fetching up to £5000 each. Due to their expense as well as their association with wealth, a pineapple was paraded in front of guests at dinner parties and then taken to the castle kitchens to be dished up. Only, they were so expensive and their taste so unknown to many guests that the pineapple would be saved for the next bishop's dinner party and spiced apple under the guise of pineapple would be eaten for dessert instead. Nowadays pineapple is probably a staple in the puddings eaten by Durham University students in the Great Hall. Those that live in the castle have their three meals served here, a far cry from my student dinners, and they even enjoy biweekly formal dinners with full gowns. It's a fine place to dine for anyone, let alone uni students.

With a few final questions, the tour ended. Rafaella took her round of applause, and the old man rattling the coins in his pocket walked straight outside past the bowl for tour tips. God, I wished a hole would grow in the depths of his pockets and those coins would run down his legs.

My intolerance of the little annoyances in life was growing so I clearly needed a sit down, something to eat, and a coffee and a quiet place to collect my thoughts. I decided a walk up the university would cure me and so crossed over the idyllic Prebends Bridge with its half moon arches made whole in the river's reflection and found my way to the university's Botanic Gardens. On my way I passed the Bill Bryson Library, named after one of my travel writing inspirations in recognition of his status as Chancellor. Bryson wrote favourably of Durham and so, he says, was given the position for that reason alone, but I doubt he's a fan of the bland, red-bricked library with its dark windows and lack of any redeeming features apart from the knowledge it contains within its walls. Sorry Durham, but I've seen car parks with more architectural flavour.

The day, though still with its creeping chill, was continuing to be bright and sunny so after a remedial cappuccino within the surrounds of Spring flowers, I walked further along the river and came to the university sports fields where two teams, I didn't know if they were both Durham or not, were engaged in a cricket match. I've only really just started beginning to appreciate cricket, only really getting into it while living in Australia where the sport is treated like a religion. I can now kind of see why twenty or so men would dedicate a whole day to standing around watching two guys bat and one guy bowl all the while hoping the ball doesn't get whacked in your direction. I joined the match with one team around 25 for one with 125 to beat and sat on a bench by the river, turning to watch the cricket at one moment and then switching to the river to watch the graceful progress of the rowers who glide along the water. It was perhaps the most bucolically British scene imaginable. All I needed was a glass of Pimm's and a top hat. When the game ended, the batting side easily catching up to the target with just one loss, I walked back up the hill to my Airbnb and settled in for an evening of writing.

Castle one day, cathedral next; that was the plan. It was fortunate really because the castle was closed for a wedding event the second day. Fine by me. There was far more to see in the cathedral. Really the World Heritage status should be named 'Durham Cathedral' and then in brackets (plus some posh house across the green) but there you are; in fairness, the two are interconnected historically. Standing proud in the centre of the tongue of Durham peninsula, Durham Cathedral has been a sight to behold for almost a thousand years. Its main selling points are the fact that it is one of the best examples of Romanesque Norman architecture anywhere, it holds the dead bodies of St Cuthbert and the Venerable Bede, and that it had Bill Bryson call it *'the best cathedral on planet Earth'*.

I'd visited briefly a few years before while passing through on my bike tour and so had fleeting memories of the awe-inspiring rib-vaults of the nave ceiling, but even prior-experience didn't stop me from lifting my head back and gorging my eyes on the view. Every cathedral makes you do this, but it never gets old, even with cathedrals you've visited before. I will never cease to be amazed by how the Normans constructed this vast complex of patterned pillars and intercrossing supports. I joined the 10.30am tour and Charles, our guide, started by sitting us down in the pews and pointing out the cutting-edge technology that the Normans were experimenting with when they set about constructing Durham Cathedral in 1093. They successfully constructed arguably the first ribbed vaults in the country and also used pointed transverse arches instead of the more typical round arches which led architecture into the Gothic period. Charles also showed us a small section of the nave wall which exhibits the red, blue and gold colours that it would have been painted with in the Middle Ages. The ceilings would also have been painted blue, but were whitewashed during Edward VI's reign and remain that way now with just the faintest patches of blue left to remind us of the colour that the cathedral was once bathed in. With the walls and pillars now the same sandy shade of stone, it is like looking at the cathedral in black and white where once there was colour.

The monarchy of the 1500s may have taken the colour out of Durham Cathedral, but fortunately Henry VIII spared it from his destruction and founded it as an Anglican Cathedral in 1541. He'd sent three commissioners to raid the Benedictine monastery as it was then, but his men were spooked by the perfectly preserved body of St Cuthbert when they opened his tomb to steal his riches. It's one of the miracles of Durham that it was left alone at such a time of destruction and pillaging of the monasteries in England. I'd seen already on my journey how the Dissolution of the Monasteries had destroyed St Augustine's Abbey in Canterbury and Fountains Abbey in Yorkshire, but Durham was spared the same fate by the very reason it was founded in the first place: St Cuthbert. Charles took us past the shrine dedicated to Durham's most famous saint, but later I walked up to its elevated platform behind the altar and looked in on the stone floor marked simply

'Cuthbertvs'. Pilgrims still come to Durham from all over the world to seek healing and spiritual guidance from this shrine; Charles regaled us with his memories of a visit from Eastern Orthodox Christians from the United States who had visited specially just to pray in front of the simple altar and the incredibly elaborate Gothic carving of the Neville Screen. It seems an incredibly strange thing to travel across continents just to be in the presence of the remains of a dead saint, but Cuthbert, presumably, is still very much the skin and bones he was laid to rest in should you believe the miracle of his incorruptibility. He's the reason Durham was started and why the cathedral is still here today. No wonder you can buy tea towels with his image on in the cathedral gift shop.

St Cuthbert may be incorrupt, but the builders behind Durham were determined to prove that they were fallible. Despite building what appears to be the perfect cathedral, they left one deliberate oversight to prove that they weren't perfect and therefore humble in front of God. The columns that support the great arches of the cathedral are sights in themselves with bold Norman patterns carved into them. Chevrons, diamonds, spaghetti lines; these patterns are one of the most distinctive features of Durham, however, close to Prior Castells' beautiful clock, the zig-zag lines of one column fail to continue in their pattern five lines up from the bottom. It's a detail I would barely have even noticed let alone considered, but Charles revealed that this is commonplace. Would the builders of this fine cathedral have made an error like this without deliberately meaning to? Surely not. It was all to show that whatever they created, they would never be as good a creator as God. This particularly struck me out of all the interesting things our smooth-speaking guide had told us. The builders and stonemasons were spending years of their lives building this huge church when really a much more modest building would have sufficed for the uses of the monastic community that were planning to live here with their old chum Cuthbert in a coffin. Why build such a huge structure? It could only be to push their God-given talents and the laws of architecture as far as their creative minds would take them. That in itself is what qualifies it for World Heritage status.

After the tour I wanted to take in the view from the heights of the towers so I enjoyed yet another tour that would guide me up the North West Tower. While Charles had been engaging and rivetingly informative, our guide for the tower was somewhat lacking in information. Quizzed on the height of the tower we would be climbing by a fellow tour member, he said it was 137 steps, but whatever that translated to in metres or feet he didn't know. In fairness, Google doesn't know either so I'll let him off that one. Fifteen of us were led up the steps to the top of the tower where we could take in two sides of a view and, well, not a great deal else apart from pigeon droppings. I descended for lunch in the Undercroft and then proceeded to the cathedral's newest piece de resistance, the much talked-about, much-advertised Open Treasure exhibition. £7.50 gained me entry to the monk's former dormitories inside which a selection of stones from monasteries were displayed and information was presented in an interactive format. I wandered politely through, impressed most by the beautiful wooden beams of the high dormitory ceiling, and then explored the Great Kitchen. Passing through sets of automatic doors that would trap you between them before releasing you like an air lock, I found the real treasures of the cathedral. St Cuthbert, despite the constant mention of him and his pride-of-place shrine, is a little difficult to get an idea of. That is until you see his gold and garnet pectoral cross displayed in the atmospheric surrounds of the dark and gloomy Great Kitchen. It's a remarkable item when you consider its direct link to the saint whose undecaying body has written the story of this cathedral and indeed this entire city. Even more intriguing are the remains of his 7th century wooden coffin which is pieced together jigsaw-style in front of a screen that tells you about the detail of the pictures carved into the wood. Crude images of saints, angels and Biblical figures though they are, the carvings really bring to life the reality of Cuthbert. This was the coffin the monks carried throughout the North East of England in search of a place to call home. It's a remarkable collection and well worth paying extra to see, though you get the feeling it's really just for the hardcore - there were none of the mums and kids who were everywhere around the cathedral.

I gave myself a few hour's break from the cathedral before reentering for Evensong. Five hours was just enough for a few tours, lunch and the Open Treasure exhibition. Outside it was warmer and still sunny. I sat by the river bank and basked in the sunlight. No wonder the monks had chosen this spot. The high banks of the river and its wooded nature ensure that there's really not much in the way of development encroaching on the river. A few bars and cafes overlook it, but on the river level there is very little, meaning that you can walk around the peninsula with just the trees and the river beside you. For a city, this is quite remarkable. Maybe it was the absence of the students who were on Easter holidays, but Durham seemed quiet and somewhat lacking in the hordes of tourists who flood other university cities in England like Oxford and Cambridge. Despite the plea of Bill Bryson to take his own car and go to Durham, it seems that not everyone has found it yet.

Indeed, entering the cathedral one last time for Evensong, I was encouraged by one of the deans to sit in the Quire to *'make up the numbers'* as he put it. In fairness, there were more than a few people around to listen to the mixed choir and reflect on some readings on a Friday afternoon. Like with Canterbury and Westminster, I had wanted to see the cathedral in action, to hear the Harrison organ being played and to listen to the echoes of the choir ring round the vast open space. Even if you're Christian or not, I think attending a service is a fundamental part of visiting a site like Durham Cathedral. Everyone is welcome and you get to see the cathedral being used for what it was built for. That's pretty rare for a UK UNESCO World Heritage site. You get mills and mines which are, of course, non-operational. You get buildings like Greenwich and the Tower of London which are pretty much just tourist attractions nowadays. Castles like in Gwynedd and here in Durham which have been repurposed. But the three churches on the list, Canterbury, Westminster and Durham, are all used daily for the exact same reason they were built. All you have to do to enjoy their use is sit in contemplative silence, standing occasionally and kneeling at some points, and gaze around at the intricate black carvings of the Quire, the Latin words inscribed on the fronts of the seats, the beautiful patterns of the organ pipes and the Norman columns, the gold leaf of the Bishop's throne, the sun piercing through the stained glass of the Rose Window and the eccentric hand-waving of the conductor as he leads the choir. It's quite a sight to behold.

After the service, we all passed out of the cathedral through the Galilee Chapel. The Venerable Bede, 'father of English history' due to his books, is buried here and there are stunning wall paintings depicting the martyrdom of Biblical characters on the walls. Most striking for me was the architecture's resemblance to Moorish mosques, like those in Cordoba, as Charles had compared them to. It harks back to the major influences that the Normans brought with them on their journey from Normandy to England. Without these influences, England would be so much poorer. Without them, Durham wouldn't have its cathedral or castle. Without the monks who adored

Cuthbert, Durham would also be bereft. I realised that without the various European influences over 2000 years, Britain wouldn't have half the heritage or culture it exhibits today.

UK UNESCO World Heritage site #18 of 28

Frontiers of the Roman Empire (1987, 2005, 2008)

On the hunt for Hadrian and Antonine

Hadrian's Wall

I was stuck on the south side of the River Tyne on a cold and terribly blowy Sunday morning. Starting from Hebburn, a suburb of Newcastle in the North East of England, I had planned to take the pedestrian tunnel under the Tyne to reach Wallsend on the other side, the start, and the end, of Hadrian's Wall. Only, when I rolled into an empty car park on my bike, I realised that the tunnel was not an option. Boarded up and protected by metal fences, it seemed pretty unusable. Later I learned that the Tyne Pedestrian and Cycle Tunnel had been this way for a number of years but was due to reopen in the summer. Typical, I was a few months too early; though given the weather, summer seemed like an age away. Fortunately there existed a shuttle bus service to take inconvenienced travellers across the water, and to ensure that they don't get the stupid idea of trying to walk or cycle through the car tunnel (it did cross my mind). Of course, I had just missed the 10am service and so waited 45 minutes for it to return back from the other side of the river. I spent the whole three quarters of an hour staring at the murky, industrialised Tyne and wondering why and how the Romans ever crossed it. Eventually the bus came round, dragging a bike trailer behind it. I hoisted my pannier-laden bike up into the air and tried to fit it into that awkward, upright position that public transport often demands when travelling with a bike. It fitted onto the trailer but inspection of the rear tyre that was supporting all the weight showed it sagging severely, the tyre pinched by the trailer and the back mudguard on the verge of snapping. It didn't look good.

'Need a hand, pal?'

The young driver of the shuttle bus reluctantly walked round to me.

'Yeah, it just doesn't look that safe. I'm just worried it will break the bike'.

'Aye, it does. We've had a fair few bikes broken on this'.

I looked at him with incredulity, not just for his honesty but also for the fact that he'd stated. There was no way I was risking my bike getting broken, and he looked like the type that would enjoy seeing me close to tears on the other side of the Tyne and thirty miles to travel to Hexham with a damaged bike. No. Way.

The cycle into the centre of Newcastle put my mind at ease that I'd made the right decision. It was a shame to miss out on the very start of Hadrian's Wall at Wallsend and the Roman fort turned tourist attraction of Segedunum, but I was now cycling through pretty city parkland on my way to finally crossing the Tyne over the ingenious curve of the Gateshead Millennium Bridge. I'd cycled past the Angel of the North the day before and here was another Northern icon to add to my collection. The pedestrian bridge curves out and then back in over the river, supported by an arch and supports that make it seem like you're crossing a harp. It fits perfectly with the other bridges in the centre of Newcastle; the mini Sydney Harbour bridge that is the Tyne Bridge, and the lighthouse topped Swing Bridge that now stands on the site of the Romans' first bridge across the Tyne.

The Romans first came to this area around 122 AD and within six years they had completed Emperor Hadrian's request to secure the frontier of the empire with a wall that stretched across England, at that time known as Britannia. There are a few common misconceptions regarding Hadrian's Wall, the main one being that it does not, and never has, delineated the border between England and Scotland. Indeed, Wallsend is a full 68 miles (109km) south of the border. It has been supposed that the Romans built the wall for a number of reasons; it wasn't just for defence against the Barbarians of Caledonia, present-day Scotland. Realistically speaking, an army could quite easily get over the wall in parts as it stretched for 72 miles (116km) and was only guarded by small garrisons in mile forts. Whether the Romans really faced much of a threat from the Barbarians is largely unknown so the other suggestions for the wall's construction seem more viable. It could have been built to assert control of immigration and trade, a way of taxing those who needed to cross between the lands. It could have also been built as a show of strength by Hadrian, a new emperor asserting his political power, and a sign to the locals of the might of Rome.

Now where have we heard this before? The parallels to President Trump's wall across the American-Mexican border seem uncanny. Indeed, great empires across the centuries have built walls as an exhibition of power as well as for their obvious defensive qualities. The Great Wall of China is the clearest example of this and, while Hadrian's Wall is significantly shorter, they are both World Heritage sites that defined great empires and have come to be recognised as symbols of their countries today, long after their respective emperors and empires disappeared.

Hadrian's Wall and the Great Wall were both inscribed at the same 1987 session of UNESCO, though Hadrian's Wall shares its status with the Limes Germanicus that run north to south for 353 miles (586km) through modern-day Germany and, since 2008, the Antonine Wall that was built by the emperor succeeding Hadrian and runs horizontally above the cities of Glasgow and Edinburgh in Scotland. I planned to cycle across both Roman walls in Britain, starting with Hadrian's before heading north to Scotland. That was if I could ever get out of Newcastle. Following Hadrian's Cycleway (occasionally signposted without the possessive apostrophe, much to my annoyance) I worked my way through street markets, business parks, busy junctions and car showrooms all while following the

River Tyne out of the city. Eventually I found the green countryside and noticed that the Tyne had become a wild and fast-flowing mistress. I stopped for a Full English breakfast (the best type of lunch) at a riverside cafe and then continued, languidly, on my way west. There's not a great deal to see Roman-wise on the way to Hexham where I had planned to stay the night, the next significant Roman fort being Corbridge just before Hexham, but the riverside riding was pleasant and, as usually happens in a country like the UK that is so packed with heritage and history, I stumbled upon a gem. Casually cycling along a simple trail I spotted a small, white cottage that turned out to be the birthplace of George Stephenson, the father of the railways who pioneered rail transportation that was key during the Industrial Revolution and has evolved into all but 32 countries in the world today having working rail transportation. Of course the railways carry us to work, but they also carry a huge amount of freight and are integral to our modern day society. This tiny cottage by a river and surrounded by fields was where the man responsible for railroad locomotives was born into a poor, illiterate family. Once again, Britain's heritage continues to amaze.

I finished the day at Corbridge, the remains of the Roman town of Coria which was the most northerly in the whole of the Roman Empire and is famous for the Corbridge Hoard which consists of armour, spears, a sword scabbard and even Roman papyrus. I was able to view a selection of the items in the museum before braving the cold and heading out to walk around the ruins of the Roman town with an audio-guide. As I paced around, shivering with the chill, I noticed a French family scrabbling in the stones by the stone foundations. Later I saw them again in the museum showing the staff some bits they had found. They seemed awfully proud of their achievement to have potentially found something Roman at a Roman fort along a Roman wall and the girl on the desk did everything to take them seriously by recording the find in a book and assuring them that they would be informed as to the result of investigations undertaken by the curator. However, once they had gone she dismissed it as nothing, just typical tourists playing archaeology. I kind of had to agree with her. What was there has now been found assumedly. It's fairly clear that Corbridge is one of many towns which the Romans set up, lived in and then departed once the empire started crumbling. You're not really going to find shocking new evidence by scrabbling around in the gravel path. I suppose people want to find more, to be explorers and discoverers, but there's precious little to discover regarding the Romans nowadays. Now we can just appreciate the sheer determination and ingenuity of the Romans for creating such successful settlements and fortifications so far from home. Despite having seen nothing of Hadrian's Wall that day, I was still impressed that the Romans bothered to make it this far north. All in the name of empire and expansion.

The next day, cycling thirty miles from Hexham to Corby, I was expecting to see the wall in full. Hadrian had his wall built on the peaks of hills so it was a fair climb up to the military road for a sunny Monday morning, but once up I was close to the wall and would be following it all day. Another assumption most people have of Hadrian's Wall is that it's still standing, but in fact most of the wall has disappeared due to time and subsequent populations repurposing the stone for their own uses. The best part to see the wall is the middle section which continues to give a sense of the grand ambition Hadrian had with the wall clearly visible as it snakes over the hills. A walking route follows it closely all the way, but Hadrian's cycleway barely gets within sight of it so I chose to leave my bike at a local information centre in the wonderfully named hamlet of Once Brewed and head out on foot to meet the wall. Giving my legs a break from turning the pedals, I launched into the six mile round trip to Housesteads, a dramatically set fort on the south side of the wall. It was hard going. The wall, just like its Chinese equivalent, soars up the steep hills and leaves you scrambling up the side of rocky mounts just to keep close to it. I climbed up one side and then was immediately sent down the next side, all while trying not to be blown away by the ferocious wind. Feeling the power of Mother Nature, I could also see the beauty of her too. The wall divides some truly dramatic landscape with lakes, collections of pine trees and peaks in the distance. Perhaps its most picturesque point is Sycamore Gap where a sycamore tree, a species the Romans introduced to Britain, stands perfectly between two sloping hills that are crossed by the relentless wall. A few families had chosen this spot for their picnics, out of the wind and with the view of a tree sandwiched in between slices of green hill to admire while they chomped on their sarnies.

I walked on through clumps of pine trees and grassy fields until I came to Housesteads. A walk around the site took me through the knee high remains of a complete Roman fort that once supported barracks, a hospital, granaries and towers. The Romans constructed these forts so effectively all over their empire but Housesteads is one, certainly amongst those in Britain, that remains fairly complete in terms of the stonework. It's certainly popular too, as the amount of people walking around it would testify. Coach loads of tour groups young and old swarmed around the site and made the stretches of the wall in the vicinity feel more like a procession rather than a walk. For some nowadays the route is part of pilgrimage. Walking back the route I had come, I passed a tall elderly man with a white beard carrying a wooden cross on his shoulders. I didn't dare stop his progress, but we exchanged smiles and I finished the walk wondering about the surprisingly large number of people who choose to hike Hadrian's Wall every year. It's a popular charity event throughout the year and one of the UK's most walked national trails. Earlier that day I'd had a chat with a walker while stopping off at the Temple of Mithras just down the road. We'd been chatting about our journeys when we saw two runners jogging gallantly westwards along the wall.

'I'd rather be cycling', I commented.

'Yes, but you miss a lot that way. Too fast'.

I'd never considered that cycling a route would be taking it too fast. Generally cycling is the best way to see the scenery. It's perfectly quiet, allows you to use pretty much any road of any condition, and is slow enough to look around or stop while fast enough to actually get you somewhere, but this walker disagreed.

'I suppose the slower you go the more you see', I offered.

'Yes, and you can feel the wall as you walk along it'.

Perhaps this is why the route is so popular. You are walking with 2000 years of history at your side. In many places, though it's discouraged by signs in some parts, you can actually get up and walk on the wall. People like that connection with history. They like to touch and feel historical items, whether it's coins, armour or even a wall. Of course, this creates headaches for conservation teams and those invested in preserving the historical item, but having just a sample of it to touch with your hands and feet is so appreciated by those who visit heritage sites. I even found myself stroking my hand along the wall as I walked, feeling the coarse stone that was laid by Roman soldiers nearly two millennia ago scrape my fingertips. It's not just enough to take pretty pictures;

we want to interact with history, and walking the National Trail or cycling Route 72 is the way to do it.

More Roman forts, turrets and milecastles awaited me so I collected my steed from the bike shed at the discovery centre and followed the undulating hills westwards again. Parts of the ride took me right next to the wall like at Birdoswald, but other times I felt disconnected from it.. Perhaps walking the wall would have been a better idea. Then again, in many parts the wall doesn't seem to exist, you are just walking where it would have been. After a night's rest in an Airbnb in Corby, a small village on the River Eden, I completed the Hadrian's Wall Cycleway by heading through Carlisle and to the coast at Bowness-on-Solway. There wasn't much else to do with Romans to see, but the stark beauty of the Solway Coast was a positive way to end a three day cycle ride that had started so frustratingly in Newcastle.

The Antonine Wall

While the general public are well acquainted with Hadrian's Wall, far fewer know about a second wall that the Romans built. Further north, a mostly turf fortification rather than stone, and with even less to see today, the Antonine Wall was added onto the inscription in 2008. Though its line is mostly covered by housing estates and roads nowadays, glimpses can be seen along the route that stretched 39 miles (63km) from Old Kilpatrick, just to the north of Glasgow, to Bo'ness which is a few miles up from Edinburgh. As the name suggests, it was the Emperor Antoninus, successor to Hadrian, who ordered its building to push north into Caledonian tribe territory, but it only lasted around twenty years, taking twelve of those years to complete, before the Romans withdrew back to Hadrian's Wall and eventually back to Rome. There were 16 forts along the Antonine Wall, but, as I was to discover, very little remains of its Roman history. Scanning across the map on the Wall's website, I noticed that the majority of the descriptions of the forts started with *'No visible remains on the ground today'*. It seemed fairly pointless therefore to religiously visit the whole wall, utilising the network of roads and railways to follow the invisible wall as closely as possible. Parts of the wall's route lie on private land and parts probably go through peoples' back gardens and front living rooms so attempting to trace the exact line would be impossible. I settled then on picking out a few of the more visible remains and taking a couple of cycling day trips out from Glasgow and then from Edinburgh to get an idea of Hadrian's younger, shyer brother.

The treasure hunt for the Antonine Wall started as conspicuously as I expected. I began in Bearsden, a satellite town of Glasgow, alighting from the train in the spitting rain and cycling through residential streets to Roman Park. Tailing a man walking his dog, I cycled along a tree-lined ridge in the park and then spotted an Antonine Wall sign. This was the 1850 year old wall, though you would never really know it or believe it. Today it's just a standard park for dogs to piss in and kids to chase a ball around. I felt a little silly. This is what I'd come all the way to Glasgow to see, a grassy mound. This is how I was spending my Early May Bank Holiday. Christ, I needed to get a life.

Thankfully the next stop was more obviously Roman related. Bearsden bathhouse is the best preserved along the wall, though I almost missed it cycling along the road. I caught a snatch of ankle high wall ruins surrounded by modern flats to my left and quickly pulled over. Though just the foundations remain, it's clear to see the various cold and hot rooms that the Romans enjoyed in their free time. A hundred infantry and cavalry men would have regularly bathed and socialised here. Though I suppose they weren't that concerned about privacy given the communal setup of the baths, nowadays they would have the residents of the blocks of flats on Roman Road gazing down on them while they sweated away in 40 degree saunas or did their business in the latrine. It's amazing that you can find UNESCO World Heritage sites in the most humdrum of places, even more so that you can buy a flat that looks down upon one. I wonder if the 'World Heritage view' adds a bit on to the asking price of 30 to 46 Roman Court, Bearsden. Walking into the baths site, you see the World Heritage sign proudly displayed by the gate, next to an information board that cheekily gives its rules about cleaning up after your dog in Latin as well as English. It's a small slice of Roman history in the midst of modernity, and proof that World Heritage can be anywhere, even in a random Scottish town just north of Glasgow.

Feeling more encouraged about actually seeing some Roman remains, I pedalled on to the next stop. So far I'd been to a park and a block of flats so I was hardly surprised when the next breadcrumb of Antonine Wall turned out to be in the middle of a cemetery. Amongst the headstones at New Kilpatrick cemetery, a chunk of the wall's stone base can be seen, clearly dug out and excavated with a sign informing visitors of its history. In many ways a cemetery seemed an appropriate place to find remnants of the Roman Empire and so I paid homage with a bunch of flowers and some quiet reflection of what was now buried in the ground. Actually, I took a walk over the stones, ticking the 'I've walked both Hadrian's and Antonine walls' box, and then quickly got back on the bike to get to somewhere that would shelter me from the increasingly heavy and cold rain.

After passing the town of Torrance, I escaped from the roads onto the Forth and Clyde Canal path and followed the calm waters to Kirkintilloch. It being a Monday, and a bank holiday too, the Auld Kirk town museum was closed, but I waited out the worst of the downpour in a comfy cafe. An hour later it was blue skies and sunshine as I ticked off the town's Peel Park (the faint shape of a ditch visible) and then continued cycling along the canal to Bar Hill where the highest fort on the Antonine Wall was constructed. Nowadays the fort and bathhouse are just outlines of various rooms, just like at Bearsden, but the spectacular view of the bare Kilsyth Hills is the same as it probably would have been in Roman times. This was truly the furthest north that the Romans came, the utmost border of one of the world's great empires. Caledonian tribe attacks on the Antonine Wall kept them from going any further, but really the Romans must have sensed that they were as far north as it was worth going. Still, their ability to initiate a series of forts and connected walls while keeping their routines of bathing in heated houses and eating fine food is remarkable. Having reached the halfway point, I cycled to Croy station and waited until the end of the week for the second half of the tale.

Friday quickly came around and now I was in Edinburgh. God I love Edinburgh. It's amazing how two major cities so close to each other can be so different. The sun was shining as my train pulled out of Edinburgh Waverley and skirted The Mound upon which Edinburgh Castle balances. I was heading to the nearby city of Falkirk from where I would cycle west along another section of the Forth and Clyde, ticking off three of the major Antonine Wall sites as I went.

First up was Seabegs Woods. I jumped off the canal path that I'd joined straight off the platform at Falkirk High and followed the B816 until I came across a line of trees planted along a mound of turf. Classic Antonine Wall clues. I was getting good at this little Roman treasure hunt. I locked the bike up to the wooden fence and walked up and down the little section of the ditch defences. Sadly the information board had been scratched unintelligible by the knife of some vandal (either they retrospectively despise the forced occupation of their native land by a brazen foreign force, or they have shit for brains) so I have precious little info about Seabegs in particular except for the fact that it now mainly serves as a place to walk your dog. Again, classic Antonine Wall. The sites of choice for the dog walkers of Scotland's central belt.

I rejoined the canal through a dank and dark tunnel that passed underneath the waterway and then pedalled onwards to meet the midpoint of the wall that I had turned around at on the Monday. Castlecary was a Roman fort along the wall and one of only two to have featured stone ramparts, but it was a right Roman pain in the arse to find. I could see the outline of a fort on Google Maps, but accessing it was another thing. Various rail lines, including one which actually bisects the fort, provided a considerable obstacle, as did the M80 which speeds alongside the west side of the fort. One possible entry point I'd identified was blocked by National Rail gates and I explored a woodland path that led me along rocks and under railway bridges. Along the way I encountered a lady wearing a Rangers FC cap walking seven or so dogs. She paused for me to pass, giving me the opportunity to ask her where exactly a few hundred or so Roman auxiliaries had built a fort around here about 1850 years ago. She was unsure, both about the directions and why on earth I was interested in seeing a field with a few stones in it, but she gave me as much useful information as she could while she held onto various leads with dogs pulling in every direction. Not a great deal closer to the truth, despite her help, I consulted Google Maps again and resolved to trying the left hand turn of a road I'd previously gone right at. It was a cul-de-sac but the Antonine Wall website had mentioned something about parking in a cul-de-sac and looking for a 'clump of trees'. I had to try it. Jeez, I thought, this Antonine Wall sure is taking me on a wild goose chase.

The cul-de-sac did indeed yield the UNESCO World Heritage site complete with an unvandalised information board, but all there was to see was a green field with a few sheep and a few stones lying under a tree. A locked cattle gate barred me from going into the site. A Scotrail train on its way to Edinburgh passed along the line on a ridge at the end of the field. That was all Castlecary had to offer. Its artefacts are now in the Hunterian Museum in Glasgow so there isn't much to see anyway except the faint outline of a fort in the grass. The railway and the road take precedent. Fair enough, I thought. Take the best bits indoors and keep the sites undeveloped for as long as you can. Fortunately World Heritage status now gives the wall sites the protection they deserve. With that said, onwards to the next.

Fortunately next on the list was Rough Castle. Though neither really that rough, nor a castle, Rough Castle is the smallest, though best preserved Roman fort on the whole wall. *'If you can only visit one location on the Antonine Wall, Rough Castle fort is clearly the best choice'* said the website, and they were more or less right, with Bar Hill running it close. There are barely any stones visible due to erosion and vandalism after its excavation in 1903, but the turf mounds show very clear ditches and the fort with its various buildings is clearly marked with signs. You have to use your imagination a bit, but the Romans clearly chose a good site for this fort and defended it appropriately. The most interesting feature is the lilias, a lily-like defence system that involves circular holes in the earth lying in wait for enemies to fall into. I couldn't help myself from jumping into the holes, nowadays filled with squelchy mud and dead leaves instead of the Roman sharpened stakes. The Romans had ingenious methods for defending their territory with ditches, pits, turf ramparts and wooden parapets all in use. If you did succeed in overcoming the natural obstacles, a ridiculously well-trained and well-armed Roman army would be waiting to teach you a lesson. In truth, most of the soldiers along the Antonine Wall were not Romans, rather they were auxiliaries hailing from a plethora of Roman occupied nations. Here at Rough Castle, Nervians from present day southern Belgium protected the northernmost frontier of the Roman Empire. The nerveless Nervians are nowadays well known as the characters of the Asterix cartoons and they were just one group of 200,000 foreign fighters that were trained the same as Roman legionaries and helped to protect Rome's interests. Soldiers as far away as modern day Syria came to Scotland to fight for Rome. The Roman weren't just great at conquest and construction, they were experts in HR too.

My final stop along the wall was as surprising a place to find the Antonine Wall as any. It seemed a theme of the two days of exploring the wall that it could be found in almost any modern day context. I'd been to residential streets, railway lines, cemeteries and public parks just to find traces of the wall, but my final location was to be the most spectacular. Callendar House is a French Renaissance chateau inspired mansion located in Falkirk's generous spread of city parkland and it has the Antonine Wall running right through it. It has a fascinating history itself, but I was more focused on seeing my last slice of Antonine Wall. Only once I'd had a cappuccino and a slab of carrot cake in the regally decorated cafe, of course. One caked and caffeined, I explored the small though informative Antonine Wall exhibition and watched a ten minute video consisting of a flyover of the wall. Even with a bird's eye view, it's hard to pick out the wall from the hedgerows and roads that modernity has dumped upon the land. Still, I was surprised to learn that the Antonine Wall was the biggest construction project in Scotland until the creation of the Forth and Clyde canal in the nineteenth century. Despite it's now depleted appearance, the Antonine Wall was the grandest man-made feature of Scotland's landscape for seventeen centuries. Though it was short-lived, it was a mighty structure with ditches and walls stretching sixty kilometres across a country, from Clyde to Forth. It required 9000 men and twelve years to build it. Of course, Hadrian's Wall is far more impressive and deservedly more famous, but the Antonine Wall is still an incredible achievement, even compared to Roman standards and all that they built. I walked out of the grand mansion in the spitting rain to walk upon the Antonine mounds, noticing their similarity to the various mounds of earth that still, 1850 years later, dot Scotland's central belt. Just like its predecessor, Antonine succeeded in building a defence from coast to coast, and it's still around today. That's something remarkable.

Having now travelled across both walls, I could find an appreciation for both. Hadrian's Wall has the fame and the tourists, but the Antonine Wall offers opportunities for discovery and surprise that so few famous sites boast nowadays. Despite the difficulty in finding some parts of it, the Antonine Wall gave me the feeling of being a discoverer. Quite a few of the sites I'd had all to myself, and what other World Heritage site can you say that about nowadays? With both walls, the overriding opinion that I'd formed was that the Romans deserve all the respect and the plaudits that they posthumously receive. The level of ambition and relentless desire to conquer kilometre after kilometre of unfriendly land was extreme, and only just about matched by the other empires that followed theirs many centuries later. Though mostly just pathways for hikers and dog-walkers to trek along nowadays, the two Roman walls across modern day Great Britain bear homage to quite simply the most organised and ambitious invaders of this island. What have the Romans ever done for us, Monty Python asked. Well, whatever they did to the natives of Britannia, they certainly left their mark.

UK UNESCO World Heritage site #19 of 28

The English Lake District (2017)

Where nature and culture collide

I don't know about you, but I love arriving somewhere I'm scheduled to be exactly on time. I'd say it's actually one of the few things I have a real knack for. Somehow, whether I mean to or not, I always seem to arrive exactly when I'm meant to. A slave to my watch maybe, but it's something that gives me some deal of satisfaction; almost an art form I suppose that I've cultivated over years of travelling, meeting and staying with people.

I'd received a message a few days before that my hosts in the middle of the Lake District were able to receive me after 5 o'clock. Perfect, I thought. My train was due to get into Windermere at 15.09 so I'd have time for a little potter around the Lake District's most touristy town and then cycle the ten miles or so along the lake and into the dales to High Park, Little Langdale. The ten miles would take me about an hour, allowing for hills and the occasional photo stop/breather.

There's always a little anxiety before a cycle into the unknown. I'd researched the route and, despite the promise of hills, was fairly confident that I'd make it all the way with my heavy panniers in tow. As lovely as Windermere is, I was pretty keen just to get on and get out of it. It had also just started to rain and so the promise of the indoors with a mug of tea was pulling me towards getting going. At exactly 4pm, I put my helmet on and rolled out of the station car park. Soon I realised that I needn't have worried much about hills, rather I should have been fretting about the traffic. Easter weekend had arrived early to the Lake District and the narrow roads were dominated by chunky 4x4s. Occasionally a cycle lane would pop up and I'd be granted some relief from grumbling motors, but it wasn't until I turned off the A593 and onto a road named Unnamed Road by Google that I was able to finally take in some of the natural tranquility that the Lake District is known for.

Though the irony of tourists flocking in their droves to escape the crowded cities exists today, the Lake District still manages to retain its quiet spots and, thanks to conservation, it still manages to provide much the same environment that drew its most famous historical inhabitants to live there and to write about it. Artists and writers have always been attracted to the Lake District, but Beatrix Potter and William Wordsworth are probably the two names mentioned most, and it was these two literary luminaries that I'd be focusing on as I spent the next ten days touring the Lakes.

As I cycled up Unnamed road, I passed a National Trust sign pointing me in the direction of High Park. This was the result of Beatrix Potter's doing. Upon her death in 1943, the author of 'Peter Rabbit' and many other children's classics donated the land and many Lake District farms that she had purchased through her book sales success to the National Trust. Potter became besotted with the idea of an organisation to protect and conserve cultural heritage while a child on holiday at Wray Castle where she met Hardwicke Rawnsley, a local clergyman and one of the founding fathers of the National Trust. Her stories were inspired by the Lake District and she wanted her legacy to be the continuation of the Lake District in its agricultural state. High Park, my accommodation for the next few nights, was one of those farms that Potter bought up and then gave to the Trust.

A rollercoaster ride on the slippery single lane road brought me to the whitewashed stone house with its small garden overlooking fields of munching sheep in the vast Langdale valley below. Dripping wet now, I was welcomed in by Tony, my Airbnb host, and warmed up with a pot of tea and a slab of fruitcake. The house was as homely as you can imagine. Wooden beams, creaky floorboards, books everywhere; I suppose it's much like Potter would have wanted her cottages to be kept: quintessential English country cottage style with the low doorways to catch your head on and the dark wood that instantly transports you back to more simple times. Tony grabbed a stack of maps for me and I spent a while perusing the vast area that was designated Britain's first National Park and one of its most recent UNESCO World Heritage sites. The protected area covers nearly 2400 square kilometres of land and holds England's longest lake, its deepest lake and its highest mountain.

Though named after its sixteen lakes, the Lake District is just as much about its hills and valleys, the local names for these revealing a unique dialect that I had to learn as I explored the map. 'Fells' are high hills, 'pike' is the summit of a hill, 'mere' is Old English for lake with 'tarn' denoting a small lake. Gazing at the mountain of maps and walking guides Tony had presented me with, I realised that in ten days I could do no more than leave the tiniest of scratches upon the surface of the Lake District. And that's just the nature. The Lake District is packed with culture too. Romans passed through, Neolithic sites have been found, mining was the major earner for centuries, farming dominates the landscape today, and then there are the inhabitants, the 40,000 or so lucky souls who call the Lake District home and the famous artists and writers who were born or led to live here. I could be here a long time, I warned Tony, but with tea and cake and the rain outside, I wasn't planning to go anywhere fast.

UNESCO has two types of World Heritage site listings: cultural and natural. UNESCO's criteria for the Lake District's inscription are all cultural. Before researching, I had assumed that the Lake District was a natural listing given its fame for its naturally formed lakes, however it's actually listed for the agro-pastoral land use, the grand houses and gardens, Picturesque and Romantic movement interpretations, and early human ideas about conserving nature. Therefore, the listing is about the human relationship with the land, not the land itself. Though we still see valleys and lakes moulded by the Ice Age, the Lake District has been changed dramatically by human activity. It is certainly not a purely natural environment, though I wonder if the 20 million tourists who visit it every year realise this. Many city dwellers seem to believe it's what nature looks like, at least this is why they visit the Lake District: to experience nature. What you see in the Lake District is not nature's behaviour, but humanity's exploitation and subsequent preservation of it. Really, the Lake District is a picture of idyll farming life, not of wild and untamed landscapes. You have to go to other parts of the world to see those.

My perhaps naive assumption that the Lake District was a natural, rather than a cultural, listing was blown apart the next day when I set out from High Park with a map, a backpack and a Full English breakfast in my stomach and took on the heights of the Central Fells. I hiked up from Wainwright's Inn until I reached a point high enough to take in the Langdale Valley behind me. It was a superlative view on a sparklingly bright morning, but I noticed, visually and aurally, that a quarry was in operation just above the village. Huge diggers were carrying tonnes of slate across a huge dusty plateau. I perfectly understand the need for slate and the myriad uses it has, and the necessary extraction methods, I just hadn't expected to find a huge quarry in the supposedly tranquil environment of the heart of the Lake District. I guess I was just surprised to see it there, in the land of Wordsworth and Potter who wax so lyrical about the quaint state of nature in this national park. There are around twelve stone quarries in the Lake District, a serious downsize from the 19th century of course, but still enough to surprise the common visitor who senses that they are entering some kind of natural theme park when they enter the green shaded areas of the map. It kind of feels like a theme park. The endless picturesque views of quaint houses wedged into dramatic hillsides, the opportunities for rowing on the lakes, the tourist buses that hog the lanes and spit out their passengers at various car parks so they can buy ice creams and t-shirts that say 'I love ewe'. They wouldn't expect quarries and intensive farming to be a feature of this most idyllic of English landscapes, and I guess I didn't either before I visited. I suppose we were in the same boat there.

Mining and quarrying aren't exactly new additions to the landscape, the stone business has been in operation in the Central Fells since the Stone Age, the stone axes Neolithic people made chopped down the virgin forest Britain was once cloaked in. Across the Lake District today there are the lifeless gaps of deforestation, though efforts have been made by the Forestry Commission to restore some woods and forests. I walked up to the top of the fells to get a glimpse of Grasmere on the other side. Walking off the trails I encountered dozens of brown Herdwick sheep, the species local to the Lake District and encouraged by Beatrix Potter who spent time as a shepherdess. A good 1000 feet up, the landscape reminded me of Daniel Defoe's 1724 quote which described it as *'the wildest, most barren and frightful of any that I have passed over in England'*. Well, not exactly wild perhaps as you still meet the occasional walker and can see villages down by the lakes, but barren yes because the sheep have gnawed through almost every square metre. In fact, it wasn't at all frightful either. The Lake District's touristic success is indebted to the fact that it is relatively accessible. The hills are low enough to be conquered by young and old alike. Wherever you go there are footpaths criss-crossing and fence stiles to be jumped over. The park has been intensively mapped as much as it has been mined. From up high you can see how human development has generally complemented the natural scenery. This was also mentioned in UNESCO's reasoning for inscription, that *'the combined work of nature and human activity has produced a harmonious landscape'*. It's quite true in my opinion. Whatever your views on conservation, rewilding, farming, and tourism are regarding the Lake District, it is almost universally agreed that the Lake District is the most beautiful corner of England. Despite the tasteless tat of tourism and the exploitation of natural resources, the Lake District, especially when viewed from the top of a rocky crag on a warm Spring day, remains objectively pretty.

Human activity isn't all destructive to the natural beauty of the Lake District. In fact it can create whole new areas of breathtaking wonder. Though the working Burlington Quarry had initially disgusted me, I was interested to learn more about the human activity in the Lake District that UNESCO has acclaimed. Descending from the hills I walked back towards High Park, but stopped off at a recommendation Tony had given me. Cathedral Quarry was formed in the 16th century but slate mining reached its peak in the 19th century when explosives were used to blast the slate free. That lady again, Beatrix Potter, bought the mine in 1929 and gave it to the National Trust who own it today, though their only influence is a sign at the entrance warning visitors to be careful and a few ropes around the deep pools. I was the only person around when I arrived, though, when I bent my head low and started walking through the dingy access tunnel towards the central chamber, I could hear the echo of sweet, melodious singing. Someone, maybe even two people, were inside, and judging by their sense of freedom to sing aloud outside of their bathroom shower, thought they were all alone.

And did those feet in ancient time,
Walk upon England's mountains green:
And was the holy Lamb of God,
On England's pleasant pastures seen!

Hating to intrude upon someone's moment, but

tempted forward by the ethereal light at the end of the tunnel, I waited within the tunnel for them to finish their singing. The high notes rang through the tunnel like angels singing.

*'Till we have built Jerusalem,
In England's green and pleasant land'*

I was spellbound, the hairs on my neck erect. I walked through nervously to discover the source of the singing and found two ladies in bikers jackets and trousers scrubbing the walls of an enormous 40 foot high cavern. I wasn't sure which to be most surprised by. First perhaps the setting. It was like being inside a giant black egg shell with jagged walls rising towards a large diamond shaped crack through which crepuscular rays were shining down like golden arrows into the reflecting pools below. Next, the ladies in leathers. They had stopped singing at the end of Jerusalem and had resumed their scrubbing of the walls. Walking closer I realised they were attempting to rub off crude painted graffiti with moss they had picked up from the rocks nature had reclaimed.

'Do you get a lot of graffiti in here?'
'Aye, unfortunately. I don't understand it myself, but we're just trying to get rid of the worst bits'.
'It's amazing in here.'
'Too right. The perfect cathedral for singing in. Where are you from?'

We exchanged the usual titbits of information. Ali and Gaynor were from Barrow-in-Furness, a town south of the Lake District, but they regularly rode their bikes up into the Lakes and had found Cathedral Quarry to be the perfect practice hall for their choir singing skills. Together, we took a look at the rest of the graffiti they hadn't been able to reach, the usual so and so loves X, thingy was here 2002 etc... and discussed why people feel the need to leave a reminder of themselves somewhere.

'*Couldn't you just get a visitor book?*', I asked, half-jokingly.
They laughed. '*I guess so, but people tend to want a visible memorial to their visit. God knows why*'.

I couldn't offer an explanation to this myself. I suppose it's as simple as just wanting their moment in a place remembered. I think I've only done it once myself. If you look under one of the sinks in the toilets by the science classrooms at my secondary school, you might spot my name and 2007. I'm not sure why I did it, it probably isn't there anymore. Perhaps I just wanted a lasting connection to a place I'd spent five years of my life at. Maybe it's the same, maybe it isn't, with these people who graffiti beautiful places like Cathedral Quarry.

Despite volunteering to erase it, Ali and Gaynor were quite sympathetic to them. We got talking as people in Cumbria are so inclined to do and then I let them take me on a little tour of the quarry. We walked out of the cave and turned left up a path that would take us up the hill to peer inside the hollowed out cavern from above. We discovered a second chamber though this one was open to the elements and found the outer side of the crack that was perfectly positioned to let the sunrays beam into the egg. Nature had certainly tried to regain the spot with moss in abundance and flowers springing from the rock face. Despite the obvious man-made destruction of a forested hill, it was a place of sheer beauty, an example of what happens when human activity is abandoned and nature is left to re-beautify it. Speaking to Tony later, he told me his grand-daughter was planning to have part of her wedding ceremony in the quarry later that year. What a spectacular place to get hitched. The acoustics were extraordinary, as Ali and Gaynor had demonstrated. After a few hours of slowly discovering the quarry and chatting about all things Lake District, I walked with them up the road and saw them off on their motorbikes down the valley. Then I had duck for dinner and a pint of local ale in The Three Shires, one of the many, many local Lakeland pubs, and walked back across the valley at sunset to the farmhouse. It was the end of a perfect Lake District day. One of those golden days filled with scenic country walking, hearty food, friendly company and a comfy bed to rest my sleepy head at the end of it. It's what the Lake District does so, so well. That night, I slept as peacefully as the lakes themselves.

After a few days I decided to see another side of the Lake District and so based myself for a week in the market town of Cockermouth, just outside the north west of the national park. It's famous as the birthplace of William Wordsworth and his sister Dorothy who helped him with so much of his poetry. Though Beatrix Potter revels in the agriculture of the Lakes, setting her stories within farms and the managed countryside of the lower fells, Wordsworth, writing a century before Potter, was very much inspired by nature in its purest state. Due to his words, he is intrinsically a part of the development of the Lake District as the UK's first national park (and indeed the worldwide idea of national parks) and was at the forefront of Romanticism in Britain that spawned some of the nation's favourite poetry and an appreciation for nature in the age of rapid industrialisation. His link to Beatrix Potter is through the National Trust. His quote in his guidebook to the Lakes that describes the area as *'a sort of national property'* inspired Hardwicke Rawnsley who co-founded the Trust and, in turn, inspired Beatrix Potter. Both writers' houses are now open to the tourist masses, Hilltop being the most famous of Potter's homes, and Dove Cottage being the most visited home of Wordsworth. The houses are less than ten miles apart in the south central region of the Lakes and, though I visited both, I failed to enter either of them.

Hilltop, it being Easter weekend, was packed with young families, so much so that queues spilled out of the front door and the country lanes were jammed with 4x4s. I witnessed one little boy of about four years come inches away from being run over at a junction and realised that this was not anything like how Potter would have wanted it. In truth, Potter didn't live at Hilltop, she only used the house for a bit of writing and painting, but it's preserved the way she left it, albeit with the addition of info signs and 'Do Not Touch' reminders.

Wordsworth's Dove Cottage was closed for renovation until the summer and the invitation of a replacement 60 minute video tour round the house (at the same price, of course) wasn't exactly appetising. Though Dove Cottage is the most well-known Wordsworth residence, he spent the largest amount of time and indeed the rest of his life at Rydal Mount, an hour's pleasant walk or so away along a bridleway. Rydal Mount is still owned by descendants of William Wordsworth and the majority of the house is open for visitors to pop in year round for a taste of Wordsworth's older years. It was here that he wrote and refined many of his poems, and in this house that he received many visitors from the literary world including Tennyson, Keats, and Southey, as well as American authors like Emerson and Hawthorne. It seems to live in the shadow of Dove Cottage and so I was intrigued to see how much I would find there.

I was the only person to get off the bus at Rydal Church and walk up the steep road towards the house. That in itself was a good sign, quite a few had got off at the scaffold-covered Dove Cottage a few stops before. As you walk up, there is a very grand mansion on the right named Rydal Hall and one can be forgiven for thinking this was Wordsworth's final home, but it actually has nothing to do with the poet. His modest cottage is rather appropriately tucked away to the left and indicated with a discreet sign and a tiny car park. There were no coach parking spaces, no queues of visitors picking their noses while they waited interminably to enter, no posh coffee vans, no kids running around going berserk. I paid my £7.50 in an out-building by the entrance and then walked up the path and let myself into Mr Wordsworth's house. It was so informal I felt like I should have knocked on the door. Nobody else was inside and so I walked around the various rooms feeling rather like I was breaking and entering. The only give away were the highly informative info boards, pin boards really with cards blutacked onto them, and a few display cabinets that housed things he no longer needs, nor anyone for that matter, including his inkstand, his breakfast condiment set, and his picnic box. I took the central staircase up onto the first floor and walked straight into his bedroom.

'Ooops, sorry Mr and Mrs Wordsworth, I seem to be terribly lost, umm...'

Fortunately there was no one in the beds to excuse myself to, but it felt like there really could have been. Other famous houses you go around have ropes around the beds or at least signs stating the obvious 'no touch' rule, but here it looked as if Wordsworth had popped out for a walk and absent-mindedly left the door unlocked. Added to the fact that I was the only person visiting at 11am during holiday time, I felt rather conspicuous as I tiptoed around, trying not to cause creaks on the wooden floorboards. I was also able to wander into Wordsworth's study and gaze out at the view the poet would have had while at his desk. It's rather perfect. Dozens of types of tree, shrub and plant frame a tiny glimpse of Windermere; the classic Lakeland view.

Wordsworth also spent plenty of time writing in his self-designed garden, more wild than manicured and providing an assault upon the nasal senses as you walk through. Walking along Dora's Terrace at the top side of the garden, you come to a sort of wooden shack with its back formed by the garden wall and a view of the slope that runs down to the grassy lawns. 'The Summer House', as it is known, is a simple, but effective hideaway. Just sitting down on its wooden bench, you feel a rush of inspiration come from the knowledge that Wordsworth himself sat exactly here and managed to wrestle the English language around the ineffable state of nature.

A few days later I visited Wordsworth's first home, where he was born and lived until the age of eight, in Cockermouth. The gardens behind the house are rather different to those at Rydal Mount, being perfectly presented and maintained, but at the far end, up on a terrace, there is a similar wooden shack in which some ingenious person has put a wind-up audio player. Turning the wheel a few times until it started playing, I could sit on the wooden bench and listen to Wordsworth's words wash over me while sitting amongst the leaves, bees, and trees. Whenever it stopped, I stood up, wound the handle again until the words started, and then sat back down. 'Daffodils' flowed with the ceaseless background music of the River Derwent over the garden wall. In the *'bliss of solitude'*, I cast my *'inward eye'* back through my time in the Lake District. Hiking up the Central Fells, cycling along the many lakes, sitting at the top of the double-decker bus, visiting the homes of England's revered writers, dodging sheep-shit in the fields; I realised that I'd developed what can only be described as a lust for the Lakes. I felt enamoured with this northern corner of the country. Suddenly, like falling in love with a beautiful girl, I'd become inexplicably invested and interested in the Lake District. I suppose the Lakes leave many first time visitors feeling the same way, perhaps explaining why it's so heavily visited. As such, I started to feel concern for the area's future. By finally achieving World Heritage status (it first tried in 1986, but as a natural listing), it looks as though the powers that be have decided to maintain the Lake District's farming culture, to keep things how they have been for the last few hundred years instead of going back thousands of years to when the area really was a natural paradise. What the impact of this will be, who knows, but for now, and I hope forever, the Lake District will continue to be just as Alfred Wainwright, famed author of extensive guides to the area, once said:

"The fleeting hour of life of those who love the hills is quickly spent, but the hills are eternal. Always there will be the lonely ridge, the dancing beck, the silent forest; always there will be the exhilaration of the summits. These are for the seeking, and those who seek and find while there is still time will be blessed both in mind and body."

UK UNESCO World Heritage Site #20 of 28

The Giant's Causeway and Causeway Coast (1986)

No camera for the causeway

Nothing. Not even a flicker. I jammed the charger in harder and wiggled it about. I checked the plug was on. I tried different USB cables. I swapped sockets. I connected it through my laptop. When every possible solution was scratched out, I looked at the amount of battery I had left. 34%. Anyone who has ever owned a phone will know that 34% of battery won't last long. Somehow I had to make it last so that I could find my way from Cockermouth to Workington on the bike, catch four different trains to Birkenhead, find the Airbnb I was staying at, then the next day find the ferry terminal to catch the boat to Belfast, then finally to get from Belfast to my next stop in Portstewart. This was to be the next 48 hours. Of course, even banning myself from taking photos, the 34%, now 33%, wasn't going to last.

It's a strangely liberating feeling to be without a mobile. My phone had died on the final train into Birkenhead, and, due to some problem with the charging port, wouldn't wake up again. I resolved to send it back to the manufacturer as it was under warranty but that meant being without a phone for the remainder of my trip. No Whatsapp, no Google Maps, no Instagram, no camera, no googling whenever a question popped into my head. I was bereft of all the advantages that modern technology has brought my generation, but, despite my loss, my overriding feeling was positive. I was a little anxious to be without such a great source of information, but at the same time keen to see how I would live without it. I realised that I'd spent the last thirteen years of my life (around half my lifetime) with a mobile phone in my left hand trouser pocket. I could feel its noticeable absence, a phone sized hole in my left thigh. Still, I was sure I could do without it. People travelled before the invention of the mobile, didn't they? They used maps and asked for directions. They consulted guidebooks and followed local advice. They didn't feel the need to update their social circles with filtered images of swirly coffee foam and selfies in front of monuments. If they could do it, so could I; though having a camera would be useful… I'd just have to use my own memory.

It was Murphy's law that my next World Heritage site was to be a natural listing and one of the most spectacular, peculiar, and photogenic sights in the whole of the United Kingdom. The Giant's Causeway is advertised rather too positively as Northern Ireland's only UNESCO World Heritage site (would they rather keep the number at one, I wondered) and is visited by over a million people each year. It's the symbol of Northern Ireland and is rightly regarded as one of the great natural phenomena of the world with ecological importance to boot, hence its accreditation as one of the first UK World Heritage sites in 1986.

It's rightly popular and protected, but many people wonder what the Giant's Causeway is. Well, there are two sides to the story of the Causeway, the geological story and the legendary story. I joined a walking tour led by the amiably Irish Jen who took us from the Visitor Centre down to the causeway via 60 million years of rock history and a myth that has perpetuated in Celtic folklore since pre-Christian times. Firstly, the rocks themselves. During the Paleocene Epoch, molten basalt formed a lava plateau on this site. When the lava cooled it contracted causing fractures down and along the molten rock. The fractures split left and right creating the mostly hexagonal pillars that we see today. There are around 40,000 of these perfectly hexagonal columns standing at various heights today, stretching like a finger out into the sea. This is where the legend of Finn McCool comes in. Finn, known to the Irish as Fionn mac Cumhaill, was a 54 foot tall giant that picked a fight with a fellow giant named Bennadonner who he could see across the water in Scotland. Finn, angered by Bennadonner's provocation, constructed the causeway to get across to Scotland as, apparently, giants don't like to get their feet wet. With his feet still dry, Finn reached Scotland to find that Bennadonner was more of a giant than he and so quickly ran back along the causeway in fear. Bennadonner chased after him, but when he arrived in Ireland, Finn's wife's quick thinking fooled the gigantic giant into thinking that Finn had gone out for a while and why didn't he come in for a nice cuppa tea while he waited for her husband? As the cunning Oonagh and Bennadonner sat round the fire with a brew, Bennadonner heard the goo-goo-ga-ga of a baby and upon discovering Finn disguised as a baby with a dummy in his mouth, decided that, given the huge size of the baby, the father must be absolutely enormous, probably even more of a giant than himself. Bennadonner fled in fear of the non-existent father and tore up the causeway as he ran back, forever destroying the land link between the Giant's Causeway and its smaller sister on the Scottish isle of Staffa.

Jen relayed the tale of Finn McCool just round the corner from the Giant's Causeway itself. As with every myth and legend, there are slight variations on the story and a fair number of holes, but it's a tale that has been told over the centuries and long before any tourists started coming to the causeway. Nowadays the winding road down to the causeway is busy with visitors going up and down, taking pictures of the cliffs and trying not to get mown down by the green bus that travels between the car park and the causeway. More than perhaps any other UK World Heritage site I had been to, the sheer variety of visitors was extraordinary. Walking down you could hear almost every major world language. There was a noticeably large number of American visitors too. Jen had to use a microphone that was broadcast into earphones for us to hear what she was saying amongst the chatter and billowing winds. We stopped a few times for Jen to point out the geological and natural features of the landscape and then we rounded a windy corner to be met by the view that thousands travel from all over the world to see.

Columns of varying dark shades of rock create a path

out into the waves, no further out than any other head, but significant because this headland is only formed of stones of mathematical perfection. As we walked closer, the honeycomb appearance of the rock formation became more apparent. As many a visitor has observed before me, the rocks look too perfect to have been formed by nature. We are used to seeing cylindrical shapes in nature with tree trunks and the like, but we seldom see hexagons, heptagons and octagons, these only seem to exist in maths class. Amongst the 40,000, Jen informed us that there's one nonagon. Where it is though she wouldn't reveal. I wasn't about to start scouring for it. It's enough to simply tip-toe from one stone to the next, being careful not to slip, and to find a spot to sit on a perfectly comfortable stone and take in the dramatic surroundings. Predictably, most people with a camera are more preoccupied with taking the perfect snap. The Giant's Causeway is a wonderful photographic subject. The waves lap over the fringes of the causeway and the puddles nestling in the concave tops of the columns reflect whatever is happening in the sky above. I'm fairly sure that I was the only person that day, perhaps that week or even that year, to have not brought a camera to the causeway. I consoled myself with the fact that I had visited a few years earlier and taken quite a number of pictures then. Indeed, I'd had one of the pictures of the causeway as my laptop background until fairly recently. Still though, whatever pictures I would have taken, they wouldn't have shown anything I couldn't already just find on Google Images. I'm a hopeless photographer anyway. I wouldn't know how to even turn on one of the fancy big DSLRs that many visitors had slung round their necks.

It was better perhaps, I reflected, that I didn't have a camera phone in my left hand trouser pocket. In fact, I think the lack of a camera forced my memory to remember the scenes more clearly. I can recall the white lichen marks on the stones, the tufts of grass growing in the ones further back from the sea and the tired, worn look of the stones on the frontline of the causeway's battle against the ocean. I can see in my mind's eye the clouds merging with the sea on the horizon, the ghosts of Scottish isles to the right, the seagulls swooping all around. I can still sense the smooth, cold feel of the basalt. Perhaps one of the reasons why people now and in the past feel that the causeway is man-made is because basalt is a common stone used in construction for building blocks and groundwork, including cobblestones in our high streets. Even the visitor's centre up the cliff is made from basalt stone, though thankfully not quarried from this UNESCO World Heritage site. The thing with photography is that you can only record the visual sense, and if you concentrate only on taking photos when you visit somewhere like the Giant's Causeway, you deny your other senses the opportunity to remember the place. We rely too much on our eyes; touch, hearing, smell and taste can be just as evocative and memorable.

Photos make a great souvenir though and it's true that everyone wants a souvenir of their time at the Giant's Causeway, or to leave a part of themselves behind. For years, right up to and probably after 1961 when the National Trust took over ownership of the site, people have taken stones away from the causeway as souvenirs. In fact, Jen informed us towards the end of the tour that around 20,000 stones, a third of the total, have been lost due to tourism. Past visitors have also left their mark on the Giant's Gate which provides land access between the two sides of the causeway by putting coins in gaps in the rock. These coins have since expanded in the heat and have caused cracks in the rock to appear. Erosion and direct human damage to natural features are the two biggest threats to the Giant's Causeway identified by UNESCO. With growing numbers of tourists, the National Trust started a year-long sustainability study at the site in 2018, the first of its scale at any World Heritage site. Photos are really the best kind of souvenir, but the lengths that tourists go to capture them have an impact on the supposedly protected environment.

I walked on from the causeway, passing Finn McCool's stone boot which flew from his foot as he ran away from Bennadonner, and then followed the path up to another unique feature of this landscape, the Giant's Organ. Here you can see the hexagonal basalt columns again, but this time there are sixty of them lined up next to each other extending 12 metres up the cliff face. Legend has it that the organ can be heard if you visit at 6am on Christmas morning, though whether anyone has got out of bed at that time on Christmas Day to hear it means it is yet to be verified. The cliffside path continues past the Giant's organ, but the way when I visited was blocked by a metal barrier. Jen had mentioned this as well. Erosion is causing many landslides to send rocks scattering down the hundred metre high cliffs. The barrier has a sign reading 'Danger' with a triangle image of falling rocks and circled images of hikers and backpackers above the words 'No access beyond this point'. It seemed a pretty crystal clear warning. Looking at the rocks at the top of the sheer cliffs along the path, it appeared to be justified.

I took a seat on a perfectly positioned rock at the foot of the Giant's organ and watched bemusedly as one group of tourists walked gingerly round the barrier and then continued along the forbidden path. The next group of tourists looked at the sign, then looked at the tourists making their way along the forbidden path, then followed them, walking round the sign carefully as it was blocking pretty much the whole access to the path. The next tourist group did the same, and then the next too. A few groups stopped at the sign and consulted each other. While some of them decided to stop and obey the sign, others chose to proceed onwards. It was obvious why many of the couples and small groups of tourists were choosing to continue along the cliff path. 70 metres or so up from the barrier there is a spot to take pictures of the causeway side on. It must make a good photo. You can stand in front of the length of the causeway with Aird and Weir's snouts in the background and the sun causing the sea below to glitter. It's the classic landscape view; also obtainable from higher up on top of the cliff, but easier to access, despite the barrier, here. While groups deliberated whether to bypass the obvious warning sign, other groups were returning from the forbidden path with no obvious sign that their cranium's had been cracked open by falling rocks. This, I suppose, provided proof to the deliberating groups that the path was perfectly safe to walk on and that the National Trust was going over the top with the Health and Safety. Most groups followed the backs of the group in front and all got their priceless photo of themselves grinning with the Giant's Causeway behind them.

It was fascinating to watch. I spent around ten minutes watching groups come and go while sat on the stone seat, making a few notes in between admiring the perfectly adequate view of the Giant's Causeway's side from in front of the barrier. A few photographers spent their time with their backs to the view, taking pictures of the towering columns of the Giant's Organ behind me. Mostly they would snap, snap, snap and then turn around and walk back down, or they would join the groups in walking round the barrier to continue along the path. After a while, putting my notebook in my bag and taking a swig of water from my bottle, I got up to my feet and started walking back down the way I had come.

'Yay, we can take pictures now!'

I stopped dead in my tracks. I stared at the man in a cap who had openly expressed his joy at me leaving.

I offered him a solution, served iced cold. *'You could just take pictures of it with me in'*.

'We already did'. The capped man's similarly capped wife snapped back.

'It's just a joke, man', the husband professed defensively.

A million retorts were caught in the filter net that guards the line connecting my brain to my tongue. I continued staring at them for a second longer and then walked past them.

'I'm not a tourist site'.

As I walked back down the path I heard the apple skin crunch of camera shutters and a cackle of laughter. *'If you're here just to take photos, you shouldn't be here at all'*, I responded to the group of tourists in my head. In reality though, there's no use replying to people like them. It's not worth the time when you could be admiring the Giant's Causeway instead.

With a slightly sour taste in my mouth, I couldn't stop thinking about that couple as I cycled the thirteen miles back to my Airbnb in Portstewart. Even though I hadn't taken a single photo of the Giant's Causeway that day, I felt that I'd experienced it enough to remember it vividly. Heading out of the Visitor Centre car park, I wound my way past mighty tour buses with licence plates from all over Europe and stopped to allow the dawdling tourists cross the road. Then I zipped down the hill and allowed the rush of air round my cheeks and ears to blow any negative feeling away. I joined the cycleway that runs parallel to the Bushmills heritage railway and followed the tracks back to Bushmills from where I could rejoin National Cycleway 93 back to Portstewart. The narrow gauge railway line was the first in the world to use hydroelectricity though it encountered many problems with the technology and so steam trains were also used. The line was closed in 1949, but has since been restored and opened again to the tourist trade in 2002. It carries tourists to and from the Giant's Causeway in style, just like it did in the 19th century, though thankfully the day I cycled along its line was a day off and so I could pass over the many track crossings without fear of being run over.

I was slowly recovering from my frustration with the camera-crazed couple until I thought of another gripe. Travelling to the Giant's Causeway using a 'green' method avails visitors of a £1.50 reduction in entry to the Visitor's Centre, a wonderful and informative facility that's well worth the money. However, of course the majority of visitors arrive by coach or car. At first I thought it was a wonderful gesture of the National Trust to give a discount, however slight, to tourists who had chosen to travel without contributing to carbon emissions. The Giant's Causeway being a natural World Heritage site and at great risk of the consequences of global warming, it makes sense to incentivise visitors to travel greenly. However, the £12.50 that car drivers pay instead of the £11.00 that I paid includes free parking. £1.50 for all day parking in a National Trust car park is unheard of. In comparison, the beach in Portstewart which is also owned by the National Trust charges £6.50 for parking. So, what's the point of trying to travel green when parking is so cheap? No wonder my bike was the only one parked in the bike parking. It all depends on how you advertise something, from which side you tell the story.

Realising this, I thought about the history and the tales of the Giant's Causeway. Geologically, the

Causeway coast is fascinating, but only to people who know their rocks. Jen had admitted this, asking whether there were any Geology students on the tour or whether she could just make up the facts as she went along. Whether it's 50 or 60 million years old, to the common man it doesn't really make a difference. Would as many people visit the Giant's Causeway if it wasn't wrapped up in the legend of Finn McCool and his beef with a Scottish giant? 'The very old volcanic hexagonal stones'; it just doesn't ring as well as 'The Giant's Causeway', does it?

As Northern Ireland's premier tourist attraction and its only UNESCO World Heritage site, it kind of has to use a bit of Irish charm to keep attracting the punters in. Then again, it's the mix of the mythology with the awesome sight of the sheer cliffs and the bemusingly regular shape of the stones that attracts over a million people here and is the reason why they all bring a camera or two. Without a camera though, it's still just as good. In fact, I spent far longer at the causeway and learned far more about it this time I visited compared to the first time I visited when I almost ran down to the causeway, took a load of pictures and then hiked back up to get a bus to the Republic of Ireland. My first visit a few years ago is the type of visit the tourist board are trying to discourage through providing other attractions in the area, and I'd also say that spending a whole day, or even five days like I did on the Causeway Coast is worth the time. Even without a camera and the memory aid it provides, I can verify that taking your time in this part of the world is worth it. Cycling instead of driving, lingering instead of rushing, taking the time to appreciate the view instead of just taking photos; the Giant's Causeway, despite Samuel Johnson's famous quote (*'Worth seeing? Yes, but not worth going to see'*), is worth the journey. Just don't be that couple in the caps with the cameras.

UK UNESCO World Heritage site #21 of 28

New Lanark (2001)

Utopia in May

I was glad to get out of Glasgow. 'Dear green place' it might be known as, but grey and dreary it appeared as I cycled along rubbish-strewn city streets to reach the Clyde Walkway. I was fortunate that this cycle route along the river would lead me all the way out of the city so that I didn't have to endure lorries and 4x4s breathing down my neck. Sadly it only took me as far as Cambuslung, and from there it was roads only. This area of Scotland, sandwiched between the major cities of Glasgow and Edinburgh, is very built-up and busy. I was heading for New Lanark, around 40 miles up the River Clyde to the south-east of Glasgow. The river is the reason why New Lanark exists, and the power source of its commercial success. By the end of the 18th century, New Lanark was the biggest cotton mill in Scotland and one of the largest factory sites in the world with over 2000 people working and living by the Clyde. While the output of these mills was colossal, it is the input of one factory manager that makes New Lanark extraordinary.

'Exchange their poverty for wealth, their ignorance for knowledge, their anger for kindness, their divisions for union'.

These are the words of Robert Owen, a Welsh textile manufacturer whose social ideas set the catalyst for so much that we know today. Free education, workers' healthcare, the eight hour day, the Co-operative movement, trade unions, child labour laws, free public libraries and museums, childcare… The list is almost inexhaustive. Owen tested many of his social reform ideas over the first few decades of the 1800s at New Lanark within his plan to make this area by the Falls of Clyde a 'Utopia'.

And it worked. New Lanark continued the success it had enjoyed when it was first set up by Richard Arkwright (yes, him from the Derwent Valley Mills) and David Dale, who happened to be Owen's father-in-law. It made Owen and others very wealthy. More than economic success though, New Lanark was the pioneering force behind so much that improved workers' conditions throughout Britain and the world. It garnered attention the world over and Owen published papers that continue to influence labour management today. New Lanark is today a symbol of work being done according to higher principles than simply making money, and for that and the ideas that were tested there, it's been a World Heritage site since 2001.

I had to work damn hard to get there though. Out of Glasgow, the Clyde had deserted me and specks of raining were pre-warning me of an imminent downpour. I was sick and tired of having engines moan behind me before their drivers shot past me with just a few inches room. Frustration, probably due to the fact that I hadn't eaten since 6.30 and it was now past lunchtime, was kicking in. I chose a quieter route into Lanark but that only yielded a series of climbs along pot-holed country roads. Gritting my teeth, I reminded myself of every other time that I've cycled a bike laden with luggage up a hill and thought *'No, I can't'*. Every time I've reached the top and realised *'I've done it'*. It was the same this time, but boy was I glad to freewheel down the side of the hills that separate modern, bustling Lanark with historic, tranquil New Lanark.

The hair pin bend of New Lanark Road brought me into view of the rows of multi-storied tenements and the monolithic sandstone brick mills that make up this much-storied model village. It was properly raining now. Thankfully the kind lady at the Visitor Centre reception desk allowed me to stick my bike in an unused conference room and I was able to start my New Lanark experience straightaway. A few minutes earlier I had been cycling in the rain, now I was sat on a sort of ski-lift in the dark that was taking me slowly through rooms filled with illuminations and holograms while a little girl talked into my ear about her life living in New Lanark. The Annie McLeod (pronounced McCloud) experience is something a little bit different for the seasoned tourist. It's a 12 minute 'dark ride' that transports visitors 200 years back in time, with lighting, sounds and smells to attract the senses. Despite giving off the appearance of a rollercoaster, the double seated 'cars' are only suspended two feet off the floor and move at walking pace so there's little chance of getting an adrenaline rush. What you do get is a rather unique way of presenting an insight into life in New Lanark back in Owen's day. Via video projections, Annie, the little ten year old girl working in Owen's mill, guides you through various aspects of life. Kids had to be educated until they were ten (something that only came into law sixty years later) and then they could earn money by working in the mill as piecers, workers who would reconnect broken threads by bravely leaning over the working machines. Annie recollected her experiences of learning a broad curriculum at school with a kind teacher who never used corporal punishment (something else Owen was also way ahead of his time with) and also spoke about the living conditions which were a marked improvement compared to other mills at the time. The ride ended with Annie's reflections on Owen, told in her sweet Scottish accent:

'As long as the wheels keep turning we keep making cotton, and that makes Mr Owen happy. Mr Owen wants us to be happy too, mind. And I think we are. New Lanark is special because of Mr Owen... Maybe sometimes his ideas can be a bit strange, maybe sometimes we don't understand him, but he is fair and he is kind. I think he's on our side'.

I was shown off the ride by the same young boy who had shown me on to the ride (maybe they still let kids leave school at ten in Scotland, I wondered), and I was back in the grey cloud filtered light and drizzle of 2019. Further along in the exhibition, there were a few pictures mounted on the walls showing groups of residents in the streets of 19th century New Lanark staring in the direction of the photographer. Old black and white photos can be hard to relate to sometimes. The lack of colour and detail with the plain white faces and old-fashioned clothes often create a distance between this world and theirs. When you look closely though, as I was doing with these pictures on the wall, you start to realise that these were real people. The stone walls of the New Lanark mills and houses were recognisable, and so were the people. They looked relaxed and happy. We're so used to thinking of these 19th century people, with their lack of modern conveniences and punishing work hours, as poor, dirty, and deprived, but there were smiles on the faces of the boys and girls and pride showing in the expressions of the women. Groups of girls in relaxed stances with their hands in their pockets. Boys with their metal hoops which they would trundle along the unpaved streets. They looked healthy, content. Owen must have been doing something right. While it was expensive and legally unnecessary to provide such standards of healthcare and education, Owen wanted to see if he could breed a society free from crime, poverty and misery. Looking at the pictures of his workers, the people living in his socialist Utopia, it looks as if he succeeded.

I continued my walk through the mills and came across a working example of the machines that would have been running in Owen's time. The spinning mule was descended from Hargreaves' spinning jenny and Arkwright's water frame, and was first assembled by Samuel Crompton. The particular specimen at New Lanark is from the late 19th century, but still uses hydroelectricity and still produces yarn, though from wool rather than cotton today. I was mesmerised as I watched the moving carriage roll forwards and back, and the yarns being spun then stretched then wound round the spindles. It was noisy, and back in Owen's day it would have been hot and dangerous for the workers, however the end product was miles and miles of yarn, enough per week to go round the world

2.5 times, that could be used for a myriad of purposes and came to be relied upon as Britain readied itself for two world wars. The machines took the really hard work out of the process and made the product cheap and open to a mass, international market, but there were still jobs to do for the women and children employed in the mill. Owen was strict with his workers as all mill owners were, but he developed ingenious systems to keep his workers motivated. His use of a publicly displayed coloured cube to review each worker's performance replaced punishment of any sort with social pressure. If you weren't pulling your weight, everyone would know it, and you didn't want to be seen as a slacker when everyone else in your community was working hard for a common cause. You didn't want to let Mr Owen down either. After all, it was him who took you out of the slums of Glasgow and gave you a modern house on a crimeless street with access to healthcare and cheap groceries. The onus was on the worker to keep New Lanark utopian.

The houses that families occupied during the 19th century are still houses today. Indeed, many of them are part of affordable housing schemes and a few were being advertised for sale at around £150,000 each. They're listed buildings so the exteriors cannot be changed at all, but you do get the privilege of being able to say that you live in a UNESCO World Heritage site. Those who visit New Lanark and wish to spend the night can do so in one of the former mills now converted into a rather plush four star hotel complete with spa facilities and fine dining restaurant. It was rather out of my price-range so I'd booked into the budget-friendly hostel which is part of a row of terraced houses called Wee Row. However, a few days before, I'd received an email from the hostel telling me they'd upgraded me to the hotel. Well, I thought, somehow they've found out I'm writing a book about them. The perks of being an author, indeed. Obviously though, however much my ego deceived me, this wasn't the reason. In fact, a large group of French school students had booked all the hostel rooms and so I'd been shunted, rather gratefully, into the hotel for the night. Needless to say, I wasn't going to kick up a fuss.

I checked in at the reception desk, and was able to leave my bike in the basement of the hotel. There are probably not many cycle tourists who stay in a hundred pound a night plus hotels so it felt pretty weird. I have to say I'm more used to Airbnbs, staying in someone's spare room with my bike in their garden shed. It can often be awkward staying in someone else's house with their personal effects all around and not wanting to impose myself on them or use their facilities excessively. Hotels are different though. You can do whatever you want in your own private space for the night and leave anonymously the next morning, safe in the knowledge that there are people trained and paid to clean up after you. You get about eight different towels, a huge, immaculately made bed to jump into, and the bonus of being able to enjoy a cup of tea without having to make small talk with a host or worry about the washing up. I kicked off my shoes, had a long, hot shower and then laid on a bed as soft as clouds and watched the TV that had automatically turned on as I entered the room. Though feeling a slight urge to get up and explore more of New Lanark, I instead just wallowed in the comfort, lazily watching Ray Mears explore the rivers and lakes of the pristine Canadian wilderness on a canoe. There was Utopia, if ever it existed. However, strictly speaking it doesn't because the Greek from which the word is derived means 'no-place'. By definition, it doesn't exist. Still, the rapids and falls of Canada, surrounded by lush pine forests and shown on the HD screen of the hotel TV, looked as close as you can get to it, even if you have to share it with Ray Mears.

Eventually, I extracted myself from the double bed's

embrace and got myself ready for dinner in the fine dining restaurant downstairs. I selected the cleanest shirt from my bike bag, ironed it, shaved my beard, did my hair, basically did the most I could to make it look as though I hadn't just spent the day (and the past couple of weeks) cycling through wind and rain. Looking about as presentable as I'm ever going to get, I still had an hour before my dinner reservation so decided on a little pre-dinner amble to the nearby Falls of Clyde, an attraction in themselves and regarded as one of the many beauty spots of Scotland. A forested path takes you along the left hand side of the river, passing three sets of waterfalls up to Bonnington Weir. It was originally a coach way for the landowners to show off the falls to visitors and so the path takes in the very best vistas as you walk up the river towards the sound of crashing water. The best vista is certainly that of Corra Linn, a 30 metre high fall that inspired writers and painters like Wordsworth (both Dorothy and William), Coleridge, Southey and Turner to describe it in words and paint. Corra Linn is certainly a sight to behold, water gushing down the gaps in the rocky tiers and plunging relentlessly into the river below. It's framed by a gorgeous assembly of foliage, part of the woodland deliberately planted by Robert Owen so that his workers could reap the benefits of being outdoors in nature. Even on the dullest of days in Scottish skies, the variety of colour of the trees injects positivity into the veins of those who walk along the riverside paths. Owen knew the value of the natural surroundings of New Lanark, not just to power his mill, but also to aid his workers' physical and mental states.

Though Owen was able to harness the power and utility of nature while keeping its beauty, it seems that it's a harder task for today's landowners. I passed by a riverside cottage that had newspaper clippings on its gate for the passing public to read. Earlier in the year, the Scottish government had rejected the latest proposal from Cemex, a Mexican building materials multinational, to extend their quarry upstream and thus encroach on the World Heritage listed land. It seems that tourism, and by association heritage, was deemed more valuable than quarried stone on this occasion. Whether it remains that way, only time will tell as pressure and the financial might of companies like Cemex has been seen to break down the will of local governments in other parts of the world. The area has also been used for its hydropower capabilities with the UK's first hydro-electric scheme used for commercial purposes being built here in 1926. The turbine runners at Bonnington Power station run up the sides of the hill from the pathway, but make up for their unsightliness by providing renewable energy for 17,000 homes. Of course, the mills also used hydropower and still do today to make the yarn that is sold in the mill shop. Not only was Owen's business socially responsible, but it was also environmentally friendly. As I wandered along, I couldn't help thinking that Owen wasn't just ahead of his time, he was also in some ways ahead of our own time today. In some ways, we still haven't caught up with Owen's progressive ideas.

Keeping an eye on the time, I turned back at Bonnington Weir and began the walk back to the hotel, passing the waterfalls once again. The scenery reminded me of the Canadian rivers and forests that Ray Mears had been canoeing along. Of course, you'd find it hard going canoeing over the Falls of Clyde, but the tall pine trees and larches hinted at a connection between the Canadian paradise on the TV and New Lanark's natural serenity. Both beautiful environments, albeit one natural and one designed, they allow the visitor to take stock and enjoy the simplicity of listening to the birds. To think of turning this into a stone quarry, it beggars belief. Humans have always sought to extract useful resources from areas of beauty, the canoeists in Canada were fur hunters, but conservation groups and protection from UNESCO have meant that there are still areas like the Falls of Clyde that can remain beautiful.

Being as beautiful as Scotland surely requires a lot of liquid sunshine. For the umpteenth time since my arrival in the country, I was getting rained on. On a bike it's a problem that you can deal with, but dressed in your smartest shirt and trousers in readiness for a posh dinner it's not ideal. It is sod's law though. I hurried quickly back to arrive at 7 on the dot but still walked into the restaurant with my hair dripping and my jacket shedding droplets of water onto the thick carpet.
The maître d' looked me up and down as I walked in through the door.

'Hello, I have a table for 7'

She furrowed her manicured brows in confusion as she looked over my shoulder.

'7 o'clock, not seven people…', I hastily clarified.

'Follow me'.

I then began that strange walk you have to do with the maître d' to your table. Which corner are they going to hide me in? Will they be kind, or will they put me next to the loud group of cackling businessmen or the family with the baby? After walking around half the restaurant, she plumped for a single table by the stairs and I sat down opposite an empty chair on a table laid for two. She removed the wine glass and cutlery opposite me and handed me a menu. Dining by yourself in a restaurant is a curious experience. Going for a coffee or even having lunch by yourself is generally acceptable, but dinner by yourself in a posh restaurant: that carries some social stigma. If you've never tried it before, I wouldn't exactly recommend it.

Time goes slowly, and the beer in front of you disappears quickly. Dining is an experience meant to be shared really, it doesn't really work when you're by yourself, but I had to have dinner somehow and this was, apart from room service, the only option available. I had my notebook for company and writing in a small black notebook while waiters pass by often puts them on edge and ensures you better service. I was politely served a pint of McLachlan's and then a good portion of Steak and Haggis pie with mash and veg. It was all delicious and, despite the company or lack thereof, I enjoyed my solitary meal surrounded by groups of diners, all of them well above my age. I retired to my room satisfied and enjoyed a peaceful slumber under the cotton covers, exhausted from a day of being rained on.

I woke up wondering how on earth I'd ended up in someone's plush hotel room, and then slowly remembered that it was my own. May as well make the most of it then, I thought. It was 7am, far earlier than I needed to be up, but the pool, sauna and steam room were already open and were begging to be used. Safe to say not many of my days visiting World Heritage sites start with a swim and a sweat, but it wouldn't be all that bad if more mornings were like this one. I could get used to this lark, at least until check out time.

After I eventually and reluctantly returned my room key, I set about completing my New Lanark passport ticket. I started in Robert Owen's house, a detached building in the centre of the village surrounded by grassy gardens. Down in the kitchens there was a video playing and a lot of information about Owen's Utopian plans post-New Lanark and the various model communities he inspired around the world. New Harmony, a community that still exists today in Indiana, was taken on by Owen when he left New Lanark for the less conservative climate of America but within two years it had proved a failure. It seems an imbalance of skills and rumbling disagreements in the community was to blame, but it didn't help Owen to prove that his socialist theories could work anywhere. Other quests for an ideal community have been started both in Europe and North America, but none have really stood the test of time.

Though the communities themselves didn't last, the ideas and practices that sprung out of them have. I visited the school room next which was built by Owen to educate the children, and the future workers, of New Lanark. Why educate mere mill workers you may ask, but Owen would have responded that education was the route out of their poverty and misery. He certainly wanted to give them a broad view of the world, providing lessons in the arts as well as the sciences. He also established the first nursery which, of course, benefited him as it meant that the mothers could work in the mills during the day while their babies were being cared for. Another initiative that Owen started was the village store which undercut the small traders already selling low quality goods at high prices. Again, there was a dual benefit with workers being kept healthy with high quality fresh produce at affordable prices while the profits were used by Owen to build his schools. We still have these ideas today in the form of free education for all, childcare, and the co-operative movement which was started by workers in Rochdale inspired by Owen's example.

Owen's legacy is considerable, but as with Titus Salt at Saltaire, there was and is criticism laid against him. He indulged in self-promotion and spent a fortune on propaganda to popularise his conviction that planned communities were the solution for society's ills. Then again, throughout his life he was always focused on ideal living rather than on profit, as opposed to the mega-rich Salt. Owen became a wealthy capitalist but lived the second half of his life as an enlightened socialist. Something deep inside Owen drove him during his whole life towards trying to make the lives of the working class better. From our 21st century perspective, it's hard to say he had a dark side. Through his essays, and the quotes dotted around New Lanark, we see Robert Owen as remarkably forward-thinking, benevolent, almost messianistic. That was the impression I got at New Lanark where his greatest achievement is preserved almost as he left it and where he is celebrated at every turn. Though he relinquished all links to New Lanark before heading to America, he's still the celebrity of the village. After Owen's departure, New Lanark passed through various groups and an inevitable decline until it was saved from demolition by the New Lanark Trust in 1983. Restoration has taken place to bring it back to its early 19th century heyday and it now attracts 400,000 annual visitors to its attractions, events, hotel and conference facilities. My guide on the tour of the village had even mentioned the popularity of getting married in New Lanark, with wedding photos on the rooftop terrace of the former cotton mills.

May is not perhaps the best month for a wedding at New Lanark though. It was still raining as the hotel receptionist brought my bike round to the front door and I loaded my bags back into the panniers. My couple of days in New Lanark had passed quickly and now Edinburgh awaited. With everything secured, I saddled up and started the climb back up the hill side towards the modern world. As New Lanark fell out of sight between the tree tops, I thought about the connection between the three textile mill listings on the UK's World Heritage list that I had now visited. They were all given World Heritage status at the same time at the turn of the millenium. Something about moving into a new period of time seemed to motivate the UK government to recommend the protection of 19th century reminders of an industry that has all but disappeared entirely from these shores. Though long gone, it was this industry, weaving cotton and wool from across the world, that powered much of the success of the British Empire, leaving an indelible mark upon our natural landscape and our cultural history at large. Arkwright, Salt and Owen were more than just mill managers, their social ideas as well as their industrial inventions changed everything from worker's rights to mass industry. It's not just the Derwent Valley, Saltaire, and New Lanark where they left their mark, it's the whole world that has experienced the effect of these three giants of the Industrial Age.

UK UNESCO World Heritage Site #22 of 28

The Forth Bridge (2015)

The three over the Forth

'*T*ickets, please'.

The booming voice just behind caused the instant ripple of passengers delving into pockets to extract their rectangular, orange passes. I had mine in my wallet so pulled it out from the front and got it ready in my fingers to present it to the guard.

'Thank you. And can I see your railcard?'

'Sure, uhh, ohh, actually I don't have my phone on me'.

I was still having issues with my phone. It was now fixed and waiting at home for me, but I wasn't at home to collect it just yet. I'd bought a crappy replacement, but had decided to return it for a refund the previous day as it was just within the 14 day returns policy. That day, while on the train north out of Edinburgh, I was sans smartphone, and it was a problem. After promising it a few years previously, the Government had actually delivered on one of their election manifesto promises and the 26-30 'Millennial' railcard had been released in January. As it's targeted at my technologically-crazed generation, the railcard is a virtual one, shown on an app on your smartphone. Great idea you may think, every 26-30 has a smartphone, don't they? Well, yes that's true. Every 26-30 year old except this one. For the next few days anyway. The guard gave me a quizzical look, like I was somehow missing an invisible limb.

'It's being fixed. The battery wouldn't charge and...'

'Well, ok son. You'll just have to pay the excess on the ticket.'

That amounted to an extra £1.95. The guard printed me off another ticket and handed me my 5 pence change. I wasn't paying too much attention though. Any minute now we'd be passing over possibly the most famous rail bridge in the world, a UNESCO World Heritage site since 2005, and the subject of Scotland's £5 notes. Ironically, this journey from Edinburgh to North Queensferry, just across the other side of the bridge, was now costing me more than a Forth Bridge decorated fiver.

The guard walked further up the train and less than a minute later the wild, thorny hedges had subsided and blue water was racing by far below us. Even though you can still hear the kerclunk-kerclunk of metal wheels on steel tracks, you get the sensation that you are floating, impossibly, above the Firth of Forth. The other passengers all looked up from their newspapers and phones. It's a pleasant sight from every seat, as you look from side to side as if watching a tennis match at the widening mouth of a mighty river. Then, from nowhere, huge blood red hulks of metal come flying at you from both sides, chopping the light into strobes that turn the inside of the train carriage into a natural, day-time disco. The rave lasts about a minute and then you're free again to see the shoreline slide under the train before arriving at North Queensferry station.

And that's the Forth Bridge. It only takes a minute or so but the 2.5 kilometres offer some of the most spectacular views from a train in the UK, and they have done since 1890. Looking right as you go north, the view probably hasn't changed too much in over a hundred years, but to the left two more bridges have been added to cater to the needs of automobile drivers. Needless to say, the Forth Road Bridge and the Queensferry Crossing are less iconic than the rail bridge, but have their merits regardless. From the train they blend in to each other to form a series of metal peaks, formed from the two trellises of the Forth Road Bridge and the three sails of the Queensferry Crossing, that in turn blend into the background of the real mountains in the distance. Together they form an awesome threesome, not just connecting two sides of the Forth, but depicting 125 years or so of Scottish engineering at its finest. It's the original bridge though, the rail one, that's really special.

I'd already seen the Forth Rail Bridge from the closest angle possible, but now I had to get back across to South Queensferry in order to continue my visit with the Queensferry museum and boat trip. Though built primarily for road traffic in 1964, the architects of the Forth Road Bridge, now the middle bridge of the three, had the generous foresight to add pedestrian and cycle paths onto both sides of the bridge. The cyclepath is particularly crucial as it forms part of National Cycle Route number 1 that runs from the Shetland Isles to Dover. I'd previously cycled along it while on my John O'Groats to Land's End trip in 2015, wobbling in the whipping breeze and being deafened by the trucks and buses screaming across it. Today I was without my bike, but also thankfully without any traffic too as the bridge was completely closed to all motor traffic so that engineers could perform repairs. There were dozens of orange jumpsuited men hammering, drilling and soldering the 50 year old structure. Without the buses and taxis that travel across it every day, the bridge was pretty quiet. The wind too was almost non-existent. I found the path onto the bridge and started the deceivingly long walk back across to the south shore.

The Forth Road Bridge has quite the medical history. Although designed to last 120 years with 30,000 cars a day, its intended capacity has been doubled and so it seems its lifespan has been halved. To that end, various actions have been taken to extend its life, but worries about its structural integrity continue to exist. One of the responses has been to build a whole new bridge, the third of the three named the Queensferry Crossing, but at a cost of £1.35 billion, the 2.7km of road alongside another 2.7km of road connecting more or less the same points wasn't cheap. Nowadays the older road bridge is reserved for public transport and pedestrians/cyclists while the 2017 bridge carries the M90 and the low hum of traffic that I could hear in my right ear as I walked over the Forth. The situation is manageable for now, I suppose. The aim of the Scottish Government in building the third bridge was not to encourage increased numbers of cars making the crossing, but to encourage public transport use. Now that two of the bridges are solely dedicated to public transport, and the third also has bus lanes, the bridges are portrayed as encouraging greener ways of travelling. All well and good until you see how busy the Queensferry Crossing is compared to the other two bridges. Well, I guess it is the newest bridge and therefore the most structurally sound. It's the one I'd want to drive over if I were in a car.

Whichever bridge you take, it sure beats getting the boat over the Forth. Ferries across the river existed from the 12th century and proposals for a tunnel under the water were first aired in 1790. I was able to get an insight into the history at the Queensferry Museum, a collection of four galleries accessed through the town's registrar's office that necessitated the ringing of a doorbell to gain entry and a hushed welcome at the top of the stairs. Once I'd been initiated, I went into the one gallery that interested me, the history of the Forth crossings, and found the collections of mid-construction photos and random items of miscellany that can be expected in a small, but passionately researched museum. The images showing the huge supports of the rail bridge standing unconnected on islands in the river exhibited the true scale of such an ambitious operation. This was a time of confidence in the nation, an era when the impossible seemed achievable thanks to the strides in engineering taken by world-leading Scotland. It had the world's longest cantilever span at the time, and still has the second longest in the world today, but the concept still needed the trust of the general populace. To demonstrate the principles, a famous photo was taken with the designers John Fowler and Benjamin Baker sat either side of construction foreman Kaichi Watanabe who is suspended by ropes held by Fowler and Baker. The men knew their idea worked, but the cost of constructing it was high, both in terms of money and men. Though Baker rather nonchalantly declared that it's '*impossible to carry out gigantic work without paying for it merely in money, but in men's lives*', there were a staggering fifty seven fatal accidents to add to the bill for £1.35 billion in today's money. There's a suggestion that many men worked drunk, having enjoyed a few too many lemonades at the nearby Hawes Inn, but even still, I thought back to the engineers I'd just seen repairing the Forth Road Bridge and all of their safety equipment and regulations. The men who constructed the Forth Rail

Bridge would have had very little of those modern-day protections, if any of them. It would have taken real balls, and possibly a little Dutch courage, to get up on those metal supports in Scottish weather and knock bolts into place.

To appreciate their work and their sacrifice further, I took a boat trip from the dock next to the rail bridge. There are a couple of companies offering 90 minute 'Three Bridges' trips and I chose the next departure, joining a slowly forming queue of tourists that had begun to get in order as the open top boat approached. It's amazing how these queues form, mostly everyone conscious of who's first and following the group in front to see where embarkation may begin. I was towards the start of a queue that I realised, when I looked over my shoulder, had grown into a snake going back all the way practically into the car park. Our vessel had sidled up alongside the dock and momentarily we were about to be allowed to board. That's when everyone around me started getting little plastic cards out of their pockets and clutching them in anticipation of having them checked. I didn't have a plastic card on me but I wasn't perturbed. I'd read in plain English on the sign by the docks that you could procure a ticket for the tour on board the boat. I readied my £15 fare instead.

'Ticket, please'.

'1 adult, please', I replied, offering the three notes with the very bridge we were standing next to emblazoned on them.

'No, you need to buy a ticket from the ticket office'.

'But the sign up there said I could buy on board'.

'No, you can't'.

I sighed. *'It's an old sign, isn't it?'*

'Yes, it is. We've been meaning to get it changed...'

'Then get it effing changed, you complete and utter...', is what I wanted to say, but instead all I did was mutter something about being at the front while turning around and making the torturous walk back up the quay towards the ticket booth that I could have sworn had been closed when I'd arrived.

'He's changed his mind, ain't he'. *'Got cold feet I suspect'*. *'Poor lad probably thought it was free!, didn't he'.* I could hear the mumblings of everyone else who had been behind me in the queue as I did the walk of shame past them. The ticket lady was idly standing by the booth as I sprint walked towards her with my fistful of notes. I really wasn't having much luck with tickets that day. Of course, though I now had a ticket, I'd lost my place in the queue and was now the last person to board. I went straight up the top deck but all the best seats had been taken long ago. Resigned to my fate, I slumped on a bench amid a forest of camera phones as we set off under the Forth Rail Bridge towards Inchcolm Island.

Without a phone of my own to take pictures with, I spent the tour sat down enjoying the views and the commentary provided over the loudspeaker. The skipper Kieran was keen to point out the sealife lurking beneath the surface and very soon we had spotted our first sea lions, puffins and even a dolphin. The sea lions provided the best photo subjects. Lazing on their sides on the buoys and tops of rocks, they seemed to pose for pictures and even provided entertainment by pushing each other off the rocks into the water. Though the tour was billed as the 'Three Bridges tour' it was as much, or even more so, about the history and wildlife of the area we were cruising in. The Forth has everything from an oil refinery to an

Augustine abbey, and below its waters there is a German U boat and the treasure of Charles I that was lost when the Blessing of Burntisland sank in a storm in the Forth in the 1600s. The treasure, with an estimated worth of hundreds of millions, is still yet to be found despite the attempts of divers and the Royal Navy.

We ventured quite far out towards the edge of the Forth's mouth, but after going round Inchcolm Island we made our way back towards the three bridges, admiring Edinburgh's skyline to the left as we passed. As well as ferries, tunnels and bridges, Kieran mentioned another past proposal that had been conjured up by the imaginative Scottish for crossing the Forth. Two men, John Jeffrey and Mathew Steele, put forward the idea of creating a dam across the Forth with a six lane road on top. The project would have created a vast lake upon which watersports would have flourished and it would have solved the problems of trying to construct wind-battered road bridges high above the water. It could also have provided hydroelectric energy and allowed ships access with a small bridged gap in the middle. Alas, it was badly timed as WW2 came along and the idea was lost to the distractions of fighting, but it's a credible idea. Instead of building over it or under it, why not build on it?

Again, Scottish ingenuity sourced close to Edinburgh, the 'hotbed of genius', enabled these ideas to become realistic possibilities. It's extraordinary that even now, over a hundred years later and with bridges over water that now span dozens of miles like the Hong Kong–Zhuhai–Macao Bridge, we still marvel at Victorian engineering. Really, bridges like the Forth Bridge are old technology. Just look at the Queensferry Crossing with its clean underside and striking pillars. The Forth Bridge looks so complicated in comparison with its multiple supports and great hulks of red steel perched on its islands. It's a bridge that nowadays just wouldn't be built, though perhaps that's the reason for its popularity. It's not just practical, but beautiful too. It looks too strong and too big just to carry two train tracks. It was built in a time when the railways were the latest in technology and, let's face it, there's far more romanticism in railways than in roads. I think the Forth Rail Bridge wouldn't be nearly as beautiful if it had thousands of cars zooming along it instead of the occasional train gingerly edging its way over. It's the reason why everyone was taking photos of the red old bridge instead of the newer grey bridges when we sailed back into the quay. Even though the road bridge is longer, and the Queensferry Crossing is higher, the Forth Rail Bridge is still the most impressive, the most eye-catching, the one everyone wants a picture with.

I was considering all of this from a comfortable armchair while looking out of a window inside the Hawes Inn. The armchair looks out at the postcard view of the bridge; an acute angle view that allows appreciation of its height as well as its span as it dominates the strip of water it crosses. The small window perfectly frames the bridge if you turn the armchair in the right direction. I thought of the other eye-catching bridges across the world I'd visited, from the Golden Gate to Sydney's Harbour, and without doubt they are all, like the Forth Bridge, wonders of the engineering world. However, the Forth Bridge edges them, I feel. Perhaps it's the aforementioned romanticism of trains over cars, maybe it's the younger brothers behind the eldest that act like a timeline of 19th, 20th and 21st century bridge building, complementing each other so fluidly. Or perhaps it's simply just that iconic desert red oxide colour known as 'Forth Bridge Red', the paint job that famously is said to never finish as once it's finished it's time to start it all over again such is the great length of the bridge. Red like the blood of the men who died building it, red like the passion for pursuing an engineering feat never before accomplished, red to wave goodbye to every goer and welcome every comer in the Firth of Forth for over a century. A symbol of a nation, and one that's still very much in use still today.

UK UNESCO World Heritage sites #23 of 28

Old and New Towns of Edinburgh (1995)

Capital of Consummate Contrasts

I always try to do a little research before I arrive in a place. I'm prone to sitting, staring out of a window on a train, but this time I at least managed to find the time to skim-read Edinburgh's Wikipedia page without missing too many fields flashing past. What I gleaned from the chapters of text is that Edinburgh appeared to be a fine city of culture, split into Old and New Towns that make up the World Heritage zone. A castle on a rocky crag, an extinct volcano, a statue of a loyal dog; these seemed to be the main cast in a city that loves, even lives, to perform. I'd visited before of course, a school trip to Make Poverty History in 2005 and a stopover on a bike tour to rest tired legs in dingy pubs, but this was to be my first visit of substance. I didn't know much, even after reading the wiki page.

'The next station will be Edinburgh Waverley'. I glanced up from my phone to watch a sheer cliff of molten black, rain-drenched rock pass by. The rock blends into brick fortifications higher up. As you pass, your neck cranes right as far as your muscles will allow, all to drink in as much of the dramatic welcome as possible. There can not be many more spectacular entrances into a city than from the west into Edinburgh. The Wikipedia page hadn't prepared me for this reception.

Outside the entrance to the station, standing on a bridge with the Old Town to my left and the New Town to my right, I let the rain soak into my waterproof jacket. It collected on my bike seat and nestled into my trousered thighs. The grand welcome felt slightly soured. Without any other option, I mounted the bike and climbed up into the Old Town, crossing over the Royal Mile where bagpipes wailed and following the map in my mind to my Airbnb. My host, Cat, welcomed me in, brushed off my apologies for dumping litres of water on her hallway floor, and then left me to wait for the torrents to dissipate.

Even in Scotland, these rain storms come to pass and, fortunately, a calm morning proceeded with bright sunlight clearing up the puddles. I was lucky as it was to stay bright and warm the whole of my stay. I was Airbnbing in Marchmont, an area of Victorian four-storey tenements popular with students that's a pleasant walk across The Meadows from the Old Town. Edinburgh looked resplendent in the morning sunshine, the green sponges of The Meadows soaking up the noise of the rush-hour traffic and allowing the many commuting cyclists to speed into the heart of the Scottish capital. Edinburgh is remarkably green, something not mentioned by the UNESCO listing though it complements the architecture it is noted for. Get this: 49% of the city's space is parkland, making it by far the greenest city in the UK. An impressive stat by itself, but mind-blowing when you compare it to other UK and world cities. For comparison, the greenest city in England is Bristol with 29% green land. Greater London has 23%. European capitals typically have around 20%. US cities even less. Half of Edinburgh is recreation space for its half a million population. Half urban, half green; a city of contrasts but one that strikes a balance.

But why does Edinburgh have so much more green space than other cities? And why does it have separate Old Towns and New Towns? The answer to both these questions lies in its history and its geography. Edinburgh was once just a long street running down a ridge between one dormant volcano and the next. The classic comparison is of the Old Town layout being like the skeleton of a fish. One long spine (known as the Royal Mile) with alleyways, known as 'closes', spread evenly along it. This dead fish was bordered on three sides by the Flodden Wall, built to keep the English out, and on the remaining side by Nor Loch which was used as the city's rubbish dump. Thanks to modern sewage systems, Nor Loch is no more, but the reek of raw sewage centuries ago gave rise to Edinburgh's less than complimentary nickname 'Auld Reekie'. Obviously, no one wants to live in a stinky city and as Edinburgh was increasing in size and importance (it had been made Scottish capital in 1437) it needed to expand. First it went upwards with wooden skyscrapers to stay within the protective walls, but after the threat of English invasion subsided with the Act of Union in 1707 it was accepted that Edinburgh could expand outwards. A New Town was needed and a competition was held to find the perfect design. One James Craig, a native Edinburgher, submitted a patriotic design that tried to mimic the crosses of the Union flag and had its streets named after kings, queens, and symbols of the newly formed United Kingdom. Today, however, the plan realised looks more like the grid systems that were growing in popularity in Renaissance cities with grassy squares bookmarking the eastern and western ends.

I joined a walking tour of the New Town, having chosen to start there rather than the Old Town like every other tourist, and our guide, a softly-spoken Glaswegian by the name of Kenny, was introducing us to the first people that would have lived in Craig's creation. As it was built to provide the wealthy with relief from the crowded and polluted Old Town, the New Town became a sought-after location for those with deep pockets and many of Edinburgh's famed writers and scientists, as well the upper-class and aristocracy, moved in. One of the most eager was David Hume, the philosopher, who used to host dinners for Europe's great intellectuals in his state-of-the-art new build. Hume has a large statue in the Old Town nowadays which, incidentally, provides two of Edinburgh's finest ironies, namely the rubbing of his right toes for luck (he was a fierce rationalist) and the nearby Jehovah's Witnesses stall (Hume has been called the patron saint of atheism). Anyway, it is the New Town, rather than the Old Town, that should be celebrating Hume as he was one of the instigators of the New Town, and Edinburgh as a whole, becoming so famous for Enlightened ideas.

Kenny led us round Charlotte Square at the West End of the New Town. Come August the normally private gardens would be full of book stalls as the centrepiece of the largest book festival in the world, but on this Sunday afternoon it was empty. Seemingly none of the local residents wanted to make use of it during a sunny May afternoon. Though Edinburgh has acres of public parks, it's still sad to see beautiful green spaces with bars and padlocks banning public access. Regardless, this end of the New Town doesn't have many residents anymore. Kenny explained that many of the properties actually contain insurance and real estate firms rather than families. Two houses in the square have different purposes though. Bute House, the central door of a neo-classical facade, is home to the First Minister for Scotland, in effect the Prime Minister for the country. *'Unlike 10 Downing Street in London, you can knock on the door and run away'*, Kenny added with a mischievous grin. It's in stark difference to the black gates and guards of Downing Street.

Next door to the First Minister's not so humble abode is The Georgian House, a National Trust restored property that offers visitors the chance to step inside and explore what living in the New Town would have been like in the early 1800s. In fact, quite a few of the properties in Charlotte Square are in the National Trust's caring hands, including Bute House which means the Scottish Government, established at the turn of the 21st century, has to pay rent, just like all twenty year olds.

A few days after the New Town tour I returned to Charlotte Square and went inside the Georgian House. It was just as Kenny had described. Large, light-filled rooms with elaborate decoration and all the mod-cons of the Georgian era. Those mod-cons however didn't extend to running water or sewage drains so the Lamont family who first occupied number 7 Charlotte Square barely washed themselves (spraying perfume liberally instead) and still did their business in chamber pots, even while engaged in conversation. We may think of them as enlightened, extravagant individuals, but they only had two baths a year and defecated publicly in bowls kept under their beds. They ate their main courses and desserts at the same time, and they kept servants to do their dirty work even when they could hardly afford them, as was the case of John Lamont. All they really cared about, it seems, was selling off their daughters to the highest bidder. The Georgians may have lived in fine houses that we still coo after, but they were pretty different to the majority of Edinburgh's population today. As far as I know, the First Minister has a working toilet in her house. You'd sort of expect it with house prices in the millions in this part of Edinburgh.

The Georgian House was one of the most informative experiences I'd had while exploring a world heritage site. Volunteers lurked in every room ready to pounce on visitors and talk nineteen to the dozen with them about every minute detail of the house and its occupants' lives. Upon entering the basement kitchen, I was given a full working tour of the instruments including the steam-powered spit roast and, while in the main bedroom, I was engaged in a discussion about everything from four-poster beds to Brexit. Usually they just serve to warn people not to touch things, but the Georgian House volunteers really wanted to talk and engage tourists in the house. It was enlightening, rather appropriately. Speaking of Enlightenment, I was humoured by the inspired use of prickly holly leaves in place of 'Don't sit on this chair' signs. I guess a prickly leaf translates into every language pretty seamlessly.
As such, I walked out of the Georgian House with my behind unprickled and my knowledge of the New

Town greatly increased.

The tour ended at the statue of James Clerk Maxwell by St Andrew's Square at the eastern end of the New Town. Maxwell was a source of inspiration for Isaac Newton and Albert Einstein and, though his name is less well known, he had just as much impact upon the modern world. Maxwell discovered electromagnetism, his equations for which underpin all modern information and communication technologies. He also presented the first colour photograph to the world. He was a direct product of Edinburgh's New Town, born on India Street, raised on Heriot Row and educated at the Edinburgh Academy and then the city's university. Without Maxwell, I wouldn't have the internet or a computer upon which to research and write about him. Maxwell is just one example of the genius that sprung out of Edinburgh's New Town. The city inspired, and continues to inspire, so many.

Resting my legs after the tour in the public gardens of St Andrew's Square, I realised that I was starting to fall helplessly in love with Edinburgh. Looking around the groups in the park on this sunny Sunday afternoon, the atmosphere was calm, and the conversations being had seemed educated. Everyone, from university students to groups of elderly friends, was sitting on rugs eating picnics or licking ice creams, engaged in friendly and fair discussion. A rare example of serenity in a city, a capital city no less. It seemed impossible. I couldn't remember ever sitting in a public park without witnessing some dramatic act of public embarrassment or annoying anti-social behaviour, but this was a first. Edinburgh seemed different, a cut above the rest without appearing pretentious, and I was falling for it big time.

This was dangerous. I'm certainly not the first, nor doubtlessly will I be the last, to fall under Edinburgh's spell. Every tourist I walked past on the Royal Mile, wherever they were from, sounded impressed at Edinburgh's liveability. *'Wow, look at that castle on the hill', 'Oh Nancy, you gotta see this cute pub', 'No way, this museum's also free!'. 'Cool, they've got trams', 'Gosh, would you just look at these houses. They're so grand!'.*

I knew I was being tricked by the warm Spring weather, but I found myself thinking: *'who doesn't love Edinburgh?'* In the attempt to quell my lust, I tried to find reasons not to like Edinburgh's Old and New Towns. There are a few to be fair, but not many. Out of the things that can be controlled (weather is not one therefore), the roads are majorly potholed and, though cycle lanes abound, the state of the roads would loosen the bolts of the toughest bikes. Then again, they're probably an improvement on the first roads in the Old and New Towns so I guess you still have to say Edinburgh's progressing, albeit slowly with regard to roads.

Then you have the tourists. The Royal Mile is effectively Scottish Disneyland, with kilts for sale, whisky experiences and the eternal whine of bagpipes. During August, the city's population triples, causing much pain and frustration for locals. Edinburgh is one of the cities where Airbnb has run wild, turning locals' houses into apartment hotels for wealthy visitors. This was one of the complaints listed in the remarkably honest World Heritage exhibition at the Tron Kirk in Hunter Square which mentioned in one example that eight flats in one building were all listed on Airbnb. Now, I'll hold my hands up and admit that I've used Airbnb extensively, some sixty different locations. However, the vast majority of my stays have been in private rooms in a local person's house, not renting the whole flat like some Airbnb listings offer. It's these whole flat listings that fire the ire of locals, and understandably so. Nobody wants a forever rotating merry-go-round of foreign tourists dragging their wheely suitcases up their apartment stairs instead of permanent neighbours who might offer community spirit and a spoonful of sugar when you've somehow run out.

I talked this over with my Airbnb host, Cat. We both agreed that Airbnb has its flaws as much as its benefits. In the act of creating a network of locals willing to host travellers, it has grown so large that it's now cutting communities apart as whole neighbourhoods get swamped by listings. There are nearly 12,000 listings in Edinburgh, over 7000 of which are entire homes. That's 7000 homes in a city with a 500,000 and growing population. Of course it creates problems. The UK is in the midst of a housing crisis and houses dedicated solely to the accommodation of tourists are not helping. The highest concentration of Airbnb listings is, of course, in the Old and New Towns. When walking down the Royal Mile, you are far more likely to hear foreign accents rather than Scottish accents as the numbers of tourists are so great and local people are priced out of the heart of their own city. World Heritage status, as one quote in the exhibition had stated, is a double edged sword. Far more attracts people to Edinburgh than just the UNESCO status (only 15% of tourists claim the WHS is the reason they visit the city), but its buffer zone denotes the tourist area as much as it defines the heritage area to be protected. The list of things not to like about Edinburgh is short, but I can imagine, like every tourist hotspot, it must get tiring for the residents of the Old and New Towns to push past dawdling tourists every day. Nowadays, the reality is that if you want to live in a beautiful and historic place, you have to share it with the camera-toting, shorts-wearing, pavement-hogging hordes. It's just a fact of life.

However, if there's a city and a country to come up with an ingenious solution for their problems then it's

Edinburgh and Scotland. Ingenuity is everywhere in Edinburgh, from the robot grass cutters that roll along the immaculate lawns to innovative buildings like the John Hope Gateway building at the botanic gardens. It's a city with weighty heritage that is moving forward at the same time. Cranes constructing new developments compete with the castle and Parthenon-esque National Monument for skyline dominance. The country of Scotland is also on a progression path. With the return of its devolved government in 1998, a new Scottish parliament building was needed and the designers were keen to be as modern, and as un-Westminster, as possible. Step forward Enric Miralles, the Catalan architect who designed a campus of low-lying buildings inspired by the connection between nature and the Scottish people within the World Heritage boundaries at the lower end of the Royal Mile. Sadly, Miralles died before its completion and much of the symbolism behind the shape of the buildings was lost with him. It means the building's curious shapes are up for debate.

'What do you think it looks like?', asked the petite lady leading the brief introductory tour at the free to enter Scottish parliament building. The crowd of us surrounding a model of the building in the visitor's lobby went silent. I decided to pipe up.

'Like shards of glass after a Friday night in Edinburgh', I offered.

Apparently most people say boats and trees, but the tour guide did say it was open to interpretation. In fairness to myself, she did ask. The buildings are (according to some) boat-shaped and do form the outline of a leafy tree, but with their glassy front and scattered formation, I felt I wasn't a hundred miles off.

Holyrood, as the Scottish Parliament is metonymically

known, is the antithesis of the British parliament at the Palace of Westminster. Also of course part of a World Heritage site, the Palace of Westminster is steeped in history, falling apart, hardly fit for purpose and full of weird rules and traditions. Oh, and also very expensive to get in. Holyrood couldn't be more different. After paying a grand total of nothing to enter, I was free to walk wherever I liked and so I visited the debating chamber, set in a hemicycle as opposed to Westminster's adversarial layout. MSPs debate the country's concerns in comfy office seats at individual desks while the general public can sit and watch just behind them in modern carved wood terraces. The building was finished in 2004, but fifteen years later looks like it was finished yesterday. Information boards clearly explain who the Scottish Parliament are and what they do, and I was left with the impression that they probably get on with a load more work than the politicians in Westminster who are surrounded by great frescoes and opulent decoration. The bill for the Scottish Parliament building came in at £414 million. Some complained over the cost, but remember that just renovating the Palace of Westminster is costing the UK Government over ten times that amount. Though not everyone's a fan of the modern look, Margery who was one of the guides at the Georgian House had named it a 'monstrosity', it does the job of keeping the wind and rain off the backs of the MPs during the short amount of time that they spend in the building each week. Though proud England would disagree, Scotland has shown that a nation's parliament doesn't need to be housed in the grandest building in the city. It just needs to be functional, and the Scottish Parliament Building works pretty well while using some rather interesting architectural design. It still looks like shards of glass to me, but to many Scots it signals Scotland becoming more independent and more in control of its future.

While one end of the Royal Mile ends with a palace

and the symbol of Scotland's future, the top end of the road is where the city's proud history is displayed. Edinburgh Castle is the centrepiece of the city's historical sites and is visited by over 70% of all the tourists who visit Edinburgh. I didn't go in. While it contains the Scottish Crown Jewels, the Stone of Destiny (of which more later) and other patriotic miscellany, it is mainly made up of military museums and army paraphernalia as it is still used by the British Army. I wasn't too interested in the inside of the castle, but I still wanted to get up close it. Fortunately I had the perfect Old Town tour guide to lead me up the slope and introduce a few of the more interesting tales behind the castle and its contents.

Let's start with the first of tour guide Angus' fine stories. The castle had been attacked many times throughout its history, but it escaped any damage in the First World War thanks to the ingenuity of soldiers based there. Seeing a German blimp in the sky they scrambled together any weapons they could find to ward off the imminent attack. All they had though were decorative cannons and blanks to use for the one o'clock gun tradition that still continues today. However, the Germans didn't know that and so the soldiers started firing blanks at the blimp from the mighty cannons around the castle. Needless to say, the Germans didn't fancy taking on a castle armed with dozens of cannons and so turned back around for home. On the way out of Edinburgh airspace they did drop one bomb but it simply hit the ground, rolled down the street and never exploded. That was, as our mustachioed Scottish-Australian guide remarked, Edinburgh's only involvement in the Great War.

It's an incredible story, even more so when relayed by the Shakespeare-trained Angus who launched into the bemusing stories with gusto and a rapidity that I could barely keep up with. Another tale he told concerned the Stone of Destiny. Sounding like a crucial object from a Harry Potter plot, the stone is also known as the Stone of Scone or the Coronation Stone because of the part it plays in the crowning of formerly Scottish now British monarchs to this day. In reality, it's just an oblong block of red sandstone weighing around 152kg, but we British love attaching ridiculous significance to simple objects so it's regarded as rather more than just a big bit of stone. In fact, it's a symbol of Scottish nationhood and was taken out of Scotland by the English King Edward I in 1296 to demonstrate that he was now King of the Scots too. That was until 1950 when the most daring heist of the century was concocted by four Glasgow University students. The foursome drove down to London, hid in Westminster Abbey, then, when it had closed for the night, attempted to steal the Stone of Destiny. Only they had rather a hard time of shifting a huge stone into the boot of a Ford Anglia. The stone broke in two during the removal and, once the authorities realised it had been stolen, the border between Scotland and England was closed for the first time in 400 years. Ian Hamilton, Gavin Vernon, Kay Matheson and Alan Stuart buried the stone in a field in Kent and eventually managed to get it back up to Scotland a few months later. A few years later the four managed to escape punishment in court, but the Stone of Destiny had already been taken back to England where it stayed until it was finally returned properly by the British Government in 1996 in a symbolic attempt to appease Scottish dissatisfaction with the administration. Now it sits in Edinburgh Castle, still just a stone but a well-travelled one at that. The story of its removal in 1950 has embellished its legend and gives actors/guides like Angus the licence to summon their inner Oscar-winner by dramatising the daring escapades of the four Scottish stone stealers while those on the tour turn around and take snaps of the castle and its views from every angle.

Though hailing from the other side of the world, Angus was in the right place. Edinburgh is ripe for a story. Its fairytale scenery with the castle looking down upon narrow, cobbled streets lends itself to tales of myth and legend. While the New Town provided the surroundings for the founding of modern science, the Old Town has inspired authors from Walter Scott to JK Rowling. It was named as UNESCO's very first City of Literature and clearly professes a love for the written word. Scott's gothic space rocket monument is the largest to an author in the world, his 'Waverley' series provided the name for the city's main rail station, and he is credited with returning kilts and whisky to Scottish culture, another great yarn that Angus performed. It's a toss up between him and Robert Burns as to which author Edinburghers adore most, though anyone who has witnessed the rounds of Burns' 'Auld Lang Syne' chorusing through the streets during Hogmanay may presume the latter edges it. Then there's Robert Louis Stevenson. Though he took himself to warmer climes in order to aid his health, he still made trips back to his home city. Inside the free to enter Writers' Museum, I explored artefacts and pictures relating to all three men. Most fascinating of all was a photo of Stevenson stood outside Skerryvore, his home in Bournemouth and where he wrote Mr Jekyll and Mr Hyde. Until I left Bournemouth to explore these World Heritage Sites, I used to eat my lunch every day in the garden of Stevenson's former home with my back to the remaining foundations of the house where he lived. It's the least touristy place related to a famous author I know. Apart from a small sign down the end of the garden, and the fact RL Stevenson Avenue starts opposite the house, you would never know that one of Britain's and Scotland's most famous authors spent time there. The only person I ever saw visit it besides myself was an elderly lady who is entrusted with the garden and who owns a very naughty dog which used to pinch my sandwiches while we talked. I gazed at the photo of a smiling Stevenson in the garden of his house and felt the unique connection that ties us.

Stevenson's most famous work, arguably, is Treasure Island, a fantastical children's story that has captured the imagination of kids for over a century. Edinburgh is also home to another author who gave children the words to open their imagination. It's hard to write about Edinburgh, especially the buildings in the Old Town, without mentioning JK Rowling. Not only did she write the Harry Potter books in the cafes and later the five star hotels of the Old and New Towns but she also inserted so much of Edinburgh's buildings and people into her books. I won't go to the trouble of repeating what countless Harry Potter tours in Edinburgh could tell you, but JK Rowling's world is much influenced by Edinburgh. The muggle world of the New Town where reason and logic were popularised, and the magical world of the Old Town where alleyways lose you and exotic treats such as deep-fried Mars bars can be sampled. The City of Contrasts once again. As Robert Louis Stevenson said of his hometown: *'Half a capital and half a country town, the whole city leads a double existence'*. The organic versus the planned, the alleys versus the wide streets, the rickety beams versus the neo-classical columns, the old versus the new.

My whirlwind romance with Edinburgh was soon to be broken apart with my imminent return to the south of England. I could sense the upcoming heartbreak, feel the pull of the city telling me not to leave. I needed one last kiss. With the sun setting on my final evening, I walked up to Arthur's Seat to witness for the final time the bewitching contrasts of this city. Named after the legend of King Arthur who is supposed to have founded his court of Camelot on these rocks (thanks Wikipedia), Arthur's Seat is a fair hike up but I made it up to the very top in time to see the sun dip behind the blue mountains, cloaking the city in a dusky haze.

Over there was the castle on the hill, tiny from up here. To the right of it, the long line of Princes Street in the New Town was lit up. Mostly though the city appeared as one. Framed by the other six of its famous seven hills and by the Firth of Forth, viewed from on high the city of Edinburgh looked snug, homely. A wind sent a chill around the exposed extinct volcano, the first I'd felt in over a week. I vowed to return as soon as I could.

UK UNESCO World Heritage Sites #24 of 28

Cornwall and West Devon Mining Landscape (2006)

A tin line between success and failure

I awoke to a mass of Cornish accents entering my carriage. It was now light, and the train was suddenly full of life. Time to open my eyes and face up to the reality of having to spend the rest of the day surviving on the very limited sleep I'd managed to get on the overnight Cornish Riviera from London. We had just stopped at Truro and were now slowly slipping through the Cornish countryside towards the end of the line at Penzance. I hazily glimpsed through sleep-dust eyes the tops of the brick engine houses that define this land, a reminder of the purpose of my visit to England's rabbit hole, the westernmost, southernmost tip of the tail of southern England. By road, Penzance is around the same distance from London as Newcastle in the north east. As you head west to Cornwall, the land width contracts, the roads become slower, the landscape becomes hillier and the undergrowth wilder.

Occasionally you see a white cross on a black background fluttering from a flap pole erected in someone's back garden. Cornwall, it is so often said, is so far from everywhere else. Far away enough to have its own distinct culture, language, flag and national dish. Largely forgotten about by the rest of the nation until the summer when thousands clog the A30 and the sandy beaches. A once a year car trip that would seemingly last forever. Bucket and spade holidays are Cornwall's present, but this now tranquil royal duchy was once one of the richest mining areas in the world, providing the metals that fed Britain's Industrial Revolution and inventing new technologies that vastly improved the efficiency and safety of mining. Cornwall did and still does affect the way that mining is conducted today, a legacy that has spread to every continent and paved the way for the modern world we live in. As with the other mining and production related World Heritage sites in the UK, the Cornish mines were victims of their own success as other countries started undercutting them, but the reminders of Cornwall's golden age, just like the mills in Derwent and the pits in Blaenavon, are kept visible and protected.

UNESCO's listing of Cornwall and West Devon's

mining landscape covers some 20,000 hectares and is divided into 10 separate zones, the two most distant apart being nearly a hundred miles from each other. Visiting areas rather than specific sites is obviously a greater challenge if you're trying to get an idea of the world heritage listing as a homogenous entity. I'd set aside a full week to cover the site, spending four days in Camborne, in the heart of Cornwall, before venturing up into Devon and staying in the Tamar Valley. Even so, I knew I couldn't hope to visit everything of worth in a week. For that reason, I chose a selection of mines, houses, landscapes and museums on the map and, after downing a coffee and a pastry at Penzance station, set about tackling the Cornish hills to reach them on my trusty bike.

It was tough going. Undulating country hills, packed panniers and sleep deprivation versus caffeine wasn't really a fair match. After huffing and puffing up the hills, via a red phone box to shelter from a passing shower, I made it to St Just and the engine houses and mines that dot this forbidding landscape. St Just's remains are the tourist brochure front cover images of stone shells with hollow windows and crumbling towers set against the endless blue waves and sky at the end of the world. They're spectacular, even in their ruined state. White waves pound the rocks upon which Crowns Engine Houses perch like birds sheltering from a storm. Cycling along the clifftop pathway you see many of these engine houses all the way up the coastline. They were used to pump water out of the mines, allowing miners to dig deeper and deeper, even under the sea. I passed a number of them either set into or on top of the cliffs before arriving at the towering headgear of Geevor Mine - a huge crane like structure that hoists men and metal up from the bottom of Victory Mine half a vertical kilometre below.

Geevor is considered a modern mine as it was mainly

operational during the 20th century until 1990, but the site also contains 18th century mines and the whole history of the area and tin mining itself is informatively told through the various exhibitions on site. The Hard Rock museum, despite bringing to mind the restaurant chain, exhibited rock of the geological kind rather than the musical sort, taking me through the association of Cornwall with tin from the earliest mention by a Greek merchant in 275BC to the present day uses for tin cans and plating metal objects. Copper was also found in abundance here with Cornwall providing two thirds of the world's copper in the 19th century, coupling it with tin to make bronze, a much harder metal alloy. The mining process was also detailed, the miners mostly employing a technique called 'stoping' which meant mining the lode (the vein of tin in the rock) as closely as possible to avoid mining waste rock. Even with this technique, one that was used throughout Cornwall, only 2% of the rock excavated contained tin. The miners would chip and blast away at the rock for hours every day, utilising electric trolleys and hoists to send the heavy rock up the surface where it would be processed, only for 98% of it to be chucked away as waste.

I thought about this fact as I toured around 'The Dry', the locker room and bath house built for the miners here which has been kept exactly how it was left since the last day of mining here on the 16th February 1990. The beginning of the end had been four years previously when hundreds lost their jobs due to a massive worldwide drop in tin prices, but it was 1990 when the very last miners arrived at work early in the morning only to be told that they were being made redundant and that the mine would be closing indefinitely. Since then, it looks as if their changing rooms, the dry refuge at the beginning and end of every shift where banter would be liberally exchanged, have remained untouched. The blasting schedule remains on the wall, posters of cartoon Thatchers on the notice boards, dust jackets hanging in the sticker-adorned lockers. The only addition seems to be the walls of photos of the men who worked down Geevor mine, every photo captioned with the names and nicknames of those men. It was humbling. I felt a lump grow in the back of my throat as I slowly walked amongst the lockers and entered into the lost world of salt-of-the-earth men who toiled deep underground for the vast majority of their lives in order to support their families. All to extract rock from hundreds of metres below the surface, 98% of which would just be thrown away. It seemed mad. Any other business that produces 98% waste wouldn't be viable. Imagine a restaurant throwing 98% of their food away, or a factory producing clothes from only 2% of the cotton they bought. It's ludicrous.

Thing is though, for many hundreds of years until other countries got in on the act, it was profitable, incredibly so. The wealth that mine owners generated bought them land and huge properties like Godolphin House and Cotehele, both of which I visited later in the trip. Back in the 19th century, conditions for the miners were poor to say the least with the average life expectancy as low as 27, but in the 20th century the mines provided well-paid jobs to the men in the community and necessitated many auxiliary industries for others. Now, all those jobs have gone. The only work available at the mine is leading tourists like me around and helping them to realise the almost unimaginable work that miners did. Geevor is one of the few mines in Cornwall that offer underground tours and so I joined a group at the Mill to go underground through Wheal Mexico. 'Wheal' is the Cornish word for 'mine', but the Mexico part of the name is, apparently, a mystery, though it's true that many Cornish miners migrated to Mexico in the 19th century taking with them their mining techniques as well as the game of football.

Our guide, a former miner at Geevor, made us don dust jackets and safety helmets before leading us, backs crouched low and following each other's arses, into the damp, dark shaft. Now, I'd promised myself at Blaenavon that I would never enter a mine again, but here I was breaking my vow just one more time. I really had meant to keep that promise too. Still, at least we weren't descending down into the depths of the earth, just the inner tunnels of the hill Geevor sits on. We walked around inspecting the lode and minding our heads as we went and twenty minutes later we were back out in the open. It wasn't nearly as intense as my previous experiences in Bolivia and Wales, but at least I'd had another brief taste of the hellish conditions in which the brave men of Cornwall would dedicate their lives to. Never, ever, ever will I go into a mine again, I promised to myself as I followed our guide out into the sunlight. Well, we'll see how long that lasts.

Fortunately it's a job I've never had to consider doing. Just being inside a mine for twenty minutes tests your mental resolve. It's hard not to think of the tonnes of rock around you and the danger you face every second longer you spend down there. The miners' coping mechanism was good, old-fashioned humour and a camaraderie that I'm not sure exists in any workplace nowadays. It was essential for the men to keep each other in high spirits while in the mine and through this they forged unbreakable friendships. At the very end of the locker room there was a display of photos from Geevor Mine annual reunions in which the ex-miners, now with less hair and wizened expressions, had their arms around each in the same way they did in the photos of their younger selves down the mines all those years ago. Friendship goes a long way, especially in the most trying of working conditions.

The lack of physical labour jobs for men since the

days of mining has had a large impact upon society. Modern men have fewer options through which to express their physical strength, and this in turn has an effect on mental health. Aside from team sports and the gym, men have experienced a loss in physical challenge, working in jobs that don't require their physical skills or lack the team spirit that spurs them on. As hard as their jobs were, reading through the personal accounts of the miners displayed in 'The Dry', they expressed a dear love for their intensely physical jobs. It gave them satisfaction to work the earth, to see the mine shafts lengthen and the amount of rock they were sending up to ground level to be sorted. There are few jobs like mining now, and I can't help but feel that this has had a negative impact upon men. There are options that partially fill the gaps left behind by the collapse in mining, like the armed forces and gym memberships, but there are many men now who find themselves at a loss because they don't have a physical outlet through which to dedicate themselves to. It's an issue that needs addressing on a national level.

Back to friendships, I had managed to arrange to meet-up with an old university mate, a real Cornishman, who had agreed to give me a local's tour of his hometown of St Agnes. Louis and I lived together in student digs for second and third year, going on countless nights out together and playing for the same university sports team. Fast forward seven years since we graduated and Louis is back in his Cornish hometown with a wife and three kids to provide for and a steady primary school job to keep him out of trouble while I'm still bumbling about with little to be responsible for apart from myself. On the surface, our lives have gone in pretty different directions but when he pulled up outside my Airbnb in Camborne I jumped into the car to find the same mate who'd once helped me to carry a stolen 'for sale' sign home amongst many other high jinks while stumbling back from another blurry student night. Four years is a long time between meetups, but like the cliche we clicked back instantly into where we'd last left each other. Louis drove us through the quaint village of St Agnes to his family home to pick up the wife and kids and then we set off on an ambitious 5 mile walk round the mining sites of St Agnes. That was once Louis and Sam had prepped the kids for the trek. Finally, after 40 minutes of being close to departing then remembering some other necessary accessory for the hike, we made it out the front door with Louis carrying 4 month old Olivia on his front and Sam supporting 3 and a half year old Sophia on her back. The eldest, Zack, ran on ahead despite the pleas of his parents to stay close.

'Never have kids mate', Louis remarked while walking with Olivia on his front, putting her left shoe on with his left hand and feeding her with a bottle of milk in his right.
'Point taken', I agreed. Impressed as I was with Sam and Louis' multi-tasking, and as cute as Olivia and Sophia were, it wasn't exactly persuading me to embrace parenthood. In no way did I envy having to lug a child up the hills of Cornwall. Of course, every parent needs their escape from time to time and Louis' way is to strap a bottle bra to his chest and run for miles along the undulating cliffs, taking in the engine houses and old mine shafts that make the St Agnes coast a World Heritage site. We were walking along one of his favourite runs with tongue burning hot Cornish pasties in hand while Louis pointed out various aspects of the landscape he's proud to call home.

'Wheal Coates down there mate, we'll walk down and explore'. He pointed down to a collection of roofless engine houses precariously perched on the edge of the land. Like at St Just, they appeared lifeless and haunting, but not so long ago they were relentlessly

pumping water from shafts reaching 185 metres down, far below the sea level. The miners dug everywhere their drills would reach, not afraid to venture under the sea bed despite the obvious dangers. Consulting cross-section plans of the land you can see layer upon layer of tunnels extending across the land and under the sea. We imagine just a few tunnels here and there but the reality is a network that in places represents the London Underground maps stacked on top of each other. The stacks and engine houses act as above ground station entrances allowing access into and out of the vast network of lode-hunting tunnels hidden beneath the tranquil cow fields and country lanes. It's hugely impressive, but also indicative of the sheer relentlessness of the mining companies to extract every last ounce of mineral out of the earth. It's amazing in some ways that there still is a Cornwall considering how much of it was transported elsewhere around the world.

When tin prices dropped, the numbers of Cornishmen seeking passage to lands overseas increased and many left to lend their mining skills to the British Empire and beyond. Poldark mine, which I'd visited the day before, exhibits a display of Cornish mining around the world. Remarkably it can be said that by 1900 there was hardly a mining site in the world without a Cornishman or a Cornish invention inside it. This is what makes the Cornwall and West Devon mining landscape a true world heritage site. It wasn't just that Cornwall was a key part of the UK's Industrial Revolution, but the skills honed in the south-west of England were key to the modern mining industry and therefore, though Cornwall has very little being mined out it these days, it is the ideas and inventions born here that are still used around the world today. Cornish culture travelled with the Cornish miners who went as far afield as South Africa, South America and Australia. Indeed, the world's largest Cornish festival is held in the Yorke Peninsula to the west of Adelaide.

Though thousands of Cornish signed up for the one way passages to the other side of the world, there's still a strong sense of Cornish identity in the county today amongst those who remained.

Bidding farewell to Sam, Louis and the kids after returning from our walk, I set out to uncover a bit of 21st century Cornish culture. Fortunately, the former mining site turned community centre at Heartlands near Camborne was hosting a one day Cornish language festival with poetry and a range of musical genres all in the reviving Cornish tongue. I was curious to see culture in action, even more so to hear some Cornish being spoken, and so entered the community hall a little apprehensive as I was assumedly the only non-Cornish attendee but very much intrigued. Sporting a festival wristband and a bottle of Knocker ale (named after the mythical folk who would knock on the mine walls to indicate lodes) in hand, I passed into the hall and settled into an evening of watching acts of folky music interspersed by poetry readings, all in the rather melodious Cornish language.

The evening finished off with a seven piece band performing Cornish psychedelic folk rock (yes, it's a musical genre) and I walked back to my miner's cottage with strains of the violins and electric keyboard in my ear accompanied by the totally unrecognisable lyrics of Cornish. It wasn't a big event, no more than a few dozen in attendance, but the Cornish language and culture is still being kept alive and nowhere else is it seen more than in the legacy that the mining industry left behind. This is the real Cornwall, away from the surf beaches and hostels of Newquay and the packed holiday cottages along the idyllic coastlines. Cornwall's soul is mining and the scattered reminders of this throughout the county tell the thousands of tourists who flock to the beaches of a time when Cornwall was not just at the tail end of

England, but was one of the centres of the industrial world.

I left Cornwall behind for the fringes of West Devon, not before running into closed heritage attractions at Heartland's World Heritage exhibition (closed due to lack of funds) and at Gwenapp Pit (the visitor centre similarly closed, this time due to 'health and safety'). This world heritage site, as mentioned, covers a vast area and the attractions are run independently, so achieving coordination and keeping the sites active, I imagine, is quite a task. The cycle trip was worthwhile though to see the bizarre ringed amphitheatre from which John Wesley, the father of Methodism, preached multiple times to the eager-eared mining population who, presumably, were only too glad to be told of another life in which they'd be rewarded for their duty to God and not have to go down a mine every day. The grassy circles, each inner circle descending down to a small centre circle, is tucked away behind people's back gardens. You'd almost never know it was there unless you manage to spot the alien-like markings shown on a satellite image. The Methodist church was strong in Cornwall with the miners, and many towns around the county have Methodist majorities - another lasting legacy of the days of mining culture in Cornwall.

I caught the train out of Redruth and hopped off at St Austell. Down the hill from the station lies Charlestown, a picturesque harbour that also had a large Wesleyan chapel, closed in 2000. The millennium was a bad time for Charlestown as it was also the year the harbour saw its last commercial load sail out to sea. Nowadays Charlestown is a well-preserved reminder of what a mining era port looked like with ships open to tourists moored up, but it now relies on those tourists for income with the buildings overlooking the water now alfresco dining and weekend break hotels. Once upon a time, the port was alive with copper from the nearby mines being shipped out, but now its walls embrace only a few tall ships and the odd local fisherman.

The trains took me further east to Plymouth and then up the Tamar River to Calstock where I planned to stay a couple of nights to take in the Devon side of the World Heritage site. The single track line up the valley to Gunnislake takes in some special views, especially those crossing the viaduct just before Calstock station where I would alight. We chugged slowly over the stone crossing; below I could see the quayside cottage where I'd be staying with my Airbnb host Tali. Off the train I sat on the saddle and let gravity take me down the hill to the water and to my accommodation with a room that led out onto a terrace over the water. Idyllic doesn't do the location justice. So green, so serene, again it's hard to believe that these areas of England were ever subject to such industry and extraction of earth and stone. Nature, aided by England's generous dosage of rain, has done everything she can to cover up the scars left by 19th century exploitation of the land. Tali showed me examples of her photography concerning the various mines in the area that dug deep for copper and arsenic mainly but also yielded manganese and tungsten. Together we made a plan to take a road trip the next day to visit the key sites and landscapes, she to capture it with her lens, I to try to describe it in ink.

After breakfast overlooking the flowing river, we departed for Morwellham Quay, a one-stop shop for the Edwardian mining village experience with traditional crafts, a farmyard and a host of other accoutrements to attract families and French school groups. Though it is 35km from the sea, Morwellham Quay was the richest copper port in the empire with 300 ton ships navigating their way up the now silted Tamar River to export the ore from nearby mines. One of those mines, though closed in 1868 due to its small size, was the George and Charlotte mine which has since been opened up for tourists to explore in cages pulled by an electric engine driven by Rick, an expert on local mining history. As they're Calstock neighbours, Tali introduced us and we got talking about the world heritage status while other passengers stooped low and boarded the caged carriages. Rick's view was that being listed by UNESCO has had little effect, both on visitor numbers and motivation to keep mining heritage alive.

'The powers that be in Cornwall are ashamed of the mining history. They want to sell Cornwall as sun, sea and sand. Forget about the mines and engine houses - they don't bring in enough people or make enough money at the end of the day. That's why we have to disneyfy places like Morwellham to attract anyone'.

It was a fair point. As with many other World Heritage sites in the UK that I'd seen, the heritage alone is not enough to keep many places afloat and they have to diversify their business. For the owners of these sites, 85% of which are small-scale private ownerships, the visitor numbers have to pay for the cost of restoring and retaining the buildings and landscape. Engine houses, stacks and mines really have no purpose nowadays, but other uses for them can be found. Of course, those that are attractive because of their position like Wheal Coates are kept as they are, but other sites like Devon Great Consuls (now mountain biking trails) and the chimney stack up Kit Hill (now a phone mast) have found modern day uses. The management plan for this World Heritage site admits that allowing new industry to develop near heritage sites would be in keeping with the industrial status, but whether that would involve a return to mining remains to be seen. Lithium mining has been talked about in the news as it's key in battery production and can be found in some of the old mines around Cornwall. Tin mining could also return to closed mines like South

Crofty as global supply has decreased and prices have risen, making it economically viable again. Lithium and tin are both used in the production of electric cars so could our trend towards green energy for transport be the catalyst for a resurgence in Cornish mining? If so, would Cornwall still feel 'ashamed' to be providing the key metals involved in the production of the latest technology?

The truth is that Cornwall should be proud of its mining history, alongside its more pleasing natural features that attract the holidaymakers. Rick drove the electric train into the mine and we passed into the darkness, water dripping from the jagged rock ceilings. Up on the ledges, illuminated by spotlights, lifesize figurines were bashing metal stakes into the rock or chipping away at the rockface with rudimentary tools. Rick stopped the train and got out to demonstrate the process of boring the rock, twisting a stake into a hole in the rock and smashing a hammer upon its flat end to send the stake a few centimetres deeper. That was the action for thousands of men, for thousands of hours over thousands of days. Dynamite could help them along the way, but there was still hard work to be done. It's still stunning to realise the toil that the miners endured for the sake of extracting a metal, the riches of which would never really be reflected on their dinner table. Now we ride around these mines on theme park trains, but the miners had to walk miles every day to get to work and to get around the mines. Rick's words, just like every account of mining I'd read while in Cornwall and Devon, resonated - so much so I didn't even realise I'd broken my 'no entering mines' promise. Oh well, no point renewing the promise if I just keep on breaking it. Really, going down mines to explore isn't so bad. I just thank God I never had to work down one.

UK UNESCO World Heritage Site #25 of 28

Stonehenge, Avebury and Associated Sites (1986)

Solstice sunset, stars, and sunrise at the stones

'*It'll be full of weirdos*', '*Why would you want to spend all night in a field?*', '*It's just a bunch of stones, right?*'.

It was fair to say I'd heard a fair few opinions on the matter of attending the Summer Solstice at

Stonehenge. The henge is one of the most striking symbols of England, and one of the most recognisable structures on Earth, but the idea of wanting to spend all night with the stones accompanied by a load of pagans and hippies, seemed pretty alien to most people's sensibilities. With around 1.5 million visitors a year, Stonehenge is one of the UK's premier tourist attractions. Those visitors pay around £20 each to park, walk around a visitor centre, then take a bus and view the stone megaliths from around 15 metres away. That's all well and good, but Stonehenge wasn't exactly built for long-range selfies and bucket list ticks. Theories range but the clearest use of Stonehenge by its Neolithic constructors was to mark the solstices, the two times of the year when the sun seems to stand still in the sky before tilting back on its axis. These solstices (from the Latin 'solstitium' meaning 'sun standing still') are some of the very few times per year when the general public are allowed to reign free at Stonehenge to celebrate the arrival of winter or summer and to practise pagan beliefs related to these seasonal events.

I had to be there for it. As I've argued before, it's far better to see these heritage sites in use and a chance to get up close and personal with the famous stones was too good an opportunity to miss. Whatever the weather, whatever the crowds, whatever the strange people that I might encounter (and isn't that part of the attraction?), the night of Thursday 20th June was to be spent with the sunset, the stars, the sunrise, and Stonehenge.

First, I just had to get there. As always, I hadn't chosen the easy option. Setting off on an afternoon cycle ride from my mate Stevo's house in Swindon (kindly hosting me pre-world heritage site again), I tackled the couple of hills going south and within an hour made it to Avebury, the first site of the World

Heritage listing on the way to Stonehenge. Arriving into the tiny village I spotted the formation of the large stone circle that surrounds Avebury, shoulder height singular rocks with a ditch running behind them. Nowadays with a large pub at its axis and an A road running straight through it, Avebury can be hard to imagine as an ancient religious site but it still attracts pagan worshippers at the solstices, a quieter experience I would assume to that at Stonehenge. Still, the Red Lion pub had security manning fences around it and the village greens were populated with large tour groups and dog walkers. On the way out after a walk around, I started counting the number of horse-drawn wagons heading towards Avebury that I passed. Cars queued behind them to overtake on the narrow country roads, but the riders, dressed in bright, flowery costumes, seemed unperturbed and in truth it was nice to see a slower pace to the usual speeding motorists on country lanes. Clearly, this bright Thursday afternoon was the prelude to a special evening in the annual calendar.

It was also the prelude to a deluge that started just as I climbed up onto the Salisbury Plains. I'm no stranger to getting wet while riding, but feeling the rain soak through the layers I'd be wearing all night brought on an attitude of 'what's the flaming point?' The weather had said it would be dry but if it was just going to rain all night then I could envision a very miserable Greg come the morning. Well, sod it. If I got wet, I got wet I told myself as I cycled on. The rain continued all the way until I got to the military camp next to Stonehenge when, miraculously, the west started to brighten and the sun broke through to create rainbows behind me. On the approach I caught my first glimpse of the world's most famous stone circle, tiny compared to the vast fields surrounding it and already thronging with revellers.

Now, before we get on to Stonehenge itself, a little

history and a disclaimer is required. When Neolithic people around 4600 years ago decided to build a stone circle to replace an earlier timber circle, they transported 80 bluestones 150 miles from south Wales to create, historians presume, a sacred burial site. Over the course of 200 years, these bluestones were joined by 30 Sarsen stones brought from Marlborough, 25 miles away, and were arranged in a 30 metre diameter circle with a ring of 30 lintel stones on top. Nowadays we can see a few lintels resting on top of standing stones, but back then there would have been a complete circle of stones almost 5 metres up in the air. How they managed to do this archaeologists still can't agree, but it's certainly a remarkable feat. The stones remained throughout the various periods of British history through Romans, Saxons and all the other rulers until its ownership passed from Henry VIII after the Dissolution of Amesbury Abbey (is there any part of English history he didn't affect?) and then into private hands until the 20th century when restoration work was started and the stones were given to the State.

The restoration work is the part of the story that many visitors don't know and never learn about Stonehenge. Though English Heritage now acknowledge that lintels were replaced and standing stones concreted during the early 20th century, they were previously accused of hiding the restoration work from the public. The truth is that pretty much every stone has been moved or restored in some way, many of them being straightened and given concrete bases which belie the belief that these stones have stood as they are since Neolithic times. What we see today is tourism motivated reconstruction, not the creation of prehistoric people. It's the reason why Constable's painting and other artwork featuring Stonehenge from the 18th and 19th centuries display a noticeably different crowd of stones from what we see today. I suppose it's to be expected. Very few of the world's ancient heritage sites have had no TLC, but it's the assumption by many who visit Stonehenge that the last people to put the lintels up on the stones were the original builders that makes Stonehenge seem a bit of a con. The information and photos are out there now, but I guarantee the majority of the British population, for whom Stonehenge stands as a national icon, don't know the half about the cosmetic surgery Stonehenge has undergone. Does it matter? Well, I guess people should be informed, but it shouldn't detract from the wonder that Stonehenge inspires. The fact remains that thousands of years ago our ancestors moved these stones into a formation akin to what we see today in order to effectively create the world's first computer, a reliable calculator of the movement of the earth. Even though we still know so little about the stones, it's remarkable, whatever the story given to us by the guidebooks.

So, now we're all informed, time to get up close to the stones themselves. I locked my bike to a fence and walked up into the field and into the stone circle where a Druid ceremony had just begun. Druids venerate nature as the core principle of their spiritualism and have performed ceremonies at Stonehenge since the early 20th century, imitating Iron Age druids who worshipped the solstices thousands of years ago. A sizeable crowd had formed around a man who, for lack of better comparison, resembled Gandalf and a few ladies who were dressed in green with garlands round their heads. They were leading the crowd in various repeat-after-me verses which involved turning to the various points of the compass and hailing the direction with calls for peace.

'Let there be peace in the north' and we'd all turn to the north and repeat Gandalf's words. It was simple enough to join in, though it did attract a fair few giggles from those who couldn't take an old bloke with a mighty white beard, carrying a staff and wearing a

white tunic seriously. In fairness, it was all treated pretty light heartedly and Gandalf saw the funny side when he was informed by a few sharp-minds in the crowd that he'd missed out the call for peace in the east after we'd moved round the other three directions. If any direction from the UK needs peace it's the east, I thought to myself. Gandalf was perhaps thinking the same a few minutes later as he launched into giving an impassioned speech about Iran/US relations and Trumpian politics to his captive audience.

While Gandalf ranted, the crowd started noticing a double rainbow appearing in the dark clouds in the east. It was quite a sight. Talk about peace in the east, there was something arguably even better. At least it allowed Gandalf to change topic and express the change in fortunes in the weather which was greatly enhancing the natural beauty surrounding the site. *'Happy Solstice everyone!' 'Happy Solstice one and all!'* We all exchanged greetings, rather like church-goers on Christmas Eve, and then the service ended with everyone wondering what on earth to do next with their lives having just seen a double rainbow and a druid ceremony.

It was now about 30 minutes before the sunset so I extracted myself from the crowd in the centre of the stones and took up a position on the ridge that surrounds the stones to see the sun descend behind the lintels, rays peeking out through the gaps and then finally dropping below a clump of trees on the horizon. The stones turned to elephant grey, but the crowd inside kept beating their drums, perched on the low stones inside the circle, while a female bagpiper puffed through 'Amazing Grace' and people around me started setting up picnics and smoking a wide variety of substances that produced wafts of peculiar smells as I walked amongst them.

I walked around the stones a few times and realised the sheer variety of people that the Summer Solstice at Stonehenge attracts. By no means it is just pagans and neo-druids. In fact, the people we most associate with this event make up a very small percentage of the attendees. There's no real majority group in truth. You get Wiltshire locals made up of families with kids, young couples, groups of friends, and teens looking to party. Then there are the visitors: the lone backpackers on their world journeys, the tourists wanting to say they've 'done' Stonehenge, the spiritualists seeking peace, the amateur photographers, the various religious groups like the loud Hare Krishnas and the helpful Street Pastors, the tribal representees like the group of Native Americans visiting, and many, many other sections of society. To be honest, I don't think I've ever seen so many different people, from so many different walks of life, at one single event. Go to a football match and you see football fans, go to a concert and you see music lovers, but the Summer Solstice at Stonehenge, it seemed to attract just about every type of person living in the UK today. It was an incredible display of the rich diversity we enjoy in the United Kingdom, and the setting, an icon of England and the oldest man-made structure in the country, seemed wholly appropriate.

Stonehenge is the heritage symbol of the UK and the one we can all group around once a year (well twice with the winter solstice, if you're willing to brace the cold), but its very heritage is at risk, according to a band of campaigners walking around with placards saying '*Save Stonehenge World Heritage Site from the bulldozers!*' I stopped to talk to them a while and to find out about the threat of a tunnel being built to carry the nearby A303 under the site. On the face of it, a tunnel to replace the sight of speeding cars zipping by Stonehenge seems like a pretty good idea. It would take away the noise of the traffic driving by and bring more peace to these natural surroundings, restoring the ancient landscape. Just from this perspective, you might have thought people would be lobbying for it, not against it. However, as I discovered, the government's plan would significantly threaten the UNESCO World Heritage status, bringing condemnation from UNESCO itself as well as many who cherish Stonehenge.

The issue is that the proposed tunnel would only extend around 3 kilometres, too short to avoid causing irreparable damage to archaeological sites under the earth that span 5 kilometres in width. Obviously this threatens Stonehenge with having its UNESCO status revoked, but there are several other interesting arguments against the tunnel such as the £1.6 billion cost and the fact that the road tunnel would take away the view that millions have of Stonehenge while driving by. Stonehenge has become an icon perhaps because of how easily it can be seen and, though the road scars the ancient landscape, it also allows millions of Brits to view the most famous heritage site in their country. I myself, previous to this visit, had only ever seen Stonehenge from the inside of a passing car, and I suspect most British people are the same. Both English Heritage and the National Trust, who are the entrusted guardians of the area, support the tunnel being built, arguably because they would benefit from increased numbers having to pay to see the henge. Widening the road would also allow more traffic to pass and therefore more potential visitors. As persuasive as the campaigners holding the placards aloft were, when reading the opposite arguments the next day I could see the advantages of a tunnel too despite my concern for the integrity of Stonehenge.

It's a hard one to call. At present the planning application has been accepted and work is due to start in 2021. Organisations like the Stonehenge Alliance are still campaigning for a rethink, but it looks like 5 years of tunnel building will commence near

Stonehenge in the next few years bar any major changes of mind. Looking behind me into the darkness, I could see the lights of cars speeding along past the site. Throughout the night, even at 3am, there were constant streams of huge trucks travelling by. It's an important artery between London and the south-west, but sadly passes so close to this extraordinarily special site. Hiding it with a tunnel seems the obvious solution, but comes with huge sacrifice and the loss of a popular view. It's the challenge that heritage around the UK and the world faces on a planet that is getting busier and more populated. What deserves to be preserved in the face of seemingly vital progress?

Even with the arguments swimming around my head, my eyelids were growing heavy and so I attempted some shut-eye on a slope in a quieter part of the site. Walking around I'd seen a few people huddled up and even some within the stone circle trying to lie down for 40 winks, but after an hour of lying on the wet grass I found it too cold and too noisy to get any quality of sleep and so resolved to passing the time until sunrise by keeping my mind active rather than trying to make it fall unconscious. I warmed my frozen feet up with a walk over to Sanger's Stage Show, the one performance tent on the site that was playing music. It made a welcome change from the constant beat of the drums within the stone circle and so I settled into watching one act after the other of varying quality keep the crowd warm with fiddles, accordions, acoustic guitars and the like. No amplified music is allowed on site, meaning that noise doesn't spread far. There are quiet areas and louder areas, depending on how you want to interact with the stones. One thing you can't avoid is being surrounded by smoke exhaled by other people, legal or illegal, and it was clear the ban on drugs and alcohol hadn't completely worked, but, I assumed, compared to previous years when alcohol had been allowed, there was a relatively calm atmosphere aside from the few teenagers who had experimented a little too far. This scene was far from the famous Free Festivals of the 1970s and 80s when tens of thousands of New Age travellers converged upon Stonehenge to party with freely sold drugs, causing destruction to a site that provided no facilities to cater for so many people. The Solstice celebrations were stopped in 1985 and only restarted in 1999. Since then the events have had their fair share of trouble, but are nowadays well-policed and well-facilitated. Rubbish collectors do rounds during the night, portaloos are bunched around the site and you can dine on vegan burgers for dinner and crepes for breakfast if you wish to bear the queues. Overall, it's a reasonably pleasant experience if you can bear the cold and annoyances of being surrounded by people all night.

After a beautiful sunset, we got the added bonus of a clear night with the stars fully visible and a red moon rising over the stones and then, around 3.50am, the main event showed signs of starting. On the horizon to the north-east, the pitch black started lightening with shades of blue, then orange. Slowly the whole sky started to colour, blue growing brighter and brighter until the full extent of the night's revelry was revealed. Heads started appearing out of sleeping bags, the rhythm of the relentless drumming in the stone circle increased, and crowds started appearing on the hills, an army of people who had woken up early to travel to Stonehenge to witness the rising of the sun. It's a strange idea really. Why do people, many of them perfectly sane and normal, feel the need to wake up at 3am on a workday to travel into the countryside to watch an event that happens every single day? Given that the 21st June has the earliest sunrise of the year, it defies logic that so many people make this day the one day of the year they purposefully wake up to witness the daily ritual of the sun rising. Every other day of the year there is no one around Stonehenge at sunrise, bar a few beleaguered lorry drivers driving past. But on the 21st of June there are around 10,000 people from all walks of life gathered in and around the stone circle waiting with bated breath for the top of the sun to appear from behind the trees on the horizon.

04.51am and a huge cheer arose from the crowd. Beyond the mist-filled fields and dark mini-forests on the top of the furthest hill, a slither of a blinding white disk emerged and over the next few minutes it rose and rose until the full circle was revealed. Witnessed through the stone circle thousands of years ago when Stonehenge was fully intact, the sun's rays would have shone straight through the 'slaughter stones' outside the circle and would have struck the altar stone in the centre with inch-perfect accuracy. On the solstice in 2019, what is believed to have been the altar stone is now recumbent and had lots of tourists and teenagers standing on it to get the best picture with their smartphones, but the sun still shone towards it as it did all those thousands of years ago when Neolithic Britons built their sacred circle. Thousands of people around me all raised their smartphones above the heads of the people in front of them to capture exactly the same images as everybody else. Such is the modern trend to film or photograph the very event that you have woken up at 3am on a workday to see, just to show to others who weren't there. The sunrise, indeed the whole event, seemed a bit like an amateur photography festival, but amongst the crunch of the shutters and the screens in your face, it was possible to appreciate the utter splendour of the very beginning of a new day on Planet Earth.

So, after waiting all night long, summer had officially begun and now the thousands in the crowds could trudge back to their cars and go to work. Others decided to continue partying or practising yoga, the Hare Krishna were still chanting and the drummers were, somehow, still going, but around 6am I decided I'd had enough. I was cold, still wet, dead tired, and had to cycle ten miles to Salisbury station to get home. So I collected my bike from the fence and cycled away from the stones to the above-ground (for now) A303.

Was it worth it? Well, for once in your life, sure. It had certainly been an experience to feel the ancient (though heavily chipped and restored) megaliths of England's prehistoric icon, and I felt fortunate to have witnessed the rare coincidence of a sunset and a sunrise at solstice at Stonehenge. I felt like the stars had aligned, just as our ancestors so perfectly aligned the stones to witness, and calculate, the sun beaming through them. Such perfection, a combination of human endeavour and natural beauty, coupled with such calculation. Perhaps it was worth the effort of dragging those stones all the way from Wales after all.

UK UNESCO World Heritage Sites #26 of 28

Heart of Neolithic Orkney (1999)

A long time ago, in a land far, far away

The prow of the Hamnavoe rose up with the huge wave and then smashed down on the sea surface. The pasty I'd eaten just after we'd set sail did more or less the same in my stomach. A second's calm and then up the prow and my stomach rose again. The queasiness sent my eyes scouring for sick bags. Swaying drunkenly through the restaurant, clutching onto anything immovable that would stop me from going arse over tit, I made my way to the sun deck at the back. Groups of passengers were sitting on the metal benches, the same shade of green as each other. I sat down on a free bench but jumped up almost immediately when I realised where the splatter of orange chunks coating the deck had come from. The ferry lurched in the unrelenting waves once again and all of us gathered in the freezing wind on the sundeck prayed for the 90 minute journey to end.

Sheltered from the worst of the elements, the arrival into Orkney's southernmost connection to the Scottish mainland was relatively calm, and I could even start to appreciate the majesty of the tub-shaped mountains around us as we cruised into the quaint harbour-side village of Stromness. With the noticeable absence of trees on the green hills, the countryside looked bleak but Stromness appeared snug and welcoming in its remoteness. I'd never been so far north in the British Isles before. Indeed, before 1472, this wasn't Britain, nor was this Scotland: this was Norway. After the failure of the Norwegian King Christian to pay the dowry for his daughter Margaret to marry Scotland's James III, the islands were annexed by the Kingdom of Scotland ending the history of Scandinavian settlers, the most famous of these being the Vikings who stayed for centuries. However, before those Vikings, in fact a long time before them, there was a Neolithic population on Orkney that left quite a mark. The most significant Neolithic remains in Western Europe are found all across the Orkney Islands, but the most important of these are the four World Heritage designated sites in the south-west of the mainland that I had come to visit.

Now I was on Orkney I just had to find a way to the sites. The four main constituents of the World Heritage site are divided into two zones. Three of the sites (the Standing Stones of Stenness, the Ring of Brodgar and Maeshowe) are within walking distance of each other, located on and near the isthmus that separates the two largest lakes on Orkney. The main road running between the two largest towns on Orkney (Stromness and Kirkwall) runs right along the southern border of the World Heritage site and buses are frequent. Getting to those three would be easy. The fourth site, the Neolithic village of Skara Brae, would be more challenging. I consulted bus timetables and found that while a bus could get me there in the morning, that bus was the only service of the day and

I'd have no way of getting back to Stromness. It would also only give me 85 minutes to enjoy the state of preservation UNESCO says is *'unparalleled for a prehistoric settlement in northern Europe'*. I was sure I'd need more time.

On the day, a windy but bright Tuesday in July, I decided that cycling would be my best bet. So I collected a well-loved city bike from a local hire company and wobbled my way down the narrow high street in Stromness to the country roads that would take me to Skara Brae. It was a good choice, despite the flat, plastic pedals and heavy weight of the frame. From the upright position on the bike I could survey the dramatic landscape of the island, cycling past bare green hills and placid lochs with the odd farm or remote house dotted around. After a while I saw a turning for Yesnaby, a place the gentleman at the hire centre had circled on my map. *'You've got to make a stop at the cliffs on the way. They're quite something'.*

I turned off the main road and followed a single track for a mile or two towards the cliffs. The beauty of dramatically shaven cliffs with seabirds nesting inside the crags was worth the detour. I walked south along the cliffs and scaled a plinth like headland with pyramid stacks of stones arranged on its highest point. A little further down, a real stack with a gaping hole in its body stood resiliently strong in the midst of pounding waves and white foam. It was stunning, but the feeling of being on the edge of the world, the sense of inhospitality with the fierce chill of the wind on a midsummer's day, was undeniable. It was remarkable, I thought to myself, that anyone would come across this land and decide to settle here.

People did though, and in their thousands. While we now tend to have a south-centric view of the UK in terms of culture and ideas, back in Neolithic times Orkney was very much the hub for innovation in

Britain. In terms of pottery and stone henges, the inhabitants of Orkney were the trendsetters for the rest of the country. What Orcadians 5000 years ago did, the rest of the British Isles copied. Of course, the innovators of 3100 BC Orkney needed somewhere to live, a place to call home and some shelter from the intense winds I was now becoming very familiar with as I cycled on up the west coast of Mainland. Nestled above an arcing sandy beach (though once ago much further inland), Skara Brae is the exceptionally well-preserved Neolithic village where our ancestors slept, cooked, talked, raised their children and, importantly, kept on top of their farming duties.

The Neolithic people built their houses and tunnels to protect themselves from the wind, but eventually it broke through, revealing their village to the relatively modern world back in 1850. In the winter of that year, a terrible storm blew the turf off the top of a small hill revealing an outline of houses without roofs. It was explored by amateur Victorian archaeologists but mostly left until the 1920s when it was properly excavated, though the question of how old it is wasn't answered until radiocarbon dating in the 1970s. The results revealed that Skara Brae had been settled from 3180 BC for a period of around 600 years making it one of the oldest surviving human settlements on earth. Why it was abandoned and what happened to its inhabitants is a matter for speculation even today, but what we can surmise from Skara Brae is that the original inhabitants were skilled masons in a time before metal had come into use. What those inhabitants looked like and what language they spoke is unknown, but what we do know about them is that they succeeded in creating an intelligently planned living space that has survived five millennia.

Leaving the bike in the car park (no need for locks, this is Orkney as the bike hire gentleman had said), I entered the visitor centre, took a good look around the cramped information boards and then walked 5000 years back in time to Neolithic Orkney. To help with the time travel, stone plaques had been placed along the 500 metre path running from the visitor centre to Skara Brae itself. I quickly passed man landing on the moon and the invention of the telephone. A few steps on and I was into the Crusades and then the fall of Rome. Into BC and the building of the Great Wall of China and the Parthenon passed me by. I was still quite a distance from the gated entrance to the village. In 2100 BC I passed Stonehenge, the World Heritage site I'd been to just a few weeks before and one that was probably inspired by the stone henges that form part of this World Heritage site. Finally, after passing the Pyramids of Giza built two thousand five hundred years before the birth of Jesus, I arrived in 3100 BC to find a site about the size of a basketball court filled with stone-lined trenches and tunnels topped with turf. It reminded me of Hobbiton; quaint, grassy rabbit-holes.

In truth, it appears this way because of the excavation work that has been done and the prettifying of the site to make it appealing to camera-toting tourists. Skara Brae is actually a village built upon multiple other older villages, as was the Neolithic way of modernising by building on top of what already exists. The people here clearly liked their mod-cons. Each house had a hearth in the middle for cooking and for warmth, and stone dressers by the walls would have contained their possessions. Bed spaces were defined, though cramped to our modern eyes as it is presumed that the Neolithic people slept in an upright foetal position. What I found especially genius was the use of covered tunnels to connect each house, meaning that the villagers could go and knock on each other's doors for a cup of sugar without having to venture outside in the wet. We still construct tunnels between buildings in cold cities nowadays, so this idea has been passed on for over 5000 years. They also recycled, using mounds of food waste, shells, and bones to stabilise the walls and provide insulation. One thing that struck me as I walked around is our usual perception of Neolithic people and how far it is from the probable truth. We see the Stone Age in cartoons like The Flintstones, and in art and films the people are often portrayed as dumb or stupid. *'Go back to the Stone Age'*, has become a common retort to people believed to have unmodern views on societal issues. However, these visions of cavemen dressed in skins hitting rocks with rocks don't allow us to appreciate the reality that these people were intelligent. Amongst all their engineering achievements, they created art by drawing patterns upon their pottery and making coloured pastes to paint their objects. These weren't the people we often think they are, and going to Skara Brae dispels our misconceptions of our ancestors. They were building these villages and stone circles before the Egyptians ever had the idea of pyramids. You try constructing perfectly designed and built stone houses that last 5000 years with no metal tools and see how you get on. For what they did, regardless of their natural environment and technology, these mysterious people were remarkable.

The clearest evidence of this is the fact that they had enough time in amongst the necessities of life to build stone circles. These were people who thought beyond their own world. They were aware of spirituality. At least we presume that this was what the standing stones at Stenness and at the Ring of Brodgar were for. My guide for the Ring of Brodgar, Martin, rounded off his tour by revealing the best explanation he'd heard for the ring of four metre high stones: poles for a washing line to dry clothes. That, and the theories of alien spaceship landing sites, can probably be safely dismissed. Most probable is that these stones had ceremonial purposes. This is clearer at Stenness, as the four remaining stones out of the original 11 or 12 surround a hearth in the middle. In contrast, the Ring of Brodgar's centre is archaeologically sterile. Its purpose is less clear, though its position on top of a hill with 31 of its original 60 stones still standing is more impressive.

As they're just a mile apart, it's possible to see one stone circle from the other. The Stones of Stenness are dated earlier and so I started with them, braving the walk on the side of the road from the bus stop to arrive at the stones with plenty of time before the free tour given by one of the Orkney Rangers. I walked around the stones, trying to decide which walk was more dangerous, the one I'd just done from the bus stop while being shaved by passing traffic, or this one around the stones with its plentiful deposits of fresh sheep droppings to accidentally tread in. Though the field with the stones in is now council-owned, apparently the local farmer likes to let his sheep graze in this field to piss off tour bus drivers who have to deal with their passengers walking up the bus with shit on their shoes.

Once a dozen of us had assembled, we started our tour a hundred feet or so from the stones at Barnhouse settlement, a collection of dwellings, though now reconstructed, that resemble Skara Brae without the tunnel passageways. One of the major differences between Barnhouse and Skara Brae though is Structure Eight, a large space with a hearth in the centre that would have presumably had a stone roof over it. How they managed to span seven metres square is a mystery, but the real question is the purpose of this very large house. Perhaps it was home to the leader of the tribe that built the Stones of Stenness, or possibly it was an indoor ceremonial site for when the weather turned bad during rituals. Anyone's guess is as good as everyone else's.

The same can be said for the Stones of Stenness,

indeed for the whole of the Heart of Neolithic Orkney World Heritage site. What was it for? The truth is we just don't know, and it's unlikely we'll ever find out. The stones that tantalise us with their mystery keep standing, albeit with plenty of lichen and bite marks from the wind. In truth, we are just fortunate they are still here. In 1814 a farmer, possibly the great great grandfather of the one who gets a kick out of shit-shoed tourists, was about to dynamite the stones as they got in the way of his mowing. Fortunately the local community stopped him. The Victorians, just like at Stonehenge, also messed about with the site by trying to reconstruct it. It appears that not everyone appreciates just leaving the stones alone, though that's probably what we should do. The stones are now part of the natural landscape and they were put here because they perfectly enhance the land. The Neolithic people didn't just build these stone circles anywhere, the sites were very carefully chosen for their visibility. The Ring of Brodgar is like a crown set on a mound surrounded by low hills, an amphitheatre it's often said. It's visible for miles around, even more noticeable because of the water on almost every side.

I walked along the lake-lined string of land that holds one of the greatest concentrations of Neolithic remains in the world to get to my next stop. Though not included in the World Heritage listing as it was discovered a few years after the inscription, the Ness of Brodgar is without doubt deserving of the title of being universally important to mankind. As often happens, the site of a vast Neolithic settlement, really a city given its size, was found in the most mundane of ways. A farmer ploughed up a stone and the archaeologists, already keen to see what was under the turf between the two stone rings, ploughed in to dig up a massive complex of Neolithic buildings as well as the associated pottery and stone tools. Sixteen years after the first find, up to a hundred diggers converge on the archaeological site for two months each year to uncover more of what many experts believe to be the key to answering many of our questions about Neolithic Britain.

'*It has the potential to rewrite every book ever written about the Neolithic Age*', Roy, our amiable guide, told the crowd of over 150 who had turned up like me to the first open day of the season. I've been on some pretty large tours in my time, but 150 people on one tour was staggering. Roy wasn't intimidated though. Armed with a personal microphone, he directed us to a scaffold platform from where a lucky 50 of us could gain a good view of the main excavation. Down below, on their muddy knees and soaked in the pouring rain, dozens of diggers worked with trowels to remove the dirt from stones jutting out of the sides of the trenches. This was archaeology in action, and it was humbling to see. Roy described what we were seeing below and what they had found so far, impressing upon us the fact that it's one of the most important archaeological sites in the world, though its lack of funding and World Heritage status wouldn't suggest so. What the diggers unearth here could dramatically change our understanding of our ancestors' culture and beliefs. It's worth keeping an eye on their progress over the summer digs to see what wonders they uncover as they excavate further down.

Of course, it's quite possible that the Ness of Brodgar will become a big tourist site, perhaps the star of the collection of Neolithic sites. At the moment the tours are led by voluntary donation and there's limited parking. The diggers seemed pretty surprised to see 150 people turn up in the rain for the first tour of the year. Perhaps it's a sign of things to come as tourism becomes an even greater financial source for projects like this. It costs around £200,000 a year for the excavation work, begging the question of why the site doesn't charge for tours. '*Well, then we'd have to provide you with toilets*' was Roy's answer.

Indeed, having facilities really would turn this archaeological dig into a tourist destination. I overheard two ladies talking to each other, one sighing to the other *'if only they had a visitor centre'*. Personally, I'm not sure I agree. I liked going somewhere historically important and not having to walk through a gift shop on the way out, or having the option to spend £3 on a frothy coffee, or being bombarded with requests to become a 'friend' of the site, or generally feeling like a tourist. It was nice to go to a working archaeological site, see it in action, listen to someone working on the project talk about it and then drop some money into a donation barrel on the way out. No fuss or frills. It felt more authentic. Then again, given the torrential conditions, I probably wouldn't have turned down a seat in a warm, glassy cafe with a cappuccino in front of me. Contradictions are allowed in these circumstances.

Next along the B9055 was the Ring of Brodgar. A grassy footpath led me into a field and then over the southern causeway that crosses the ditch around the stone circle. Though built at a similar time, Stonehenge and the Ring of Brodgar are really quite different. Brodgar has a much larger circumference, more stones (though none with lintels) and possibly even more mystery surrounding it. It too has had alterations made by humans (many fallen stones were placed back into their sockets in 1908) and by nature as lightning strikes have toppled two of the stones in the last hundred years. Our guide, the warm and vastly knowledgeable Martin, told us of the day in 1980 when he'd visited the stone circle after a huge storm and saw how one of the stones had been sliced by lightning, a huge shard of stone sent flying into the centre of the circle. It has since been placed in the grass next to its mother, but it's a reminder of the power of nature, as well as the exposed position of this stone circle right in the centre of a cauldron of hills.

Another significant alteration since Neolithic days is the addition of graffiti. Now before you start tutting, some of this graffiti (not the additions made by vandals earlier in the year mind) gives us a valuable insight into the history between now and the 4000 year old stones. Martin pointed out twig runes which suggest that a Viking called Bjorn once thought to inscribe his name upon the stones. Seven centuries later the stones drew many Victorian tourists who also enjoyed leaving their mark, significantly though as they were showing off their new found ability to write at the time of the passing of the Education Act. Again, just like at Stonehenge and on many other ancient objects around the UK, graffiti is etched, proving that these sites have drawn visitors for centuries to come and wonder at the meaning behind what Britain's prehistoric people left behind.

In some ways you can't blame them. Graffiti can actually add to the story of an object. Nowhere is this more true than at Maeshowe, my fourth and final stop for the day. I'd seen where Neolithic people lived, where they supposedly worshipped, and now appropriately I was off to see where they were buried. At least that's what experts assume Maeshowe is. A burial chamber is the most educated guess as to what purpose this stone chamber served. To get there I had to trek along the main road again, away from the chambered cairn itself, to reach the visitor centre where I was greeted by two bantering blokes on the front desk who printed off my reservation and told me to wait for the bus to the site. Maeshowe requires a reservation as the chamber, and the bus to the site, can only hold 25 people at a time. There were a fair few groups of tourists who walked in while I waited and were told that they'd have to book a tour for tomorrow as today was sold out. Some turned back around resignedly, others got a little incensed as if their whole holiday plans had been ruined, but I hope they all found time to visit Maeshowe in the end for it's truly a unique and fascinating experience.

Getting off the bus down the road, you are herded across the main road and onto a fenced path that leads up to a turf covered mound. Bending down as if walking into a mine (the entrance is only a metre high and is nine metres long), you follow the arse in front of you until you are able to straighten up inside a square, stone-walled chamber. Immediately you notice the difference between the precisely measured, corbelled walls of the chamber and the white painted mess of bricks that make up the ceiling. The walls are Neolithic, the ceiling is Victorian. The original would have had a roof but this was first broken into by Vikings and then completely removed by Victorians, both of whom were looking for treasure that they never found. Strangely for a tomb, nothing of note has really been found in Maeshowe; no bones, no gifts to the Gods, no clues at all to the true purpose of this curious chamber.

The Vikings didn't take anything, but they certainly left something. Our guide Jack dimmed the lights in the chamber and shone his torch on the walls for us to see the vast amount of Viking graffiti left by Earl Harald's band of warriors. As told in the Orkneyinga saga, they were sheltering from a winter snowstorm in the cairn and they passed the time by writing some rather crude and boyish inscriptions upon the walls. Indeed, quite a few of the runes pass sexual comments about various women known to the men. Other graffiti shows a game of 'Who can write the highest' going on as the highest example of graffiti reads '*Tholfir Kolbeinsson carved these runes high up*' just above similar remarks with different names. Another theme of the graffiti is the promise of treasure in the north-west, as well as crosses from the recently christianised Vikings and a depiction of what appears to be a dragon. We shuffled around the chamber marvelling at these direct links to a group of people who usually we learn about in school and then mostly forget.

Though these Vikings clearly left their mark, Maeshowe's original marvel is the most stunning, though we were about six months too early to see it. Maeshowe's front entrance is perfectly aligned to allow the light of the setting sun on the Winter Solstice to pass through the entrance passage and illuminate the whole chamber. It's a spectacular event, viewable on Youtube, but one that I can imagine can only really be appreciated in person. Jack admitted that he'd only ever seen it on the internet, and given Orkney's poor winter weather there is only about a one in twenty chance of the clouds parting and the sun's rays being let into the chamber, but it has to be one of the most special events on the planet. An event that the Neolithic builders of Maeshowe perfectly engineered so that they could tell when the winter tide was turning back towards the prosperity of summer. As I have never, and likely never will see the winter solstice at Maeshowe, I'll give you this beautiful account of it from Orkney's famed poet George Mackay Brown.

> *The winter sun just hangs over the ridge of the Coolags. Its setting will seal the shortest day of the year, the winter solstice. At this season the sun is a pale wick between two gulfs of darkness. Surely there could be no darker place in the be-wintered world than the interior of Maeshowe.*
>
> *One of the light rays is caught in this stone web of death. Through the long corridor it has found its way; it splashes the far wall of the chamber. The illumination lasts a few minutes,*

then is quenched

Winter after winter I never cease to wonder at the way primitive man arranged, in hewn stone, such powerful symbolism.

George Mackay Brown could hardly be more right. Primitive though we describe them compared to ourselves in the Technology Age, the Neolithic Age people were able to achieve remarkable symbolism from stone, all while getting along with the necessities of life. Though we have so many questions to answer about them, the four (with the Ness of Brodgar should be five) sites in UNESCO's Heart of Neolithic Orkney inscription are clearly of monumental value and importance in our attempt to discover where we came from and who our ancestors were. Their legacy, their stones, cairns, and houses, have stood for so long, and we're only just beginning to understand and appreciate who and what they were. Hopefully, if only for the sake of the archaeologists digging in the rain soaked dirt at the Ness of Brodgar, we will get some answers one day.

UK World Heritage Sites #27 of 28

Jodrell Bank Observatory

One muddy festival for man, one giant telescope for mankind

'**B**ad news Greg - new world heritage site in UK announced today. Now 28!'

It was this Whatsapp message from my aunt that was the first to inform me what many friends and family would later notify me about. It had been 27 for 27 for almost a whole year. Going round the 27 UK World Heritage sites while 27 years old had seemed like the perfect coincidence, but now, just three weeks shy of my 28th birthday and the last of the list to visit, that list had been added to by UNESCO at their annual conference in Baku.

'It'll just have to be 28 for 28', I texted back.

Indeed, it would now have to be 28. Very fortunately the site that UNESCO had newly inscribed is located not a million miles away from the summer school I was teaching at. I worked out the timings between Sedbergh in Cumbria and the newly listed Jodrell Bank Observatory in Cheshire and found that it could be done without too much of a fuss on my weekly day off. Easy peasy. I'd squeeze it in the weekend before my trip to St Kilda in the Outer Hebrides and then I'd still be able to see all the sites in 365 days. The quest was still on! To Jodrell Bank and beyond!

Of course, things never work out simply like you plan them. Visiting the Jodrell Bank website a few days before the weekend I discovered that the whole site would be closed for the weekend. The annual Bluedot festival would be taking over the area around the radio telescope and so only those with a ticket for the festival would be able to visit. Just my luck. The one weekend I had to visit it and the ticket would set me back ten times what it usually costs to visit Jodrell Bank. It had to be done though. Reluctantly I shelled out for a Sunday ticket, reserved the cheapest hotel in Manchester for the Saturday night and organised the various trains I'd have to catch to get to the remote corner of the Cheshire countryside that the observatory is located in.

I've never really been one for festivals. Every summer I've worked in summer camps or schools and the time off that I've had I've tended to dedicate to going to football tournaments. Glastonbury, Latitude, Creamfields, Reading and Leeds; all the famous British summer festivals have simply passed me by.

Plenty of friends have gone to them but I've always been too busy (and too disorganised in October when tickets go on sale) to attend. Bluedot isn't nearly on the scale of the larger UK music festivals, but it still attracts tens of thousands to a muddy field in the middle of nowhere for a weekend of drinking, debauchery and doing your business in squalid conditions. Though Bluedot has plenty of the above, its theme is more bent towards the realm of science and space exploration. One of the world's most famous radio telescopes provides the setting for a long weekend of science talks, stalls, exhibitions and science-themed musical acts. This particular year being 50 years since Neil Armstrong jumped around on the moon meant that there would be some extra special events and celebrations of man's finest achievement. It was promising; a once-in-a-year opportunity to see the pioneer of radio space exploration surrounded by a festival of science and the latest addition to the UK's growing list of World Heritage sites. Moreover it was also an escape from teaching English day after day to sleepy teenagers while the summer days burned away outside the classroom windows. Anywhere on my day off would do, but Bluedot at the newly World Heritage inscribed Jodrell Bank would do very nicely.

Now that Jodrell Bank is part of the World Heritage set, and will inevitably attract more tourists because of this, something might have to be done about getting public transport to the site. For those without a car, there are no public buses in the area and the nearest train station is a good two and a half miles away. I chose to get the train from Manchester (once Northern Rail had helpfully cancelled the first one of the morning) to Goostrey and then walked the country roads to Jodrell Bank, forgoing the suggestion of getting a taxi. In the end, it was actually the taxi that got me. Walking along the left hand side of the narrow road I heard a vehicle approaching from behind. At

the same time a small truck appeared on the other side. Both cars slowed as the gap between them and me closed, but the vehicle behind me shaved my right arm with his wing mirror as it passed. In fairness, I hardly felt it. The vehicle, a black minivan taxi, was going pretty slowly, but even so, he had hit me. I clutched my arm in feigned pain, wincing convincingly and rubbing the area where the wing mirror had brushed me. Cristiano Ronaldo would have been impressed. The taxi stopped a little way ahead and waited for me to catch up. As I passed, the driver shouted out the window at me.
'Sorry pal! Did I hit you back there?'

'Yeah...

'Get in. I'll give you a lift to the festival'.

We passed by plenty of other people walking along the side of the road on our winding way through the country lanes. Many cyclists too. Once we got to the main car park I jumped out, thanked the apologetic taxi driver, and headed for the mud bath of the wristband checkpoint. It was squelchorific. Step on the wrong part and your foot would sink inches into the enveloping mud, covering your shoes and not letting go. Everyone else had wellies on. Amateur mistake on my part. I stepped cautiously up to the entrance, allowed a steward to slip a wristband onto my wrist (now I could be one of those cool kids who wear festival wristbands and never take them off) and then hot-footed it across a sea of churned up earth to the path.

It was easy enough to find the centre of the festival. Even while walking from the train station and in the taxi, every time I looked around or ahead of me there was this shape, like a white egg cup, towering above the landscape. It can be seen from the train too. It's captivating, alienic, bewildering. An ordered mess of steel supports holding up a bowl, 89 metres high, to the sky. I hastened towards it and found myself in the middle of one of the thoroughfares of the festival, right up against the gate that encircles it. Now almost at its base I could appreciate its mighty scale. Built in 1957, it was by far the biggest radio telescope in the world at that time and is the world's third largest even today. In layman's terms, the Lovell Telescope basically picks up radio waves coming down to earth from distant galaxies, black holes and exploded stars inside its parabolic dish (imagine an upturned contact lense). The white panelled contact lense reflects these waves onto a small object called a focus box which is located at the top of a tower in the centre of the dish. The focus box converts the radio waves it receives into electrical signals which travel down the telescope and into the control room which can then interpret the data and tell us what's going on in outer space. It's all a little hard to imagine but a good example of the telescope's ability is that it would be able to detect the signal from your smartphone if you were standing on Mars. Pretty smart stuff. Being a huge dish pointed up at the sky means that the fainter signals from space can be received and thus we can stretch further out into the galaxy and beyond to send and receive radio signals. In radio science, size is everything, and the Lovell Telescope's sheer size has meant that it has been used to conduct everything from alien life research to tracking American and Soviet space missions.

All this from a metal dish in the middle of a field just outside of Macclesfield. While its location may seem random, it's actually in a perfect position. When Sir Bernard Lovell wanted to move his radiowave research out of the centre of Manchester in the 1940s, the University of Manchester granted him their potato fields in the spot where the Lovell telescope now stands. The idea to position a telescope under some of the cloudiest skies on a famously cloudy island has been questioned by many before, but as the telescope is a radio telescope it doesn't matter at all what Manchester's weather is like. It's apparently one of the most common questions visitors have though, according to James, a student at the university and our guide for the first telescope walking tour of the day. A few dozen of us gathered around the meeting point holding our noses as the festival toilet team sucked the sewage out of the nearby portaloos. James graciously moved us towards the first stop on our 45 minute walking tour which covered probably no more than 100 metres in distance. Our geeky guide led us with his umbrella from info board to info board, stopping every twenty metres or so to regale us with the history and science of Jodrell Bank. The telescope shot to fame in 1957 when it was thrust into the action of the Space Age, tracking the Russian's intercontinental ballistic missile rocket that shot Sputnik up into space. A decade later and Jodrell Bank was able to steal the Russians' thunder by intercepting the first ever pictures from the surface of the moon transmitted from the Soviet Luna 9 Lander. These were printed in British newspapers before the Russians had a chance to show their success to the world. Nowadays it is used by science research teams who bid for time to use it for whatever research they want to conduct.

However, as James explained in answer to a question about going up the telescope, it is now closed for maintenance for around ten months as its surface panels need replacing, the refurbishment being carried out by the same company restoring Ironbridge Gorge which I'd seen covered in scaffolding in the Autumn. At other times it's possible to take a trip up in the lift to the sheds hanging off the sides of the structure and then climb inside the dish, blinding your eyes with the white panels that swoop upwards at an unscalable angle. It would be a little like being trapped in a porcelain fruit bowl. For the things that do find themselves in the bowl (namely rain and snow) there are holes and pipes to permit escape and the dish is able to turn enough on its side for snow to pour out onto the ground below. The telescope is actually pretty flexible, able to tilt almost 90 degrees and to be steered around 360 degrees on a circular railway track. This gives it the ability to be pointed any direction the scientists want, honing in on a particular area of the sky to pick up the radiowaves that help us to understand a little bit more about who we are, where we are, and where we came from.

It will also be one of the first places in the world to discover if there is an intelligent alien lifeform out there. Part of Jodrell Bank's remit is to aid SETI, the search for extraterrestrial life. The telescope can be used to send signals out into space in the hope that aliens have a similar device to us that can receive these radio waves and is able to send radio waves back. Of course, that requires the Lovell telescope to be operational and always listening for the eureka moment when/if we do hear from extraterrestrials. This raised a rather pertinent question from a member of our tour about whether hosting a festival like Bluedot at the telescope was actually sabotaging our attempts to find alien life. What if this is the weekend they decide to drop us a line? Usually visitors to Jodrell Bank are required to turn off their mobile phones as the signals mess with the telescopes and cause the data to skew. James had mentioned a past story of scientists believing they had found alien life when in fact the increase in radio waves had been caused by someone microwaving their dinner in the staff canteen. Reassuringly, by enjoying ourselves at the festival, James said there was really no negative effect on the research being performed at Jodrell Bank. Rather, with some of the profits going towards Jodrell Bank, the festival is a boost for the coffers, especially as it was only a decade ago that Jodrell Bank was faced with closure due to shortfalls in government agency budgets. There are other radio telescopes around the world who would pick up the signals from aliens if the little green men really did start to send them.

The search for alien life, and many other aspects of the research that Jodrell Bank is used for, is strengthened by the many organisations and collaborations that the centre has formed with similar projects in the UK and abroad. Jodrell Bank is these days also a symbol of the world working together for a common goal. The centre is a key part of the UK's MERLIN project connecting Jodrell Bank to six other radio telescopes in the UK which can combine to create higher resolution images from space. Jodrell Bank is also the headquarters for SKA, a highly ambitious (and costly) project to create square kilometre wide telescope fields in South Africa and Australia that will be able to survey the sky thousands of times faster than ever before. More than 60 years later after its construction, Jodrell Bank is still very much at the forefront of our attempts as a human race to see what is out there beyond our blue planet. Its history is still being written, even while its heritage is being celebrated.

The tour finished with a few more questions and then we all dispersed back into the festival, happy that we'd enjoyed a bit of science and could now resume our head banging and beer swilling. I walked back round the telescope taking in its magnificence and then decided to see what else Bluedot had to offer me. I first stumbled upon an eight-foot tall robot named Titan and a man dressed in a suit named Dave giving a show to an audience of mums, dads and kids. Titan walked mechanically around the audience, picking on particular audience members and making jokes about them then squirting them with water from his eyes making the kids erupt into squeals. Though the sceptical among us would like to remind others that this was just a robot suit with a man inside, it was superb entertainment. They talk about robots taking our jobs, and if I were a comedian I'd be looking over my shoulder a little worried.

As Bluedot is primarily a music festival I headed over to the main stage to catch a few songs and join in with the majority of people who were here for the bands. As we collectively nodded along to the psych-pop lyrics of female-fronted She Drew The Gun, I looked around to gauge the crowd who had made it to this remote symphony of science and psychedelic sounds. Glitter and NASA shirts seemed to dominate, as did kids running around with space-themed toys. By the telescope earlier I'd seen lightsaber classes being given to the kids by fully-trained Jedis. At some of the stalls you could see 3D printing in action, buy astronaut food, and try out your own science experiments. Walking round, it had struck me how much of a commercial industry space science is. The message seemed to be that science is cool, but it's also a marketable product. It's spawned and inspired genres of music, created celebrities out of scientists, influenced fashion and cult costumes. It seemed totally logical therefore that there should be a British summer festival dedicated to the geekier side of us. Really, Bluedot is an outdoor science museum with a striking balance between the serious talks on space projects and the availability of purchasing blow-up plastic Martians. In the space of a minute I walked from a thought-provoking talk from astrophysicist Eamonn Kerins about the possibility of Plexit, the idea of humans leaving earth for other planets, to witnessing the totally bizarre, out-of-this-world performance from Henge, a group of dancers dressed in alien jumpsuits led by a bearded man with a plasma ball on his head jumping around in deranged fashion to cosmic disco beats. That is the glorious contradiction of Bluedot; on the one hand you have scientists denying the possibility of Martians existing while humans dressed as Martians walk around with a craft ale in hand. As humans (and I suppose also as humans pretending to be aliens), we love the myths as much as we love the facts. Does it really matter if we find alien life if so many of us are just as happy assuming they're green slimy creatures with swollen heads and long fingers?

With this in the back of my mind, I continued my weird but wonderful festival tour around the serious science of the Lovell telescope. I rocked out in the Nebulus stage to the excellent (though sadly human dressed) Talkboy, stepped into various stalls and tents to listen to the state of our world and the universe, and witnessed the gymnastic performance of Strong Women demonstrating the forces that govern us to eager-eyed kids. Balancing chairs on their chins and standing on each other's shoulders, they did more to explain physics to me than five years of lessons at secondary school. It was science, but simplified. I'd finally found my level at the kids-aimed hands-on science tent. In many ways though, this is what science needs to be. To be appreciated by future generations it has to be accessible to them, and for that it was uplifting to see so many kids at the festival. The advantage of Jodrell Bank becoming a UNESCO World Heritage site is that it will become more widely appreciated, its importance (now recognised as being of universal value to mankind) will see greater amounts of funding (and ultimately its future) secured and, especially with the new visitor centre being built, Jodrell Bank will be in a better position to attract more visitors and inspire more minds. Opening its doors to a festival like Bluedot attracts people with different interests, whether those be musical or otherwise, to the site, enabling greater appreciation for the projects that are of interest to every human on the planet. If we ever get those answers to where we came from or what is out there, it will be because we invested money, time and interest in the scientists that use facilities like Jodrell Bank. Becoming the UK's 32nd

World Heritage site (28th in the British Isles) validates the importance of Jodrell Bank's history as well as its future to come. Now, let's see what they find.

UK UNESCO World Heritage Sites #28 of 28

St Kilda (1986)

Birthday with the birds on the lonely isle

Waking up on a birthday is different to waking up any other day of the year. Automatically your brain informs you, like a smartphone notification, that today is the anniversary of your mother giving birth to you. For everybody else it's just a normal day, but for you there's the strange sense of one year being added to your scorecard. You look at your phone and already the Whatsapp messages and Facebook posts have started to trickle in. Friends and family sending their wishes before they go to work. When I was younger and living at home, I would scamper downstairs to find a pile of presents and cards on the kitchen table. The excitement was palpable. The present opening was just the start of a day dedicated to me. We'd go out to my favourite restaurant, eat a cake that I'd chosen, sing a song with my name in it. As you get older though, birthdays start to fade in significance and excitement. You wake up early for work, cringe at the embarrassment of being sung to in various out of tune chords, and go to bed with the nagging feeling that you're now a year older and really you should get on and do something with your life.

So, it was strange then that I awoke on Monday 29th July ages before my 7am alarm and was so excited that I couldn't get back to sleep. I laid in bed and thought about the day ahead. For once I was neither at work nor near any family on my birthday. Exactly a year ago I had been on a summer school trip to the Tower of London, my first of the 28 World Heritage sites. A year later, while still in the British Isles, I was almost as far away from London as possible. I had woken up in a four bed dorm room in a bunkhouse in the small Outer Hebridean village of Leverburgh. In an hour or so I would be walking down to the pier and boarding a fast boat to the remotest chunk of land belonging to the British Isles, a dual World Heritage site, and my 28th and final site on this quest to visit all of the UK's World Heritage sites between my 27th and 28th birthdays.

Not being able to stand the anticipation much longer, I got ready for the day, read the family birthday cards I'd brought with me, and then slung my bag with lunch and notebook inside around my back and set off down the road on a warm and calm summer's morning.

Perfect conditions. The previous week had seen quite a few of the trips out to St Kilda cancelled due to adverse weather. I'd been terrified that the same fate would befall my birthday trip, so the text I'd received the previous day from the boat company had caused me to punch the air in delight.

Hi. We are looking to do your St Kilda trip on Monday. We meet at Leverburgh pier for 7.45am. Regards, Seamus, Sea Harris.

I'd been on the seven hour bus between Glasgow and Uig on the Isle of Skye when I received the confirmation that the trip I had planned months ago would indeed be happening. Just getting to the Outer Hebrides from England in less than a day had been an achievement. Connecting with the bus, the ferry from Uig took me to Tarbert on the Isle of Harris, but as it was a Sunday there were no buses to take me the 20 miles to Leverburgh and few, if any, taxis available. The only option was to stand on the side of the road to Leverburgh with my thumb out and hope some kind soul would stop and offer me a lift. It took about 40 minutes and around 15 cars zooming past my outstretched thumb before a pair of friends slowed down and invited me to hop in. Joan and Peter were off to catch the ferry to Berneray from Leverburgh Pier so they could drop me right next to the bunkhouse. We talked about St Kilda on the way.

'Aye, it's an incredible place alright. I went there once meself. The birds, the cliffs. Just incredible. I'd love to spend a night there one time. Just to see what it's like, y'know. The isolation, the loneliness....'

Isolation and loneliness are the two words most often associated with St Kilda. It's the 41 miles between the Outer Hebrides and St Kilda that have given the archipelago the nickname 'The Lonely Islands'.

At exactly 8am, with twelve passengers including myself on board, we set off from the tiny village pier and after passing a sea of islands the mountains started to fade until they were no more. About an hour into the journey there was no sign of land in any direction. It was just us and the ocean. The trip would take us only two and a half hours at a speed of 22 knots, but this would have been a voyage of three or four days in the past, depending on how treacherous the sea decided to be. Being surrounded only by water is something that really tests the human resolve. Nowadays we have GPS maps and the like to show us where we are going, but the people heading out to St Kilda hundreds and even thousands of years ago would have had only blind faith that the sea would carry them to the volcanic outcrop. That, and the accompaniment of birds who we could see skimming the calm waters beside us. Half way through the journey a thick blanket of mist descended, obscuring our vision of the horizon and anything more than ten metres ahead of us. We ploughed on regardless, the mist parting as we skimmed through it. Then, after an hour of blindness, the mist suddenly disappeared, the sea turned back to blue, and we slowed down to cruise past the tiniest island of the archipelago, Levenish; a 200 foot stack that welcomes visitors from the east to St Kilda with its cliff face silhouette in the shape of a human face. It was like finding a secret island with a treasure map and a red cross etched into the middle of the sea.

Soon the main island of St Kilda, Hirta, came into view, its mighty hills with their near vertical slopes imposing and dramatic. The finger thin island of Dun guides you in on the left hand side, protecting Village Bay where all boats dock. We slowed down to a stop well within the bay and then transferred to a dinghy to reach the pier. Once all twelve of us had been brought over to the pier, we made our way onto the island and took in our surroundings. The first thing you notice when you arrive at St Kilda is that it's far from deserted. If you were imagining an untouched paradise, well, Hirta at least is not really it. Humans lived here for up to four thousand years of course and the stone remains of houses from the 1830s wrap around the bay. Then there's the more modern infrastructure. We were here at a historic moment in time, the ranger of the island John informed us. Within a few months the dark green cabin-like buildings from the 1950s would all be gone. Good riddance I thought as I looked over at the ghastly flat-roofed buildings. John pointed out their replacements, a smaller set of single storey, wood-clad walled and turf roofed buildings that men in hi-vis jackets were working on while we listened. An improvement, that's for sure. But why are these buildings here anyway? No one lives on St Kilda any more, do they? Well, not permanently. Since 1957 the Ministry of Defence has used St Kilda as a missile tracking base with masts up on the highest peaks and accommodation down in Village Bay. Scientists also stay on St Kilda to do research into the Soay sheep, a unique breed on the island, and the National Trust for Scotland also has people working and volunteering on St Kilda such as our kind ranger John who gave us each a map, told us to just use our common sense and then let us roam the island at our leisure.

'Oh, but one thing, don't venture into the nesting areas of any Arctic Skewers. If you do, they will attack you as they think you're trying to steal their eggs. If one does attack you then simply find a stick and hold it up above your head as they'll only go for the highest part of you. All right everybody. Well, have a lovely day. The gift shop open at 2.30 and the boat will pick you up at 3.30.'

With that, we were released. As the mist had descended again, cloaking the hills, I decided to start with the buildings in Village Bay. Near the pier there is a small church with a classroom attached. I popped in for my first taste of what life was like for the St Kildans who endured the solitude and harsh conditions here before their voluntary evacuation in 1930. For centuries the people here had hosted visiting ministers, but it was Rev John MacDonald, 'the Apostle of the North', who instigated a religious fervour in the 19th century. St Kildans took their religion so seriously that it's said their island duties suffered as a result of four hour long preaching sessions and masses. They would sit on the hard wooden benches like those in the church today and listen attentively to an extreme form of Presbyterianism from the hard-line ministers. The school children weren't much happier, judging by the scowls on the faces of the black and white class photos displayed on the classroom wall.

Their homes with their families were stone buildings built next to each other but not joined together in a single line along The Street, facing out onto the bay. After relocation within Village Bay in 1830, each new-built home was given a plot of land and the islanders would store their food in stone mounds known as 'cleits' which are dotted throughout the island. Food was mainly derived from the plentiful sea birds who visit St Kilda. A limited amount of crops could be grown and cheese was made from sheep's milk, but the islanders didn't tend to go fishing given the rough nature of the water surrounding their home. We might view their life as harsh, but the islanders lived freely in peace and without crime. Every day the able-bodied men of the village would gather on The Street to discuss the tasks to be done that day and this came to be known as the St Kilda parliament. The Scottish writer Martin Martin noted in his 1697 book about the island that the residents were *'happier than the generality of mankind as being almost the only people in the world who feel the sweetness of true liberty'*.

However, this near-Utopia couldn't last forever. The evils of the rest of the world eventually arrived on St Kilda and when they did they spelled the beginning of the end for the St Kildans. Diseases from visitors to the island such as tetanus killed off the majority of new-borns. Tourists started arriving in the late 19th century bringing money into the society for the first time. The First World War brought a German submarine to the island which destroyed a signal station erected by the Royal Navy, though fortunately there were no casualties bar one sheep who was hit by the shelling. On the back of young men leaving the island and a series of crop failures, the decision to evacuate was made and on 29th August 1930 the 36 remaining St Kildans departed their island home for Morvern, a peninsula on the west coast of mainland Scotland where they lived until the final St Kildan, Rachel Johnson, died in 2016.

Thus St Kilda severed all ties to a human population that lasted millennia. It's this population that contributes to St Kilda nomination as a cultural World Heritage site alongside being a natural World Heritage site. UNESCO inscriptions are divided into natural and cultural listings, but a few very special places around the world are dual World Heritage sites, being nominated both for their natural as well as their cultural universal value to humanity. Of over a thousand World Heritage sites, only 39 are dual sites like St Kilda. Some of St Kilda's peers include Uluru, Cappadocia and Machu Picchu, meaning that St Kilda is in a very exclusive club of the sites most cherished around the world.

The other half of St Kilda's inscription concerns the natural setting of the islands and its attraction to the bird life of the North Atlantic. Europe's largest seabird colony is of monumental ecological importance attracting thousands of gannets, fulmars, puffins and many other species which in turn attract many twitchers to view this paradise of bird-watching. The birds are everywhere, circling and swooping throughout the island, following the boats as they enter the bay and nestling on the rocky ledges of some of Europe's highest sea cliffs. After inspecting the partially restored dwellings in the village, I consulted the map the ranger had given me and decided to get across to The Gap, a dip between the two highest hills on the island that affords spectacular cliff edge views. I was already fairly high up on the slope that leads to The Gap from the bay so I decided to cut across the land and join the slippery tracks around half way up. It was warm now so I took my thick jumper off and enjoyed the warm breeze in just a shirt. Shirt weather in the North Atlantic, who would have thought?

Whoosh! The sound of rushing air made me turn around just in time to see a pair of outstretched gnarly claws sail over my head, scratching my scalp as they passed. I turned around and saw a dark red bird with a mighty body and large wings turn back on itself in mid-air and launch another attack. Three, two, one, impact. The claws scratched my head again like a hairbrush of nails. As the Arctic Skewer did a 180 degree turn and prepared to strike a third time, I remembered the advice that the ranger had given us that morning.

'If one does attack you then simply find a stick and hold it up above your head as they'll only go for the highest part of you'.

St Kilda is a totally treeless island. There are no sticks on the ground only, swoosh, I ducked just in time to avoid the skewer's claws, only stones and those wouldn't do much good. They'd surely only make it angrier. Again the skewer came for me, twisting in the air and then dive bombing with vengeance, its wings pointed and stream-lined. I ducked again this time and felt only the air passing above my head. Quickly I retreated down the slope, but the skewer wasn't giving up until I was well out its territory. Four more times it came for me, and four more times I ducked just in time to avoid having my scalp ripped off the top of my skull. Finally, after making it down to the village wall, I saw the bird turn around and head back to its chicks.

'Thanks for that! I hadn't spotted an Arctic Skewer until now'.

'No worries. Any time.', I responded through gritted teeth to the nearby bird-watcher who had witnessed the whole charade.

After the escape from the bird attack, I needed a little rest so I hiked up to the top of The Gap and sat down on the cliff edge to take in the near-impossible view of sheer cliffs dropping hundreds of metres down to the azure sea. I get vertigo from places like these so I stayed a little back from the very edge but still the view of gannets soaring and diving next to the almost mythical cliffs was mesmerising. My appreciation of birds that don't attack me was quickly returning. The mist rolled up the slope from the village and then cascaded down the drop. Sea birds screeched and yelled as they flew overhead, performing acrobatics in the air for what seemed like the sheer hell of it. The twists and dives they were performing could serve no other purpose than pleasure. I was being treated to a show.

Eventually, after consulting my watch and discovering I'd already spent half my allotted time on St Kilda, I trudged back down the slope past the numerous cleits towards the walls and roofless houses of the village. You can't go very far on St Kilda without some calf-straining climbing on wet grass, but I chose to explore the other side of Conachair, the highest hill on St Kilda at 430 metres, by using the concrete road that runs from the MoD buildings to the collection of masts on top of Mullach Mor. I started the climb up the road, pausing for a break while the mist came, covered and then cleared before continuing. A little way up a jeep appeared behind me and a kind MoD worker, Kenny with ginger hair and an almost incomprehensible accent, offered me a lift up to the masts. I jumped into the passenger seat and we talked while he drove the jeep up the steep roads to the summit. He was in the second week of his monthly rotation, and said he actually quite enjoyed coming out to St Kilda. The food and accommodation in the MoD building weren't bad, there was a lively crowd in the Puff Inn some nights, and, so long as you didn't mind the conditions, the natural scenery was a perk of the job. Of course, he wasn't too willing to go into details about what exactly the MoD are working on at the moment, but the test missiles that are fired in the Deep Sea Range in the Outer Hebrides are tracked by the radar stations on St Kilda. To a simple member of the public like me, the radar station consisted of two brown footballs on top of supports and a tall tower. Surprisingly I was allowed to just wander around the missile trackers like the free roaming sheep on the island, but Kenny did drop me off a little before the main buildings so that his boss didn't see.

In truth, I wasn't really that interested in whatever the radars are tracking. I'm not much of a threat to national security, although I was being extra careful to not trip over and upset the many wires and cables laid on the grass between the facilities. Rather it was the spectacular view from on top of Mullach Mor that caught my attention. From this position I could see more or less the rest of the main island. The military road travels up the spine of Hirta giving you views of both sides. The village and The Gap on your right as you go up and the even remoter western side of Hirta and the island of Soay on your left. With the low mist channeling through gaps in the hills, it wasn't too hard to imagine being castaway on an Atlantic island if you just ignored the hum of the generators and the large masts behind you. To the north west I could see the island of Boreray and the stacks that surround it. It too was still cloaked in cloud, though you could clearly see its peaks rising above the mist like a castle in the sky. I had to get back to the boat pretty sharpish for the tour around Boreray so I walked quickly down the road back to the village, stopping occasionally to appreciate the truly remarkable views of the scattered cleits and line of houses below.

Even if you've been to many of Scotland's islands, or you've visited Norway or Iceland, St Kilda is still quite something. It's the magic of finding a place this ruggedly beautiful teeming with bird life in the absolute middle of nowhere that is spellbinding. Take away the radar masts and the MoD buildings and you'd have an almost pristine island, though the MoD's presence does of course enable and fund conservation work. In fact, the MoD's presence is vital to the National Trust for Scotland's work and the threat of the MoD leaving the island given the advances in technology would make conservation work very difficult for the Trust. Though many visitors on tour boats like mine probably bemoan the ugly MoD buildings in the village and the unsightly tower that stands atop of Mullach Mor, it's vital to the continuation of St Kilda as a place to visit. Short of getting the descendants of the last St Kildans to return to their ancestral home and resume some sort of primitive life, the integrity of the island as a place of heritage is high, even with the sound of diggers and drills reverberating round the hills.

Though the people have left, the birds certainly haven't. Judging by my encounter with the Arctic Skewer that morning, I'd wager that the birds haven't forgotten about the people who used to nick their eggs. Back on the boat we were treated to tea and a slice of gingerbread homemade by the company owner Seamus' mother and then we set off for a spin around Boreray. There are birds on Hirta, many in fact, but nothing compares to the skyscrapers of birds perched on the craggy cliffs of Boreray. It's the Empire State Building of birds within the city of birds that is St Kilda. We were able to get up close and personal with the stacks that teem with gannets, kittiwakes, shags, fulmars and puffins. With no meat-eating predators to worry about (after the last St Kildans left, that is), the sea birds flourish here with the rich sea life to feast on and provide for their young. The St Kildans, whose main food was the sea birds, would go to great lengths to catch the birds for their meat and steal their eggs. Our guide on the boat pointed out the ledges that women would often scale to get up and down the cliffs to raid the nests of the birds.

Though there's no flat land on Boreray, humans have spent a fair bit of time here. In one famous story from 1727, there were three men and eight boys who had gone to Boreray to capture birds. As there is no place to dock, the custom was to drop the hunters off and come back in a few days to pick them up with the fruit of their labours. However, while the boat had been absent, a smallpox epidemic broke out amongst the islanders on Hirta killing all the adult inhabitants. The 11 islanders on Boreray had to survive 9 months on the sheer rocks living off sea fowl and a few sheep before they were found and rescued by the steward. Not knowing that there had been a smallpox outbreak on Hirta and that everyone had died, they must have been pretty peeved by the time they were rescued. Sitting, waiting on a lonely rock in the middle of the ocean for nine months would have been torturous. No fire, no boat, just the clothes they were wearing and the knowledge of how to survive off wild birds.

Thankfully we weren't getting off the boat. Jaw-dropping as it is, the thought of being stuck on Boreray is almost unimaginable. We pootled around the island and the stacks, gazing up at the mass of sea birds flying overhead and spotting the varieties of birds nesting cheek by jowl on the ledges. The rocks were literally covered in birds, thousands upon thousands of them. One of the most difficult habitats for humans to survive in, but one of the best for birds. The captain of the boat led us through narrow gaps between stacks, past caves that seemed to bore deep into the inside of the rock and into turquoise waters you'd never believe were real until you see them for yourself. The cliffs of the stacks are just under 200 metres high and Boreray's highest peak is nearly 400 metres above sea level. Below the water the cliff faces can stretch around 50 metres down. When you're directly below them, the cliffs command respect, but still the St Kildans were hardy (and hungry) enough to start climbing them in just their bare feet and homemade rope. When viewed from afar, Boreray is the spitting image of a mythical island shrouded in mist and mystery. Like the whole of the St Kilda archipelago, it's the kind of place you can't stop yourself audibly saying 'wow' to, even if no one else is listening.

Sadly, after an hour of cruising round the various stacks, it was time to make our way back to civilisation. We turned around and sped off into the mist. I took my seat back inside and reflected on a journey that had been months in the planning, and the end of a project that had taken me exactly a year to complete. St Kilda was, in many ways, the perfect site to save till last, and a wonderful, inspirational place to spend a birthday. Oh yeah, it was still my birthday. My mind had been elsewhere during bird attacks, hikes up hills and trying not to get in trouble with the Ministry of Defence. I looked at the time on the boat's dashboard. 18:14. The exact time I'd been born. Now I was officially 28 years old. Of course, I felt no different for turning from 27 to 28, but with the completion of the 28 UK World Heritage sites, it felt like a chapter ending. What would the next chapter bring? Well, I have a few, slightly crazy, ideas...

Printed in Great Britain
by Amazon